Community Corrections

READINGS IN CRIME AND PUNISHMENT
Michael Tonry, *General Editor*

What Works in Policing
David H. Bayley

Criminology at the Crossroads
Feminist Readings in Crime and Justice
Kathleen Daly and Lisa Maher

Incarcerating Criminals
Prisons and Jails in Social and Organizational Context
Timothy J. Flanagan, James W. Marquart, and Kenneth G. Adams

Community Corrections
Probation, Parole, and Intermediate Sanctions
Joan Petersilia

Community Corrections

Probation, Parole, and Intermediate Sanctions

Edited by

Joan Petersilia

New York   Oxford

OXFORD UNIVERSITY PRESS

1998

Oxford University Press

Oxford   New York

Athens   Auckland   Bangkok   Bogota   Bombay   Buenos Aires
Calcutta   Cape Town   Dar es Salaam   Delhi   Florence   Hong Kong
Istanbul   Karachi   Kuala Lumpur   Madras   Madrid   Melbourne
Mexico City   Nairobi   Paris   Singapore   Taipei   Tokyo   Toronto   Warsaw

and associated companies in
Berlin   Ibadan

Copyright © 1998 by Oxford University Press, Inc.

Published by Oxford University Press, Inc.
198 Madison Avenue, New York, NY 10016

Library of Congress Cataloging-in-Publication Data
Community corrections
p.   cm.
ISBN 0-19-510542-7.—ISBN 0-19-510543-5
1. Community-based corrections—United States.
2. Probation—United States.   3. Parole—United States.
HV9279.C62   1998
364.6'8—dc21   96-54062
                                                  CIP

Printing (last digit): 9 8 7 6 5 4 3 2 1

Printed in the United States of America on acid-free paper

For my husband,
Steve
You're the most wonderful husband and
the best friend I'll ever have.
I am so thankful to be sharing my life with you.

Contents

Preface

Community corrections' populations have experienced tremendous growth in recent years—from about 1.4 million persons in 1980 to just under 3.6 million adults and 600,000 juveniles by 1997. According to the Bureau of Justice Statistics, 3.2 percent of *all* U.S. adult men and 0.6 percent of adult women Americans are currently on probation or parole in state and federal jurisdictions. Today, fully 72 percent of *all* identified U.S. criminals are not in prison but rather are serving sentences in the community.

Not only has the size of the community corrections population risen, but the clientele has become increasingly serious if judged by the offender's criminal record, current conviction crime, or substance abuse history. Today, community correctional administrators estimate that nearly 40 percent of the persons they supervise need close, intensive supervision—yet fewer than 10 percent receive it.

Funding is simply inadequate to support the kinds of services that would protect the public or encourage offender rehabilitation. In fact, most jurisdictions have experienced recent budget *declines* in order to fund increased jail and prison capacity. Today, although nearly three fourths of correctional clients are in the community, only about *one tenth* of the correctional budgets goes to supervise them.

Despite all of the public and media attention paid to probation and parole—mostly when an offender is rearrested for a heinous crime—there is relatively little scholarly literature on the subject. The student or policymaker who wishes to answer the most basic questions—for example, who receives probation or parole, what services are provided, at what cost, to what effect—will find that the information either does not exist, is of questionable quality, or is not easily accessible. The best information is scattered among government reports, agency evaluations, and obscure professional journals.

I wanted to compile a reader that would allow someone quickly to get "up to speed" on the issues, data, and programs that comprise community corrections. I have used materials in this reader that, for the most part, I had originally used to supplement my undergraduate and graduate "community corrections" courses at University of California, Irvine. Over time, packets of these assembled articles began to replace the standard textbook I had assigned.

I wanted this reader to be self-contained, in that it could serve as the sole text for a class or corrections training conference. As such, I commissioned several articles specifically for this reader where I felt there were serious gaps in the available literature (an example is Norm Holt's review of the state of parole in America), or some important new information had yet to be published (e.g., Susan Turner and Doug Longshore's evaluation of Treatment Alternatives to Street Crime). Some previously published articles needed updating, and the authors obliged (e.g., Mark Dean-Myrda and Francis Cullen's article on the evolution of community corrections). Most of the selections from published materials have been edited to facilitate the page limit and reader accessibility. Readers who are sufficiently intrigued by the excerpt can follow up by obtaining the original source.

I believe there is great unrealized promise in community corrections. My hope is that the information in this volume can be used to bring us one step closer toward realizing that potential.

JOAN PETERSILIA, PH.D.
Professor, Criminology, Law, and Society
University of California, Irvine

Community Corrections

CHAPTER **1**

The Evolution of Community Corrections

INTRODUCTION

"Community corrections" is a somewhat ambiguous concept. It is a legal status, an alternative to incarceration, a service-delivery mechanism, and an organizational entity. But, to most, the term *community corrections* refers to two types of criminal sanctions, probation and parole, although community corrections also includes halfway houses, residential centers, work furlough, and all other programs for managing the offender in the community.

Probation and parole are commonly confused with one another, especially in the media and political discussions. *Probation* is a sentence the offender serves in the community while under supervision, in lieu of a prison or jail term. *Parole* is the conditional release of an inmate from incarceration under supervision after a portion of the prison sentence has been served.

While probation and parole have been a part of sentencing practices since the 1800s, they have always been subject to controversy over their effectiveness and to criticism that they represent undue leniency toward criminal offenders. When the United States embraced rehabilitation as the primary goal of corrections in the 1960s, probation and parole were in great favor. Caseloads were reduced to manageable levels, new programs were instituted (mostly with federal funding), and confidence in the ability of the justice system to change offenders was strong. Probation and parole professionals were encouraged to provide offenders with counseling and job training. But when the nation's mood turned punitive beginning in the 1980s, probation and parole services fell out of favor, budgets were slashed, and public confidence declined considerably. Officers were encouraged to redirect their efforts toward offender surveillance and monitoring, with community safety rather than offender rehabilitation as their primary goal. A whole new array of community corrections programs emerged, known as "intermediate sanctions," where the focus was on close surveillance and stricter supervision.

Mark Dean-Myrda and Francis Cullen put these shifts in thinking about community corrections' purpose and activities in perspective. They discuss the early rationale for incorporating "community" in corrections, and how the pendulum has continued to shift back and forth since its inception between the helping and punishing role that communities and community corrections can play. Moreover, they caution that the nation's approaches to crime control have sought simplistic solutions, when no such solutions exist. They write that our search for silver-bullet fixes to the crime problem hampers our efforts to accumulate solid research evidence to guide practice, further contributing to the nation's ever-changing crime control policies, which have ultimately proven ineffective.

This is a critically important article, in that it suggests that the current "lock em up" fervor is not new and it too shall pass. The challenge for community corrections is to ensure that the next time the public and those who fund corrections take a close look at community-based options, there are programs and policies that make good sense in terms of balancing public safety, offender rehabilitation, and system costs.

Dean-Myrda and Cullen point out that one reason community corrections has not fared well recently is that practitioners have not taken the time to articulate what they are doing, evaluate their effectiveness, or take a proactive stance in educating the public about appropriate directions. Without this information, the public and, in turn, elected officials, act instead on information garnered from politicians and the media. Public opinion can be influenced by probation and parole professionals, but there has to be a message, a plan, and a policy that is clearly articulated and readily understood. The authors believe that when the pendulum swings back in favor of community-based corrections, current program administrators will be in a better position to be proactive, arguing for programs and policies that have shown to be effective.

Community-based sentencing programs are going through particularly difficult times right now, but there are signs that the pendulum is beginning to sway back in favor of incorporating community-based options. In reality, the best crime control policy will be one that reflects an appropriate balance between institutionalized and community-based corrections. We must continue to imprison violent offenders. It is a false dichotomy to argue between tough law enforcement and community-based crime prevention. The choice is not one or the other—it must be both. We need to create enough prison space to incarcerate those who are truly violent and also support programs to reduce the tide of criminals that currently flood our society. The challenge is to develop a more balanced approach that will make better use of taxpayer funds, an approach that recognizes that incarceration may have an impact, albeit limited, on crime rates; that focuses imprisonment on those most likely to pose a threat to society; and that redirects some resources into promising community based programs so that offenders who can benefit from rehabilitation programs are given the opportunity to do so.

The Panacea Pendulum: An Account of Community as a Response to Crime

MARK C. DEAN-MYRDA
Cook County Juvenile Court

FRANCIS T. CULLEN
University of Cincinnati

America's efforts aimed at controlling and preventing criminal wayward-ness, reveals James Finckenauer (1982), have been dominated by a futile search for panaceas. This "panacea phenomenon," as Finckenauer calls it, is characterized by a cycle of unrealistic expectations, failure and dissatisfaction with the proposed cure-all, and ultimately a renewed search for yet another foolproof elixir for the crime problem.

Intimately connected with many of the panaceas embraced over the years has been the notion that the "community" is an integral component to a final solution of the crime problem. Reformers of differing generations, however, have manifested little consensus as to whether this crime-eradicating community lies within the larger society or within a specially created institutional environment. Policymakers have also disagreed on whether such a community should be fundamentally benign or, alternatively, punitive in its orientation. Criminal justice reforms have therefore followed a pendular path, swinging between opposite extremes on these two key dimensions.

In light of these considerations, the intention here is to present a historical account of the role that the concept of community has played in the search for a cure to the ostensibly intractable problem of crime. We will investigate in a beginning way how "community" has been involved in the panacea pendulum that has long prevailed within the arena of American correctional policy.

"The Panacea Pendulum: An Account of Community as a Response to Crime" by Mark C. Dean-Myrda and Francis T. Cullen has been revised and updated. It was originally published in *Probation, Parole, and Community Treatment*, edited by Lawrence F. Travis, © 1985. Reprinted with permission from Waveland Press.

COMMUNITY PUNISHMENT

The concept of community as a factor in American criminal justice policy can be traced back to the prerevolutionary colonial period. At this time, however, the community was viewed neither as a cause of criminal behavior nor as an all-encompassing cure for it. Rather, the colonists inherited from England a religious explanation of deviance (Rothman, 1971, p. 15). Criminals were often thought to be possessed by demons or evil spirits, or to have made pacts with the Devil through such things as witchcraft, black magic, and sorcery. Punishment was harsh, therefore, not so much because there was confidence that the wicked could be easily transformed into upstanding citizens—"rehabilitated" in more modern terms—but because it proclaimed the evil of sin and the sanctity of God's laws.

Equally significant, the majority of these sanctions were carried out not behind the high walls of an institution but in the community itself. Public punishments and executions provided an important opportunity for the rest of the community residents to reaffirm their commitment to one another and to reestablish bonds of mutual trust (see also Erikson, 1966). By the community binding together to inflict a sanction that rectified the victimization of an individual citizen, social ties among the residents were strengthened.

This community-based punishment involved such "curious" practices as tarring and feathering, branding, mutilation, forcing the criminal to wear a scarlet letter, banishment, and the use of the pillory and the stocks (Earle, 1969; Newman, 1978, pp. 112–113). But these sanctions served a social purpose integral to colonial communities. As Rothman (1971, p. 49) observes, in colonial times "the offender was held up to the ridicule of his neighbors, a meaningful punishment and important deterrent where communities are closely knit." He further notes that the use of such punishments "presumed a society in which reputation was an important element in social control, where men ordered their behavior in fear of a neighbor's scorn" (1971, p. 50).

As the colonies prospered and population centers emerged, the colonists' ideas of crime causation, and consequently of crime suppression, began to change. This change is largely attributable to the Enlightenment (or Age of Reason, as it is alternatively labeled), an ideological movement that took place during the last half of the eighteenth century. In a nutshell, Enlightenment-era philosophy said that traditional authority—including religious authority—should be closely scrutinized and discarded whenever it seemed irrational.

This social climate allowed Cesare Beccaria, father of the Classical School of criminology, to interpret crime in a political fashion, rather than simply attributing it to demonic possession. In 1764, Beccaria published an attack on the legal system of the time, asserting that it was arbitrary and overly severe. He believed that criminal conduct was an expression of individual freedom, and that the only justification for curtailing such freedom was that society would be unable to function if crime were left unpunished. According to Beccaria, the purpose of punishment was deterrence, both of the offender and of potential offenders. Therefore, the legal code and the penalties for breaking it had to be made public knowledge and had to be universally applied to all citizens without regard for power or wealth. Only if the punishment was certain would it be an effective deterrent (Duffee et al., 1978, pp. 253–255). Rationality, not custom, should inform the construction of the justice apparatus.

INSTITUTIONAL TREATMENT: THE RISE OF THE THERAPEUTIC COMMUNITY

The paradigm of the Classical School set the stage for the first true crime panacea in America. When crime was attributed to a person's innate sinfulness and Satan's schemes, there could be little hope for eradicating it. However, if crime were viewed as the product of free and rational choice, then a simple manipulation of punishments could be used to render such a choice unfeasible, and crime could be virtually wiped out.

Following the American Revolution, policymakers in the United States readily embraced Classical School values and turned to the task of setting differential penalties for various crimes (Barnes, 1972, p. 121). However, many of the punishments that had previously been imposed with regularity were beginning to fall by the wayside. Banishment from the community was eventually abandoned because the growth of cities made it impractical (Rothman, 1971, p. 50). Corporal punishment was also denounced, partially because industrialization created a demand for human labor, thereby increasing the value of human lives and limbs.

Reformers needed a new punishment to use in place of those that were being discarded. The Pennsylvania Quakers furnished a plausible alternative for intervening with offenders: imprisonment. Indeed, the Quakers were instrumental in establishing prisons as the primary criminal sanction in the United States. Until the late 1700s, imprisonment was rarely used as a penalty for common law violations. Instead, for all but the exceptional, offenders were institutionalized only until a court hearing could be arranged or, if convicted, until the punishment could be meted out.

By contrast, the Quakers were enthusiastic supporters of incarceration as a regular reaction to crime. In the face of social forces that were rapidly precipitating the modernization of society, they felt that the very fabric of their community was coming unglued. This subsequent anxiety over the attenuation of their traditional way of life lent much legitimacy to the conclusion that society's ills—including crime—were firmly rooted in the disorder now burdening their community. This reasoning suggested that the cure for the criminally wayward lay in removing this population from the corrupting influences of a disorganized communal existence (Rothman, 1971).

The panacea for crime thus was manifest: place offenders in the controlled environment of an institution so as to isolate them from the moral depravity that they had not yet learned to resist. Such a therapeutic community would indoctrinate the inmate into the values of religion, hard work, and discipline, and then return the offender to society as a useful, productive, law-abiding citizen. Clearly, then, the Quakers optimistically felt that a comprehensive solution to crime was possible if only a special community based on traditional moral values were to be created and vigorously promoted.

The Quakers believed that this therapeutic community, which they called a "penitentiary," could best be achieved by placing offenders in solitary confinement where they could read the Bible, contemplate their sins, and do penance. Reformers in New York offered the competing "congregate" system at their Auburn prison, which isolated inmates in the evening but allowed them to gather—under the rule of silence enforced by the whip—for meals and for work. In this period, the two sets of reformers engaged in heated debate, but in hindsight they were arguing over details and not central principles: they both endorsed the idea that criminals would be saved by removing them from a criminogenic society and placing them within an exquisitely designed, purifying, orderly institutional community.

In the end, the Auburn congregate system flourished, mainly because of economics: inmate labor was more productive if offenders could congregate to participate in industrial work (Fogel, 1975). This model promised to cure criminals and earn a profit to boot. Events in the succeeding years, however, did little to foster the conclusion that the penitentiary would in fact achieve the grand designs claimed for it by reformers only a few years before.

As is common today, the population of offenders eligible for incarceration quickly outstripped available cell space. The resulting overcrowding undermined the capacity of prison authorities to enforce a regimen of total silence, particularly as offenders were double-celled. But this was not all. Those sent to prison proved less malleable than reformers had anticipated; indeed, the task of reformation was made difficult because habitual criminals—not first offenders as the reformers had hoped—were being housed in the state's institutions. Further, the social characteristics of the wayward were changing; prisons were crammed with immigrants and native poor. Many citizens were unsure that such people, who did not share their heritage or social standing, were reformable. Thus, the public grew comfortable with the mere fact that the members of this "dangerous class" were being caged where they could not prey on the innocent.

In this context, the notion that the communities prevailing within the prisons were anything approaching panaceas seemed increasingly untenable. Rather, it was evident that institutions were fulfilling the social function of incapacitating treacherous offenders, many of whom were seen as biologically defective. If "the promise of reform had built up the asylums," observes

Rothman (1971, p. 240), "the functionalism of custody perpetuated them." Indeed, the very places that had been established "to exemplify the humanitarian advances of republican government . . . were actually an embarrassment and a rebuke . . . the evidence was incontrovertible that brutality and corruption were endemic to the institutions" (Rothman, 1980, p. 17).

In 1870, the first Congress on the National Prison Association met in Cincinnati to discuss the crisis besetting America's prisons (Mitford, 1971, pp. 35–36). Admitting that the system had been distorted by abuses of authority, they reaffirmed the idea that a proper prison community could effect the reform of criminals (Rothman, 1980, p. 31). To help accomplish this task, they proposed a revolutionary sentencing policy: the indeterminate sentence, in which offenders would not serve a fixed term but would earn their freedom only when they had shown their rehabilitation. Stating that "hope is a more potent agent than fear," the Declaration of Principles drawn up by the Congress called for "peremptory sentences . . . to be replaced by those of an indeterminate duration—sentences limited only by satisfactory proof of reformation" (Fogel, 1975, p. 32). In theory, this took the decision of sentence length away from the keepers and placed it in the hands of the kept. Threats and harsh discipline would no longer be needed, since the convicts would enthusiastically and energetically work toward their own rehabilitation and consequently their own release.

This blueprint to renovate correctional practice, however, did not take hold immediately. The seeds for reform were laid, but the social context was not ripe for their blossoming. Reformers would have to wait three decades before American society would enter a period, called the Progressive era or the Age of Reform (Hofstadter, 1955), in which their panacea for solving the crime problem would direct a fundamental reshaping of the correctional system.

THE BEGINNINGS OF COMMUNITY CORRECTIONS

By the latter part of the nineteenth century, rapid social and economic change was seen as posing a threat to the nation's stability. As technology and the pressures of demand increased production, wave after wave of immigrants poured into urban areas seeking employment. These immigrants, with their strange languages and foreign customs, tended to settle next to one another, forming little ethnic pockets in poorer sections of town. Immigrant neighborhoods soon became characterized by high crime rates (Shaw and McKay, 1931, p. 11).

Progressive reformers sought to address this threat to order by turning the nation into a "melting pot." Through education, the immigrants would be persuaded to give up their backward ways and would be taught English. They would then be inculcated with the values of honesty, hard work, thrift, and hygiene. Fully Americanized, they would finally be able to overcome their shortcomings and rise into the ranks of successful middle-class citizens. They would no longer have any reason to engage in criminal activity, and crime would be largely eradicated (Rothman, 1980, pp. 48–49).

Within the correctional system itself, Progressive designs were characterized by three features. The first was a focus on treatment rather than on punishment. This view was largely an outgrowth of the Positivist School of criminology, established by Cesare Lombroso in the late 1800s. Whereas the Classical School saw offenders as exercising considerable individual freedom and weighing the costs and benefits of crime, Lombroso's view took a much more deterministic view of human conduct. After enumerating various determinants of behavior, especially those of a biological nature, Lombroso concluded that criminals were incapable of exercising free choice and therefore it made no sense to punish them. Instead, "punishment should be replaced by scientific treatment of criminals calculated to protect society" (Duffee et al., 1978, pp. 257).

An insistence on individualized treatment was the second hallmark of Progressive criminal justice reforms. This stance was largely a by-product of the positivist emphasis on determinism. As Rothman (1980, p. 53) explains, the "reformers believed that the environmental causes of crime were so varied that no one general prescription could fit all cases. Only a one-to-one approach could uncover the slums' effects on the offender" (see also Barnes, 1972).

This concern for the individual offender dovetailed nicely with the third factor that distinguished Progressive intervention in the lives of law violators: an implicit trust in the state to do good. "Ameliorative action," notes Rothman (1980, p. 50), "had to be fitted specifically to each individual's special needs, and therefore required a maximum of flexibility and discretion." Consequently, Progressives were willing to give tremendous discretion and power to the state, primarily because they foresaw no reason for the state to abuse it. The government would no longer be punishing criminals but would be responsible for reforming them into upwardly mobile citizens. The resocialization of criminals seemed to Progressives to be a win-win proposition, in which the offender was helped by the state to find his or her niche in society and as a result was no longer driven to victimize others (Rothman, 1980, p. 60).

Fueled by their ideological fervor and buoyed by a favorable social climate, the Progressives embarked on a campaign to renovate the criminal justice system. In notable contrast to the thinking of the Quaker and Auburn reformers of nearly a century before, the Progressives did not hold a dark vision of the prevailing social order. To be sure, certain areas of the city were seen as distinctly criminogenic, and it was agreed that it was not safe to leave everyone free in society. Nonetheless, unlike the founders of the penitentiary who felt that the cure-all for criminality rested in the re-creation of traditional orderly communities within the impenetrable confines of the penitentiary, Progressives neither looked backward for solutions nor manifested a fundamental mistrust of the principles that were now being used to organize sociopolitical arrangements.

It is thus instructive that attempts to construct a therapeutic prison environment took one of two paths. On the one hand, there was a complete acceptance of the new, scientific view of a "rational" response to the criminally wayward. Such deviants should not be the focus of vengeance, but rather should be placed in hospital-like settings where they would be treated just as any other sick patient would be. A community fashioned after the "medical model" would allow for the individualized treatment of the malady that drove the unfortunate beyond the confines of the law.

On the other hand, some reformers were less enthralled with the magic of medicine. But, again, they did not see past times as holding answers for the special problems of their day. Rather, they felt that the panacea for crime lay in transporting the dominant community and its values into the prison. The task was not to insulate offenders from the larger society per se, but to introduce them to the wonders of true American citizenship. It was clear to the Progressives that inmates—many of whom were not native stock—could not become contributing citizens unless they lived in a prison environment that approximated a normal community on the outside. Imposing strict silence and rigid discipline would only foster unnatural social interaction and dependence and retard successful reintegration into society upon release from the penitentiary. A truly "progressive" solution thus involved creating a vibrant and thoroughly American social order within the institution (Rothman, 1980).

The reformers of the day, however, did not halt their reasoning here. Their faith in the ultimate goodness of the American order furnished them with the belief that not all offenders need remain incarcerated or even suffer this fate initially. With proper supervision by a state official who could be both caring and stern when necessary, many offenders might be taught to conform within the confines of their local environment. Indeed, the policies of parole and probation were trumpeted as important innovations and won implementation across the nation. Between 1900 and the middle part of the 1920s, the number of states with parole rose from a handful to forty-four (Cavender, 1982, p. 37), while probation was instituted in two thirds of all states for adults and in every state for juveniles (Rothman, 1980, p. 44). Notably, these reforms signaled the emergence of the idea that treatment *within* the community—as opposed to the artificial creation of a therapeutic prison community or, for that fact, punishment within the community as obtained in colonial times—was an integral part of the cure for America's crime problem.

For the Progressives, parole went hand in hand with the indeterminate sentence, which accomplished two interrelated purposes: the length of sentence could be manipulated to correspond to the needs of the individual offender, and control would be maintained over offenders until they had been rehabilitated. The alternative policy of determinate sentences and hence of mandatory release from prison was of much concern to the Progressives. Parole represented the successful completion of the prison treatment program, and it provided for additional supervision while the transition to life outside was made. Mandatory release, on the other hand, risked returning convicts to society regardless of their condition. Having been isolated from society and lacking the prospect to earn a shorter sentence through genuine self-improvement, it was little wonder that such offenders were unable to readjust upon reentry and eventually recidivated.

For offenders whose violations were not serious enough to warrant the intensive therapy of incarceration, Progressives advocated the use of probation. They believed that probation, which approximated parole without a prison sentence, would provide the guidance and supervision needed to reform those who had only begun to dabble in crime. Probation proved to be a popular reform, soon replacing suspended sentences as the normative sanction for most misdemeanants and first-time violators.

THE FLOURISHING OF COMMUNITY CORRECTIONS

The reforms undertaken during the Progressive era succeeded in popularizing a blueprint for criminal justice that has informed correctional policy until recent times. To be sure, the grand hopes of the Progressives to create a system that could simultaneously regenerate and control offenders was never realized. All too often, bureaucratic interests and custodial convenience took precedence over the treatment needs of those brought within the grasp of the state's correctional apparatus. Nevertheless, until the late 1960s there was substantial agreement that the final solution to crime in America lay in hastening the construction of the "therapeutic state" (Menninger, 1966; cf. Kittrie, 1971).

Many still believed that there was nothing wrong with the theory of justice espoused by the Progressives; rather the real problem was in the failure to implement this theory—in the lack of resources allocated to carry out the task of giving offenders individualized treatment. Moreover, not all was bleak. Despite many failures, progress had been made. The past century had witnessed the firm entrenchment of rehabilitative thinking and had advanced the idea that the establishment of therapeutic milieus within the prison was essential to eradicating the deviant inclinations that offenders imported into the society of captives (McKelvey, 1977, pp. 299–348).

Such optimism regarding the curative powers of the panacea offered by the Progressives was not to last. The linchpin of the design of individualized treatment was that the state could ultimately be trusted to do good for offenders. The events of the late 1960s and early 1970s, however, made it difficult to sustain this notion. In particular, the civil rights movement, the Vietnam conflict, the shooting of students at Kent State and Jackson State, and finally the Watergate scandal caused many on the left to suspect the intentions and integrity of the government. Within the realm of criminal justice, the bloody suppression of the uprising at Attica, in which unarmed inmates were shot down by officers storming the prison, revealed the extent to which the state would go to reinforce its order. In the face of this reality, it became common to speak of the "legitimacy crisis" confronting the state's exercise of authority (Friedrichs, 1979) and to force consideration of the "limits of benevolence" (Gaylin et al., 1978).

Not everyone, however, was prepared to conclude that the search for a cure to crime was a fruitless enterprise. The mistakes of the Progressives could, in fact, shed light on where the real panacea might be found. By extending an inordinate amount of trust to the state, the Progressives had fostered the erroneous view that the most coercive instrument at the state's disposal—the prison—could be transformed into a community capable of effecting the humanistic treatment of convicts. In light of Attica, such a conception seemed utopian at best and tragically ludicrous at worst.

This reasoning led to a new policy agenda: if the notion, inherited from as far back as the Quakers, that the prison community was curative must be forfeited, then the solution to crime must lie outside the penitentiary's walls, in a place where the state's coercive potential is minimized. Offender rehabilitation must be undertaken not in artificially created milieus but in the heart of society. Indeed, all logic pointed to the fact that "community corrections" was the long-awaited panacea for crime.

While the prevailing social context made this thinking plausible if not compelling, the community corrections movement drew added legitimacy from the criminological writings of the day. Research on recidivism rates, for example, revealed that prisons did little to diminish criminogenic predispositions. Theoretically, the appeal of community corrections was bolstered by the emergence of "labeling theory," which contended that the real cause of illegal conduct had less to do with deviant psychological and environmental forces and much more to do with the way in which the legal system reacted to those whom it labeled as criminals.

According to labeling theorists, prisons were brutalizing, they deepened criminal values by forcing inmates into close association with one another, and they made reintegration into normal societal roles more difficult by stigmatizing offenders. Thus, trying to save the wayward by placing them in institutions inevitably had the unanticipated consequence of trapping offenders in a criminal career. The most rational policy was thus to start programs that would "divert" offenders from the formal legal system and into the community where they could receive the help they needed. At the extreme, authors such as Edwin Schur (1973) called for reformers to embrace the policy of "radical non-intervention." As he urged with regard to problem adolescents, "leave the kids alone whenever possible" (1973, p. 155).

Disturbingly, investigations into the actual conditions of institutions ostensibly confirmed that they fell far short of the humane therapeutic communities the Progressives had envisioned (Nagel, 1973; Wooden, 1976). Prisons were now called "houses of darkness" (Orland, 1975), and more than a few commentators advocated the "end of imprisonment" (Mitford, 1971; Sommer, 1976). This call gained credence when, in the early 1970s, Jerome Miller closed Massachusetts' juvenile reformatories without causing an upswing in delinquency (Miller, 1991).

Community-based corrections was suddenly hailed as the cure for all the problems facing the criminal justice system. The state would not exercise complete power over offenders as occurs in prison but would control only limited aspects of their lives, such as through probation and parole supervision. The halfway house would replace the closed institutions of the past and would operate under the watchful eye of the community. Reduced program size would lend itself well to therapeutic techniques and therefore would be more successful. Offenders would have an opportunity to become resocialized with the community, rather than being forced to adapt to the artificial environment of the institution. And all of this would be done at a substantial savings to the taxpayer, since the offenders would be able to partially support themselves through employment in the community, and because resources already available in the community (public schools, social services, recreational facilities) could be utilized in the therapeutic enterprise. The transition from panacea to panacea was undertaken with great hope and enthusiasm.

COMMUNITY PUNISHMENT REVISITED

The prospects for a comprehensive community corrections movement initially seemed bright. The policy of treating offenders in the community promised to be cost effective, fundamentally humane, and a therapeutic panacea for all but the most sociopathic among us. But, remarkably, the appeal of this policy agenda was not sustained for long.

Conservatives, as might be anticipated, criticized such notions as diversion and deinstitutionalization as merely more attempts by liberals to coddle offenders and rob the criminal sanction of its deterrent powers. Unexpectedly, however, commentators on the political left also launched an attack on the concept of community corrections. Sensitized to the ways in which past reforms had been corrupted, they were quick to scrutinize community-based programs and to illuminate their shortcomings. In their most fundamental attack, they claimed that the community corrections movement was merely a new and subtle means by the repressive state to expand social control over citizens.

In an analysis that typified liberal thinking, Austin and Krisberg's (1982) review of research led them to argue that the community corrections movement was best characterized as an "unmet promise." "In each instance," they observed of community-based programs, "the nonincarcerative options were transformed, serving criminal justice system values and goals other than reducing imprisonment" (1982, pp. 405–406). In particular, these "reforms" typically expanded state control. They pointed, for example, to the phenomenon of "net widening," in which community programs developed as alternatives to incarceration were in fact used mainly for offenders who otherwise would have been placed on probation or given a suspended sentence.

In the matter of a few years, then, liberals had reached the conclusion that not only was it foolish to imagine that crime-curing communities could be fashioned within the prison but also to anticipate that prevailing realities would ever allow for humanistic and efficacious reforms outside the penitentiary's walls. It was manifest that "nothing works" (Martinson, 1974), and that well-intentioned criminal justice reforms unwittingly were "dangerous" undertakings (Doleschal, 1982). With hopes of curing criminality dashed, the best that could be done was to try to ensure that offenders would be treated justly both before the courts and while incarcerated (Fogel, 1975; von Hirsch, 1976). Beyond this, meddling in criminal justice matters simply risked making things worse.

This line of thinking, however, had its own unanticipated consequence. Now bereft of a panacea for crime, those on the political left were reduced to advising that nothing works and that all reforms were doomed to failure. But this was hardly a persuasive blueprint for making society safer and did little to address the genuine concerns citizens had about the nation's high crime rate. Indeed, liberal thinking on crime was so impoverished that it opened a huge policy chasm that conservatives filled with confident, if often misguided, proposals for ending lawlessness (Travis and Cullen, 1984).

"Law and order" conservatives did not ponder the root causes of criminality or the complexities of crime control, but rather set forth a clear panacea for stopping the victimization of innocent citizens: put offenders in prison for lengthy sentences. "Getting tough" would deter criminals and those contemplating illegal conduct by teaching that "crime does not pay." At the very least, lengthy stays behind bars would ensure that the dangerous did not roam free in the community. In particular, it was claimed that if the most chronic offenders were selectively incapacitated, substantial savings in crime could be achieved (Wilson 1975; cf. Gordon 1980).

On the surface, the conservatives' agenda was a resounding success: in the last two decades or so, prison populations increased five-fold, with well over a million offenders incarcerated on any given day. But two glitches beset the prison panacea. First, the crime rate remained stubbornly high despite the huge financial investment required to imprison large numbers of offenders. Although some crime savings undoubtedly occurred, prisons hardly were a panacea for the nation's lawlessness (compare Logan and DiIulio, 1992, with Clear, 1994, Currie, 1985, and Irwin and Austin, 1994).

Second, states lacked the capacity to lock up every offender. In fact, prisons quickly became overcrowded and corrections expenditures soared, consuming larger and larger chunks of state budgets. Conservatives in the late 1980s and 1990s thus faced the dilemma of how to remain "tough on crime" while also staving off prison crowding and avoiding the bankruptcy of the government treasury.

An ingenious solution was at hand: punish and control offenders *in the community* through the use of "intermediate sanctions"—penalties that lay between prison and probation (Morris and Tonry, 1990). To be sure, prisons were not abandoned as the linchpin of the conservatives' crime-control agenda. Nonetheless, intermediate punishments had all the signs of a complementary panacea. These sanctions would reduce crime and alleviate the prison crowding problem by controlling offenders in the community—and do so at a cost savings! Even the liberals were enticed on board the intermediate punishment bandwagon: offenders might be punished, but at least they would escape imprisonment.

But how was such community control to be accomplished? Intermediate sanctions, answered the conservatives, would not be used to rehabilitate criminals, the chief goal of traditional community corrections, but rather would be used to supervise offenders closely and to punish them if they dared to depart from the law. Thus, offenders might be placed under home confinement where they would be monitored electronically; they might be intensively supervised by probation and parole officers—policed, so to speak—while in the community; they might be given drug tests to ensure that they stayed "clean"; or they might be given these (and other) sanctions in combination.

As with previous panaceas, however, intermediate punishments were much oversold and now appear to be an "unmet promise" (see, for example, Byrne and Pattavina, 1992; Cullen et al., 1996; Petersilia and Turner, 1993). They did not seem to work any better than other sanctions in reducing recidivism—and sometimes performed worse. They were most effective, in fact, in catching offenders for minor indiscretions—"technical violations" of probation or parole conditions. Officials then faced a dilemma: not to punish offenders by returning them to prison would rob the intermediate sanctions of their supposed deterrent value; to punish offenders would contribute to the very problem—costly overcrowding of prisons—that the sanctions were devised to solve.

BEYOND THE PANACEA PHENOMENON

In an era in which virtually every political campaign is replete with sound bites promising simplistic answers to virtually every social and economic problem, including criminality, it would take much hubris to predict that we are likely to see the panacea phenomenon be replaced by mature, civil discourse on how to solve the crime problem. Even so, reasons exist to conclude that panaceas may not have the shelf life they possessed in the past.

Criminologists are one reason: with the organized skepticism of the discipline and the growing number of scholars capable of conducting evaluation research, today's criminologists are in a position to show the limits of cure-alls. Practitioners also are becoming more sophisticated consumers of research, more involved in collaborative evaluations with scholars, and less likely to embrace simplistic ideas (Petersilia, 1996). And there are signs, perhaps permanent, perhaps only transitory, that political extremism is being rejected in favor of more moderate approaches to social policy that can build a broad consensus among the American electorate.

Within corrections, we propose that a more reasoned approach—one capable of building consensus—would seek both to control and rehabilitate offenders (Gendreau et al., 1994; Petersilia, 1995). In the past, these two strategies were pitted against one another, conservatives calling for greater punitive controls and claiming that treatment was a euphemism for leniency, liberals calling for greater rehabilitation but fearful that control would invariably corrupt attempts to reform offenders.

In fact, both are essential components of a judicious corrections. Many offenders deserve and require restraint in prison or surveillance in the community. The evidence is mounting, however, that the behavior of offenders, including serious criminals, can be changed by rehabilitation programs (see, for example, Andrews et al., 1990; Palmer, 1992; Prendergast et al., 1995). It is noteworthy that public surveys reveal that citizens endorse using both punishment and treatment to respond to lawbreakers (see, for example, Cullen et al., 1990; McCorkle, 1993).

Regardless of where correctional policy heads, the concept of community will be implicated. Within the prison, we will debate how life in institutional communities reduces or exacerbates recidivism. In the wider community, we will face the sticky issues of deciding which offenders should remain among us and then how best to achieve the protection of citizens and the reform of the wayward. These are difficult challenges that will require continuing research, discourse, and informed policy and practice.

The lesson we can gain from history, however, is that panaceas are unlikely to help in this endeavor. Panaceas are not fully without value, since they have the potential power to energize reform and to reshape social institutions in need of change. But their continuing downside is that they enforce a kind of political correctness that obscures the complexity inherent in social issues (such as crime) and that cuts off reasoned debate. We often end up with strident and silly public policies that may strike a chord with public frustration over crime but ultimately fail to deliver on the promise to make the nation safer (Finckenauer, 1982). In the end, we should contemplate the wisdom of entering a post-panacea period in which simple solutions are forfeited in the pursuit of meaningful, if incremental, progress in an arena—crime control—that has been stubbornly resistant to the quick fix.

REFERENCES

Andrews, D. A., Ivan Zinger, Robert D. Hoge, James Bonta, Paul Gendreau, and Francis T. Cullen. 1990. "Does Correctional Treatment Work? A Clinically Relevant and Psychologically Informed Meta-analysis." *Criminology* 28:369–404.

Austin, James, and Barry Krisberg. 1982. "The Unmet Promise of Alternatives to Incarceration." *Crime and Delinquency* 28:374–409.

Barnes, Harry Elmer. 1972. *The Story of Punishment: A Record of Man's Inhumanity to Man.* Montclair, N.J.: Patterson Smith.

Byrne, James M., and April Pattavina. 1992. "The Effectiveness Issue: Assessing What Works in the Adult Community Corrections System." In *Smart Sentencing: The Emergence of Intermediate Sanctions,* edited by James M. Byrne, Arthur J. Lurigio, and Joan Petersilia. Newbury Park, Calif.: Sage, pp. 281–303.

Cavender, Gary. 1982. *Parole: A Critical Analysis.* Port Washington, N.Y.: Kennikat Press.

Clear, Todd R. 1994. *Harm in American Penology: Offenders, Victims, and Their Communities.* Albany: State University of New York Press.

Cullen, Francis T., Sandra Evans Skovron, Joseph E. Scott, and Velmer S. Burton, Jr. 1990. "Public Support for Correctional Rehabilitation: The Tenacity of the Rehabilitative Ideal." *Criminal Justice and Behavior* 17:6–18.

Cullen, Francis T., John Paul Wright, and Brandon K. Applegate. 1996. "Control in the Community: The Limits of Reform?" In *Choosing Correctional Options that Work: Defining the Demand and Evaluating the Supply,* edited by Alan T. Harland. Thousand Oaks, Calif.: Sage, pp. 69–116.

Currie, Elliott. 1985. *Confronting Crime: An American Challenge.* New York: Pantheon.

Doleschal, Eugene. 1982. "The Dangers of Criminal Justice Reform." *Criminal Justice Abstracts* 14:133–152.

Duffee, David, Frederick Hussey, and John Kramer. 1978. *Criminal Justice: Organization, Structure and Analysis.* Englewood Cliffs, N.J.: Prentice-Hall.

Earle, Alice Morse. 1969. *Curious Punishments of Bygone Days.* Montclair, N.J.: Patterson Smith.

Finckenauer, James O. 1982. *Scared Straight! and the Panacea Phenomenon.* Englewood Cliffs, N.J.: Prentice-Hall.

Fogel, David. 1975. *"We are the Living Proof. . . ": The Justice Model for Corrections.* 2d ed. Cincinnati: Anderson.

Friedrichs, David O. 1979. "The Law and the Legitimacy Crisis: A Critical Issue for Criminal Justice." In *Critical Issues in Criminal Justice,* edited by R. G. Iacovetta and Dae H. Chang. Durham, N.C.: Carolina Academic Press, pp. 290–311.

Gaylin, Willard, Ira Glasser, Steven Marcus, and David Rothman. 1978. *Doing Good: The Limits of Benevolence.* New York: Pantheon.

Gendreau, Paul, Francis T. Cullen, and James Bonta. 1994. "Intensive Rehabilitation Supervision: The Next Generation in Community Corrections." *Federal Probation* 58 (March):72–78.

Gordon, Diana R. 1980. *Doing Violence to the Crime Problem: A Response to the Attorney General's Task Force*. Hackensack, N.J.: NCCD.

Hofstadter, Richard. 1955. *The Age of Reform*. New York: Alfred A. Knopf.

Irwin, John, and James Austin. 1994. *It's About Time: America's Imprisonment Binge*. Belmont, Calif.: Wadsworth.

Kittrie, Nicholas N. 1971. *The Right To Be Different: Deviance and Enforced Therapy*. Baltimore: Penguin Books.

Logan, Charles H., and John J. DiIulio, Jr. 1992. "Ten Myths About Crime and Prisons." *Wisconsin Interest* 1:21–35.

Martinson, Robert. 1974. "What Works? Questions and Answers About Prison Reform." *The Public Interest* 35 (Spring):22–54.

McCorkle, Richard C. 1993. "Punish and Rehabilitate? Public Attitudes Toward Six Common Crimes." *Crime and Delinquency* 39:240–252.

McKelvey, Blake. 1977. *American Prisons: A History of Good Intentions*. Montclair, N.J.: Patterson Smith.

Menninger, Karl. 1966. *The Crime of Punishment*. New York: Penguin Books.

Miller, Jerome G. 1991. *Last One Over the Wall: The Massachusetts Experiment in Closing Reform Schools*. Columbus: Ohio State University Press.

Mitford, Jessica. 1971. *Kind and Usual Punishment*. New York: Random House.

Morris, Norval, and Michael Tonry. 1990. *Between Prison and Probation: Intermediate Punishments in a Rational Sentencing System*. New York: Oxford University Press.

Nagel, William G. 1973. *The New Red Barn: A Critical Look at the Modern American Prison*. New York: Walker.

Newman, Graeme. 1978. *The Punishment Response*. Philadelphia: Lippincott.

Orland, Leonard. 1975. *Prisons: Houses of Darkness*. New York: The Free Press.

Palmer, Ted. 1992. *The Re-emergence of Correctional Intervention*. Newbury Park, Calif.: Sage.

Petersilia, Joan. 1995. "A Crime Control Rationale for Reinvesting in Community Corrections." *Spectrum* (Summer):16–27.

Petersilia, Joan. 1996. "Improving Corrections Policy: The Importance of Researchers and Practitioners Working Together." In *Choosing Correctional Options that Work: Defining the Demand and Evaluating the Supply*, edited by Alan T. Harland. Thousand Oaks, Calif.: Sage, pp. 223–231.

Petersilia, Joan, and Susan Turner. 1993. "Intensive Probation and Parole." In *Crime and Justice: A Review of Research*, Vol. 17, edited by Michael Tonry. Chicago: University of Chicago Press, pp. 281–355.

Prendergast, Michael L., M. Douglas Anglin, and Jean Wellisch. 1995. "Treatment for Drug-abusing Offenders Under Community Supervision." *Federal Probation* 59 (December):66–75.

Rothman, David J. 1971. *Discovery of the Asylum: Social Order and Disorder in the New Republic*. Boston: Little, Brown.

Rothman, David J. 1980. *Conscience and Convenience: The Asylum and Its Alternatives in Progressive America*. Boston: Little, Brown.

Schur, Edwin M. 1973. *Radical Nonintervention: Rethinking the Delinquency Problem.* Englewood Cliffs, N.J.: Prentice-Hall.

Shaw, Clifford R., and Henry D. McKay. 1931. *Social Factors in Juvenile Delinquency,* Vol. 11. National Commission on Law Observance and Enforcement, Report on the Causes of Crime. Washington, DC: U.S. Government Printing Office.

Sommer, Robert. 1976. *The End of Imprisonment.* New York: Oxford University Press.

Travis, Lawrence F. III, and Francis T. Cullen. 1984. "Radical Non-intervention: The Myth of Doing No Harm." *Federal Probation* 48 (March):29–32.

von Hirsch, Andrew. 1976. *Doing Justice: The Choice of Punishments.* New York: Hill and Wang.

Wilson, James. 1975. *Thinking About Crime.* New York: Vintage.

Wooden, Kenneth. 1976. *Weeping in the Playtime of Others: America's Incarcerated Children.* New York: McGraw-Hill.

CHAPTER 2

The Current State of Probation, Parole, and Intermediate Sanctions

INTRODUCTION

It is surprising that we know so little about the current operations of probation and parole agencies. After all, they are responsible for supervising three-fourths of all criminal justice clients in the nation. But, prisons and jails get most of the public and scholarly attention.

Part of the reason for the lack of attention paid to community corrections is the fact that, until recently, probationers and parolees were not seen as posing particular serious risks to public safety. This was particularly true for probation populations. Probation is commonly assumed to be a sentencing alternative for misdemeanant (less serious) offenders, not felons. Historically this was true, but no more. Today, as the article in the next section discusses, nearly half of all offenders granted probation have been convicted of *felony* crimes, not misdemeanors. Many of these rather serious offenders are not required to participate in treatment or work programs, and few have stringent reporting requirements. Of course, this is not surprising when one considers that, on average, we spend about $200 per year per offender for probation and parole services. And, as Norm Holt and Patrick Langan discuss in their articles, even when probation and parole violations are discovered, incarceration is unlikely due to a number of administrative and budgetary constraints.

But the news is not all bleak. All three of the articles in this chapter review the emerging evidence that community correctional programs *do* work. When probation and parole programs are targeted to appropriate clientele, and when the programs are delivered consistently over several months and incorporate both treatment and surveillance activities, offender recidivism can be reduced.

The articles in this chapter, taken together, can be viewed as providing "state of the art" reviews of the three components of community corrections—probation, parole, and intermediate sanctions. The articles discuss client characteristics, program services, costs, and impacts. The reader should view these articles as providing the "facts" and analytic framework around which to debate the costs and benefits of incarceration versus community alternatives.

A Crime Control Rationale for Reinvesting in Community Corrections

JOAN PETERSILIA
University of California, Irvine

In 1994, Congress passed the most ambitious crime bill in our nation's history, the Violent Crime Control and Law Enforcement Act of 1994. It allocated $22 billion to expand prisons, impose longer sentences, hire more police, and to a lesser extent, fund prevention programs. But in 1995, as part of the Republicans' "Contract with America," the House significantly revised the Act, and the money allocated to prevention programs was eliminated. The amended bill, passed by the Senate, increased the overall price tag to $30 billion and shifted nearly all of the $5 billion targeted for prevention programs into prison construction and law enforcement. As a *Los Angeles Times* op-ed concluded of the whole matter: "what started out last legislative season as a harsh and punitive bill has gotten down right Draconian" (*Los Angeles Times*, 1995).

What is wrong with these proposals? Some argue that they are racist, or that they cost too much; however, nearly everyone agrees they have one major flaw: they leave the vast majority of criminals, who are serving sentences on probation and parole, unaffected.

In 1993, there were just under five million adults under correctional supervision—or about one in every 39 Americans. Seventy-two percent of *all* identified criminals were not in prison, but serving sentences in the community, on probation or parole supervision. Even though the number of prisoners has quadrupled in the past decade, prisoners are still less than 1/5 of the convict population, and the vast majority of offenders remain in the community amongst us (Bureau of Justice Statistics, 1995). If we are to effec-

"A Crime Control Rationale for Reinvesting in Community Corrections" by Joan Petersilia, from *The Prison Journal*, Vol. 75, No. 3, 1995, pp. 479–504. Reprinted by permission of Sage Publications, Inc.

tively control crime—as opposed to exacting retribution and justice—we must focus our efforts where offenders are, which is in the community reporting to probation and parole officers.

WHO IS ON PROBATION AND PAROLE? A PROFILE OF THE POPULATION

The public misunderstands the safety risks and needs posed by offenders currently under community supervision, particularly those on probation. Many erroneously assume that as prison populations have grown, the probation population will have declined and those remaining in the community will have become increasingly less serious, and hence less in need of supervision. But populations in all four components of the corrections system have grown at record rates since 1983, and the 3:1 ratio of community-based to institutional populations has remained relatively stable for more than a decade.

It might seem logical that since prison populations have quadrupled over the past decade, those remaining in the community are increasingly less serious offenders—since the more serious offenders have been skimmed off and sent to prison. Unfortunately, this is not true. Analysis shows that the probation population has become increasingly serious if judged by their prior criminal record, current conviction crime, or substance abuse histories. The truth is that the overall US population has grown, more citizens are being convicted, and all corrections populations have increased simultaneously.

The Bureau of Justice Statistics (BJS) tracks the sentences handed down by the courts in felony convictions. They report that in 1986, the courts granted probation to 46% of all convicted felons. They also report that about 30% of the defendants were required to serve some jail time as part of their probationary term. Considering different crime types, about 6% of murderers were placed on probation, as were 20% of convicted rapists. Twenty percent of convicted robbers and 40% of burglars were similarly sentenced to probation rather than active prison terms. The average sentence to probation was just under 40 months, and an average jail term (for those where it was imposed) was six months.

To gauge the public safety risks of probationers and parolees, it is useful to consider the population as a whole in terms of conviction crimes. This information is provided in Table 1, which shows the conviction crimes of all adults under correctional supervision during 1991.

Table 1 shows that about 16% of all adult probationers were convicted of violent crimes, as were 26% of parolees. This means that on any given day in the US in 1991, there were an estimated 435,000 probationers and 155,000 parolees residing in local communities who have been convicted of violent crime—or over a half million offenders. If we compare that to the number of violent offenders residing in prison during the same year, we see that there

TABLE 1
Adults Under Correctional Supervision in U.S., By Offense 1991

Most Serious Offense	Percent of Adult Offenders			
	Probation	Jail	Prison	Parole
All offenses	100	100	100	100
Violent offenses	16	22	47	26
Homicide	1	3	12	4
Sexual assault	2	3	9	4
Robbery	2	7	15	11
Assault/other	10	8	10	6
Property offenses	34	30	25	36
Burglary	7	11	12	15
Larceny/theft	16	8	5	12
Auto theft	1	3	2	2
Fraud/other	10	8	6	6
Drug offenses	24	23	21	30
Trafficking	8	12	13	18
Possession/other	16	11	9	2
Public-order offenses	25	23	7	7
Weapons	1	2	2	2
DWI/DUI	16	9	NA	3
Other	9	14	5	3

Source: Census of Probation and Parole, 1991; Survey of Inmates in Local Jails, 1989; Survey of Inmates in State Correctional Facilities, 1991.

were approximately 372,500 offenders convicted of violent crime *in* prison, and approximately 590,000 *outside* in the community on probation and parole! Overall, we can conclude that nearly three times as many violent offenders (1.02 million) were residing in the community as were incarcerated in prison (372,000). These numbers make painfully clear why a failure to provide adequate funding for community corrections invariably places the public at risk.

Of course, the type of crime an offender is convicted of doesn't necessarily equate with his/her risk of recidivism. Patrick Langan at BJS tracked for a 3-year period a sample representing nearly 80,000 felons granted probation in 1986. Just over 40% of the probationers were classified by probation departments as needing either "intensive" or "maximum" supervision—meaning they appeared to be at a high risk of recidivating based on their prior criminal records and need for services. If probationers are growing in numbers and becoming more serious, they are in need of *more* supervision, not less. But less is exactly what they have gotten over the past decade.

Despite the unprecedented growth in probation populations and their more serious clientele, probation budgets have not grown. From 1977 to 1990, prison, jail, parole, and probation populations all about tripled in size. Yet only spending for prisons and jails had accelerated growth in overall government expenditures. In 1990, prison and jail spending accounted for two cents of every state and local dollar spent, twice the amount spent in

1977. Spending for probation and parole accounted for two-tenths of one cent of every dollar spent in 1990, unchanged from what it was in 1977 (Langan, 1994). Today, although nearly *three-fourths* of correctional clients are in the community, only about *one tenth* of the correctional budget goes to supervise them.

The increase in populations, coupled with stagnant or decreasing funding, means that caseloads (the number of offenders an officer is responsible for supervising) keep increasing. While the 1967 President's Crime Commission recommended that ideal caseloads would be about 30:1, national averages for probation are now approaching 150:1, and for parole, 80:1. And in some communities, caseloads are much higher. In Los Angeles County, for example, where nearly 70,000 adults are on probation, funding cutbacks have resulted in caseloads reaching several hundred and few direct services. A recent report noted that 60% of all Los Angeles probationers are tracked solely by computer and have no contact with an officer (U.S. Advisory Commission, 1993). Texas reports that it has about 400,000 adults on probation, and 95% of them are on regular supervision, which means they are only seen once every three months.

Nationally, BJS reports that three out of five felony probationers see a probation officer no more than once a month, at best, because actual contacts are often less than the number prescribed. Because of underfunding and large caseloads, probation supervision in many large jurisdictions amounts to simply monitoring for rearrest.

But neglect in funding has had serious consequences. As caseloads rise, there is less opportunity for personal contact between officer and offender, limiting any ability of the officer to bring about positive change in the offender, or refer the offender to appropriate community-based resources and programs (which incidentally are also being reduced). Langan (1994) found that about 90% of probationers are required to do one or more things as a condition of their community-based status—pay restitution to victims, stay under house arrest, perform community service, participate in substance abuse counseling, and so on. But about half of them never comply with the terms of their sentences, and only a fifth of the violators ever go to jail for failure to comply—all of which adds to probation's tarnished image as being too lenient and lacking in credibility.

Lack of services and supervision undoubtedly contributes to high recidivism rates, since it has been continually shown that there is a "highly significant statistical relationship between the extent to which probationers received needed services and the success of probation." (Comptroller General, 1976:25). As services have dwindled, recidivism rates have climbed. In the national BJS study mentioned earlier, Langan and Cunniff (1992) found that within three years of sentencing, nearly half of all probationers were convicted of a new crime or abscond. Among probationers with new felony arrests, 54% were arrested once, 24% were arrested twice, and 22% were arrested three times or more. The total group of some 79,000 probationers was responsible for nearly 34,000 arrests, including 632 arrests for murder, 474 for rape, and 5,500 for robbery and assaults. By the end of the three year period, 26% of the probationers had been sent to prison, another 10% to jail, and an additional 10% were designated absconders with unknown whereabouts. Overall, 46% of felony probationers were classified as "failures." It is no wonder—the same study shows that while 53% of the sample was characterized as having a drug abuse problem, only 14% of the sample participated in any required drug treatment during the 3-year follow-up period.

Parolees fare no better. BJS statisticians Allen Beck and Bernard Shipley (1989) tracked 108,580 parolees released from prison in 1983. The sample represented more than half of all released State prisoners that year. They found that within 3 years, 62% of them had been rearrested for a felony or serious misdemeanor (23% for a violent crime), 47% were reconvicted, and 42% were returned to prison or jail. By year-end 1986, those prisoners who were rearrested averaged an additional 4.8 new criminal charges.

Another means to gauge the contribution of probationers and parolees to the crime problem is to examine the "criminal justice status" of offenders at the time they committed or were arrested for their current crime. Numerous BJS reports provide that information, and the relevant figures show that about 28% of felony arrestees are on probation or parole at the time of their arrest, as were 40% of jail inmates, and nearly 50% of prison inmates. A BJS survey reports that 31% of all persons on death row in 1992 report committing their murders while under probation or parole supervision.

Indeed, about 12% of all persons arrrested for all violent crimes in the U.S. are out on pretrial release for a previous charge, 7% are on parole, and 16% are on probation. Thus, about a third of all violent crime is committed by persons who are technically "in custody." Leaving probationers and parolees "unattended" is not only bad policy, it leaves many victims in its wake.

The high failure rates of probationers and parolees also contribute significantly to prison crowding. Current estimates show that between 30 and 50 percent of all new prison admissions are community supervision failures (Parent et al., 1994). Indeed, offenders who fail under community supervision are the fastest-growing component of the prison population.

WHAT CAN WE DO? A PROPOSAL TO DEVELOP AN INTEGRATED TREATMENT/CONTROL PROGRAM FOR DRUG OFFENDERS

The grim situation described above is known to most of those who work in the justice system or study it. Until we curb the criminal activities of the three-fourths of criminals who reside in the community, real reductions in crime or prison commitments are unlikely. But just as there is growing agreement about the nature of the problem, there is also an emerging consensus about how to address it.

We need to first regain the public's trust that probation and parole can be meaningful, credible sanctions. Once we have that in place, we need to create a public climate to support a reinvestment in community corrections. Good community corrections costs money, and we should be honest about that. We currently spend about $200 per year, per probationer for supervision. It is no wonder that recidivism rates are so high. Effective treatment programs cost at least $12,000–$14,000 per year. Those resources will be forthcoming only if the public believes the programs are both effective and punitive.

Public opinion is often cited by officials as the reason for supporting expanded prison policies. According to officials, the public demands a "get tough on crime" policy, which is synonymous with sending more offenders to prison for longer terms. We must publicize recent evidence showing that offenders—whose opinion on such matters is critical for deterrence—judge some intermediate sanctions as *more* punishing than prison. Surveys of offenders in Minnesota, Arizona, New Jersey, Oregon, and Texas reveal that when offenders are asked to equate criminal sentences, they judge certain types of community punishments as *more* severe than prison.

It is important to publicize these results, particularly to policymakers, who say they are imprisoning such a large number of offenders because of the public's desire to get tough on crime. But it is no longer necessary to equate criminal punishment solely with prison. The balance of sanctions between probation and prison can be shifted, and at some level of intensity and length, intermediate punishments can be the more dreaded penalty. Of course, some might suggest making the "prison" side of the equation more punitive—by lengthening terms or providing fewer services to prisoners. But states can ill-afford the enormous costs associated with lengthening prison terms, or the court costs likely to accompany trying to limit constitutionally protected inmate services.

Once the support and organizational capacity for community corrections is in place, we need to target the offender group that makes the most sense, given our current state of knowledge regarding program effectiveness. Targeting drug offenders makes the most sense for a number of reasons. Drug offenders weren't always punished so frequently by imprisonment. In California, for example, just 5% of convicted drug offenders were sentenced to prison in 1980, but by 1990 the number had increased to 20%. The large scale imprisonment of drug offenders has only recently taken place, and there is some new evidence suggesting that the public seems ready to shift their punishment strategies for low-level drug offenders.

A 1994 nationwide poll by Hart Research Associates reported that Americans have come to understand that drug abuse is not simply a failure of willpower or a violation of criminal law. They now see the problem as far more complex, involving not only individual behavior but also fundamental issues of poverty, opportunity and personal circumstances. A study by Drug Strategies (1995) reported that nearly half of all Americans have been touched directly by the drug problem, and 45% of those surveyed in the 1994

Hart poll said that they know someone who became addicted to a drug other than alcohol. This personal knowledge is changing attitudes about how to deal with the problem: seven in ten believe that their addicted acquaintance would have been helped more by entering a supervised treatment program than by being sentenced to prison.

It appears that the public now wants tougher sentences for drug traffickers, and more treatment for addicts—what legislators have instead given them are long sentences for everyone. The Drug Strategies group, who analyzed the Hart survey, concluded that "Public opinion on drugs is more pragmatic and less ideological than the current political debate reflects. Voters know that punitive approaches won't work." So, in that vein, the public appears willing to accept something other than prison for some drug offenders.

The public receptiveness to treatment for addicts is important, because those familiar with delivering treatment say that is where treatment can make the biggest impact. A recent report by the prestigious Institute of Medicine (IOM) recommends focusing on probationers and parolees to curb drug use and related crime. They noted that about one fifth of the estimated population needing treatment—and two fifths of those clearly needing it—are under the supervision of the justice system as parolees or probationers. And since the largest single group of serious drug users in any locality comes through the justice system every day, the IOM concludes that the justice system is one of the most important gateways to treatment delivery and we should be using it more effectively.

Moreover, those under corrections supervision stay in treatment longer, thereby increasing positive treatment outcomes. The claim that individuals forced into treatment by the courts will not be successful has not been borne out by research, in fact just the opposite is true. The largest study of drug treatment outcomes (TOPS) found that justice system clients stayed in treatment longer than clients with no justice system involvement, and as a result, had higher than average success rates.

However, as noted above, quality treatment does not come cheap. But in terms of crime and health costs averted, it is an investment that pays for itself immediately. Researchers in California recently conducted an assessment of drug treatment programs, and identified those that were successful, concluding that it can now be "documented that treatment and recovery programs are a good investment." (Gerstein, et al. 1994). The researchers studied a sample of 1900 treatment participants, followed them up for as much as two years of treatment, and studied participants from all four major treatment modalities (therapeutic communities, social models, outpatient drug free, and methadone maintenance).

Gerstein et al., (1994:33) conclude:

> Treatment was very cost beneficial: for every dollar spent on drug and alcohol treatment, the State of California saved $7 in reductions in crime and health care costs. The study found that each day of treatment *paid for itself on the day treatment was received*, primarily through an avoidance of crime.

CONCLUDING REMARKS

Current federal efforts to curb crime seek simple, politically attractive solutions where simple answers do not exist. There are no silver-bullet fixes to the crime problem, nor are there any hopeful signs that lead us to expect a spontaneous decline in the problem in the absence of dramatic policy action. If anything, the indicators point to increases in violent youth crime, a trend that will likely continue unless effective steps toward arresting it are taken.

This article argues that current federal efforts are misguided, and do not focus on preventing the crimes of the next generation or de-escalating the criminal careers of those on probation and parole. Dr. Dean Ornish, the guru of the low-fat road to cardiovascular health, shows a cartoon at the opening of his lectures that has application far beyond the topic of cardiovascular disease. The slide shows a crew of doctors frantically mopping up a floor that continues to be flooded by an overflowing sink. The problem, of course, is that no one has turned off the faucet.

Current crime policy is similarly focused. Short-term strategies have held sway at the expense of long-term prevention programs. We remain so consumed by the overwhelming challenge of providing cells for those imprisoned that we have little energy (or money) to address the more fundamental question of how to deter the ever increasing number of young people who choose to enter a life of crime, or dampen the escalating criminal careers of probationers and parolees.

Of course we must continue to imprison violent offenders. It is a false dichotomy to argue between tough law enforcement and community-based crime prevention programs. The choice is not one or the other—it must be both. We need to create enough prison space to incarcerate those who are truly violent and also support programs to reduce the tide of criminals that currently flood our society.

It will not be easy, so we had better start now.

REFERENCES

Beck, Allen and Bernard Shipley, "Recidivism of Prisoners Released in 1983," Bureau of Justice Statistics, Washington D.C., 1989.

Drug Strategies, *Keeping Score*, Washington D.C., 1995.

Gerstein, Dean R, Robert A. Johnson, Henrick Harwood, Douglas Fountain, Natalie Suter, and Kathryn Malloy, *Evaluating Recovery Services: The California Drug and Alcohol Treatment Assessment (CALDATA)*, Department of Alcohol and Drug Programs, State of California, Sacramento, California, 1994.

Institute of Medicine, Committee for the Substance Abuse Coverage Study (D.R. Gerstein and H.J. Harwood, eds.), *Treating Drug Problems*, Vol. 1, A Study of the Evolution, Effectiveness, and Financing of Public and Private Drug Treatment Systems, National Academy Press, Washington D.C., 1990.

Langan, Patrick and Mark A. Cunniff, "Recidivism of Felons on Probation, 1986–89," Bureau of Justice Statistics, Washington D.C., 1992.

Langan, Patrick, "Between Prison and Probation: Intermediate Sanctions." *Science*, Vol. 264, 1994: 791–794.

The Los Angeles Times, March 15, 1995. Vincent Shiraldo, "Some Gift—For $1.4 Billion, We Pay $31 Billion." B13.

Parent, Dale, Dan Wentwork, Peggy Burke, and Becky Ney, *Responding to Probation and Parole Violations*, National Institute of Justice, Washington D.C., July 1994.

U.S. Advisory Commission on Intergovernmental Relations, *The Role of General Government Elected Officials in Criminal Justice*, Washington DC, 1993.

U.S. Bureau of Justice Statistics, "Correctional Populations in the United States, 1992," BJS Bulletin NCJ-146413. Washington, D.C., April 1995.

U.S. Bureau of Justice Statistics. "Probation and Parole 1991." BJS Bulletin NCJ-146412. Washington, D.C., June 1994.

U.S. Comptroller General, Government Accounting Office. *Probation Services Need to be Better Managed.* Washington, D.C., 1976.

The Current State of Parole in America

NORMAN HOLT
California Department of Corrections

Parole is both a procedure by which a board administratively releases and returns inmates to prison and a provision for post-release supervision. Parole has gone through two decades of turbulent change. Indeterminate sentencing and discretionary release came under near fatal attack in the late 1970s as the cohesive philosophy of rehabilitation, and the accompanying coalition of powerful interest groups who supported it began to dissolve. State after state enacted sentence "reforms," which stripped parole boards of their most important powers. This article is the story of how parole has changed in response to these pressures and the critical issues and opportunities it now faces.

PAROLE IN A RAPIDLY CHANGING ENVIRONMENT

Earlier attacks on parole focused on its shortcomings in practice and its failure to live up to its lofty ideals. But in the 1970s, the attacks were also against the basic principles and assumptions of parole and indeterminate sentencing.

Attack on Parole Board Practices

The traditional criticisms of parole boards and their releasing practices grew louder as the old faultfinders found some new liberal friends. Critics pointed out that there were seldom any professional requirements to become a board member, and when legislative guidelines were established they were usually ignored in favor of patronage. Boards were viewed as meeting in secret, operating beyond public scrutiny and exercising unfettered discretion while refusing to provide the simplest documentation of the reasons for their case decisions. Absent any standards, direction, or feedback, parole decisions were often arbitrary, capricious, and inherently flawed. What was intended as a systematic, scientific inquiry in practice was the simplest of common questioning having little to do with the causes of crime. The parole dockets (preboard reports) were threadbare documents in many states; often little more than an arrest report. It was probably just as well. In a lawsuit against the California parole board in 1974, board members gave depositions that they relied heavily on the psychological evaluation in making their release decisions. When the plaintiff's attorney read excerpts from typical reports in open court, none of the members could explain what the excerpts meant. But the deficiencies of the dockets were overshadowed by the speed with which cases were dispatched—three to six minutes was not uncommon (Rothman, 1980, p. 165). Even more detrimental was the charge that there was no scientific basis for determining readiness for release in the first place.

Attacks on Field Supervision (the Other Parole)

Field supervision practices did not stand up to scrutiny much better. Caseloads were often outrageously large, well beyond most agents' abilities to provide a reasonable semblance of supervision. The national average budgeted caseload in 1979 was seventy-one parolees. Computations of the agent's available time, after administrative duties, usually revealed only a few minutes a month for each parolee. A study of federal probation showed seven minutes a week per case. Another in Georgia showed eight minutes per week. Moreover, most were superficial contacts in the office amounting to little more than empty formalities (Rhine et al., 1991, p. 24). Outsiders and control agencies were often told that parole work was so esoteric it could not be explained to laypersons. In practice, it often resembled a set of customs or traditions more than science or craft. Management was by sporadic case reviews combined with a detailed sifting of major parolee incidents to discover any agent errors in judgment (McCleary, 1978; Simon, 1993).

Still, most agents had some formal casework training, saw themselves as professionals, and were well paid compared with county probation officers or local police. The disorganization, although considerable, may not have been as detrimental in practice as it seemed at a distance. Parole supervision during this period is probably best described as operating on an "assistance model," brokering services from the wealth of federally funded War on Poverty and Great Society programs.

Intellectual Foundation for a Retribution Model

While the demise of indeterminate sentencing was probably due largely to various shifting social currents, the intellectual foundation for its demise was laid by a few academics. The results were alliances of liberal and conservative legislatures each using the abolition of parole to pursue very different ends. For liberals, the problem was the unfettered discretion of parole boards. A justice model seemed more honest and humane. For conservatives, it was the early release of inmates and frustration over the inability to enact legislation with a real impact on prison terms. It seemed senseless to enact laws increasing penalties when the results were neutralized by parole board decision (Burke, 1988; Holt, 1995).

"Nothing Works"   Robert Martinson struck the first serious academic blow in 1974 with an article titled, "What Works? Questions About Prison Reforms." The article summarized the results of a larger work that reviewed the effectiveness of 231 treatment programs and found little or no evidence of positive effects. The equivocal result from treatment programs was known and documented for some time but failed to find a receptive audience until the mid 1970s (Kassebaum et al., 1971; Robison and Smith, 1971). Martinson's overdrawn and strident conclusions were widely and regularly paraphrased as "nothing works," a position he refuted himself in 1979, particularly in reference to the use of probation and parole as alternatives to incarceration (Martinson and Wilks, 1977). The broad dissemination and acceptance of Martinson's earlier conclusion dealt a near fatal blow almost overnight to the rehabilitation concept. If rehabilitation could not be legitimated by science, there was nothing to support the "readiness for release" idea, and therefore no role for parole boards or indeterminate sentencing.

"Just Deserts"   What was needed for the final blow was a seemingly neutral ideological substitute for rehabilitation. The concept was furnished in a report by the Committee For the Study of Incarcerations, authored by Andrew von Hirsch. The report, entitled *Doing Justice: The Choice of Punishments* (1976), argued that the discredited rehabilitation model should be replaced with a simple nonutilitarian notion that sentencing sanctions should reflect the social harm caused by the misconduct. Certainly justice requires consideration for differences in culpability and blameworthiness, but the sanction should fit the offense, not the offender. Criminal conduct similarly situated should suffer similar results.

Determinate Sentencing

The promise of equitable sentencing was necessary because there was no logical reason why doing justice should lead to expanded sanctions. One might even think a system devoid of any rehabilitative pretenses would deprive fewer people of their liberty for shorter periods and be even less expensive. But, under determinate sentencing structures, the conservative just deserts allies were rapidly increasing the number and length of prison sentences to the point of dangerously overcrowding prisons. Determinate sentencing was intended to solve the capriciousness of sentencing and to ensure that defendants served the time intended. Most observers would agree it has done neither. Sentencing went from a "stealth" system well insulated from daily politics and the passions of the moment to a structure that was very visible and easily changed. Some critics feared that determinate structures would become a "Christmas tree" for legislators to hang their favorite crime bills on like shiny ornaments and would raise in lawmakers the endless and irresistible urge to "tinker." States that adopted determinate sentencing discovered they also lost their ability to equalize justice between jurisdictions and manage unusual or heinous cases. Equally important, along with the loss of releases, the states lost their safety valve to prison overcrowding.

Major Changes in Sentencing Structures

Between 1975 and 1985 the criminal justice system went from a system in which the sentencing codes of every state had some form of indeterminacy to a situation where every state had revised, replaced, or seriously considered replacing its codes with determinate sentencing. Between 1976 and 1979, seven states abolished all or most of the paroling authority's discretion (Ringel et al., 1993). These were joined by six more states by 1990. New Jersey and Pennsylvania abolished indeterminate sentencing without abolishing parole. From 1990 to 1993, three additional states had considered but rejected abolishing parole (Burke, 1995, p. 16). Illinois, California, and Minnesota, among the first to alter parole, are examples of states that adopted fixed sentences but retained post-release supervision. Connecticut, Washington, Maine, and Florida abolished both discretionary release and field supervision. Delaware abolished determinate sentencing in 1990.

Decrease in Parole Release Authority Short of abolition, many legislatures continue to decrease the authority of parole boards by changing sentencing rules. Changes take several forms.

1. Parole consideration has been prohibited until the inmate serves all of the minimum term, such as in Michigan and Massachusetts.
2. Sentences of life without parole for certain offenses have been mandated in five states and the District of Columbia.

3. "Three strikes" laws requiring extremely long minimum terms for certain repeat offenders have been enacted by the federal government and several states such as Washington and California.

4. Laws requiring that a specified proportion of the total sentence be served in prison have passed in many more states, such as Missouri, Nebraska, Montana, and Texas. Maryland recently increased the 25 percent requirement for parole to 50 percent of the sentence.

5. Some states have increased prison time requirement for violent offenses to as much as 85 percent in order to qualify for construction funds under the Federal Violent Crime Control and Law Enforcement Act of 1994. This not only effectively eliminates parole but also most "good time."

   In the last five years, a dozen parole boards have lost some or all of their releasing authority. In 1993, Kansas developed sentencing guideline grids for drug- and nondrug-related crimes and Arizona abolished discretionary release. Virginia and North Carolina abolished parole releases in 1994. Mississippi and North Carolina followed suit in 1995. Ironically, the Ohio parole board, whose releasing authority ended July 1, 1996, was to assume a new role of extending terms for prison misconduct (National Institute of Corrections, 1995). Adding time, of course, is just the opposite of where parole boards began in the 1800s.

Current Status of Parole Release   In November 1995, thirty-five states retained some form of discretionary release of inmates but nineteen of these were limited to certain kinds of offenses. In New York, for example, the board's discretion over second-term violent felons was curtailed. Sixteen other states have paroling authorities that continue to hear only those cases committed before indeterminate sentences were abolished. Although parole release was largely abolished in only seventeen jurisdictions, several are among the largest (California, Florida, Illinois, plus the U.S. Parole Commission) (National Institute of Corrections, 1995, pp. 3–10). This, combined with increasing restrictions placed on numerous other boards, caused the dramatic decline in the percent released by way of parole from 71.9 percent in 1977 to 38.8 percent in 1993 (Table 1).

   Release by parole remained the most common form of release in 1993 but by only a slight margin. By the end of 1996, parole releases was less frequent than mandatory supervision.

RESPONDING TO CHANGES

"Abolish parole" became a popular political slogan and began to symbolize a wide variety of complaints with the criminal justice system and the demand that offenders be held strictly accountable for their crimes. As a campaign slogan, "abolish parole" is simple; abolishing parole in practice is very

TABLE 1
Type of State and Federal Prison Releases by Year in Percentages

Release type	1977	1983	1988	1993
Parole	71.9	47.9	40.3	38.8
Mandatory supervision	5.9	26.2	30.6	31.7
Probation	3.6	5.0	4.1	5.4
Other	1.0	2.4	6.0	7.7
Term expired	17.6	18.5	19.0	16.4
Total	100%	100%	100%	100%
Total under post-release supervision	82.4	81.5	81.0	83.6

Source: Rhine et al., Bureau of Justice Statistics, Sourcebook of Criminal Justice Statistics, 1984 and 1994, p. 119.

complicated. Parole departments reacted to the attacks first by increasing accountability for what both boards and field supervisors did and why. Boards became more open, promulgated formal policies, adopted term-setting guidelines, and made special efforts to open the process so that victims could have their say. Virtually every board now has procedures to notice victims of hearings, decisions, and release dates and to take and consider their testimony in release decisions. Some provide for victim attendance at release hearings. Parole field agencies developed new parole supervision models and programs.

Parole Term-Setting Guidelines

The parole release and supervision decisions were traditionally arrived at by the case study method, also referred to as clinical judgments. In this process, the board member, caseworker, or parole agent collects as much information as possible, combines it in unique as well as traditional ways, mulls over the results, and arrives at a decision (Holt and Glaser, 1985). The problems with this method and the superiority of statistical prediction have been known for some time (Wiggins, 1973), and criminologists had urged parole boards to use actuarial devices (Glaser, 1962).

Early Guidelines The U.S. Parole Commission's Salient Factors Score was the first of a new generation of such "risk assessment" or predictive instruments (Hoffman and Adelberg, 1980). The score was arrived at by summing the points assessed for various background factors. This total was then combined with an offense severity scale to form a matrix or grid. Those inmates sentenced for the least serious crimes and also the least likely to reoffend (statistically) were the first to be released, and so forth. The federal system was followed by a National Institute of Corrections (NIC) term-setting model that was widely disseminated in the 1980s (Burke et al., 1989). By 1988, virtually all boards had developed or borrowed some system of guidelines or other devices to make parole decision-making more objective

(Champion, 1994, p. 62), and 40 percent used a risk prediction instrument. Guidelines may also be a few simple written but nonbinding rules.

Problems Applying Guidelines It is unclear, however, just how these devices are used (Rhine et al., 1991). To be effective, instruments should be uniformly applied and consistently followed, except in very unusual cases. Merely adding a statistical prediction as one more piece of information to a clinical judgment process does not work. Even the most structured decision-making allows for exceptions, which tend to increase to the point where they become the rule. For example, parole decisions in Utah in 1985–1986 departed from the guidelines 61 percent of the time and mostly for longer terms (Rhine et al., 1991, p. 74). Members sometimes feel that using numbers and checking boxes trivializes the important decisions they must make. New members sometimes feel they represent special constituencies and bring a long overdue fresh perspective to the board, and they may take pride in making different decisions. There may be a structured instrument in place but members are told, as in New York, that the ranges of time "are merely guidelines." Whatever form they take, guidelines require that decisions be audited to be most effective. But it is doubtful whether more than a few systems collect and aggregate information in a way that would allow actions of hearing panels or individual members to be systematically examined.

Value of Guidelines Nevertheless, at a minimum, guidelines direct the members' attention to specific crime-relevant information and away from idiosyncratic concerns in decision-making. They also make some standard for decision review possible, provide a basis for consensus building, raise relevant policy issues, and help members appreciate their role as policymakers as well as case reviewers.

The Changing Role of Parole Boards

Parole boards have always served as "back door" population managers in times of crisis. Few observers missed the fact that states that were quick to abolish discretionary parole soon had major prison overcrowding problems. The population crisis became the single most important factor derailing the movement to eliminate parole in the 1980s (Burke, 1988). It probably still is. The board's role in helping to manage the population crisis is more important now than ever. This is done formally through laws and administrative changes or informally through directions from the governor and members' personal concern for the crisis.

Managing Overcrowding Michigan became the first state to pass emergency overcrowding legislation in 1981. By 1988, twenty-one states had adopted an Emergency Powers Act, while Florida, Hawaii, Oklahoma, and Rhode Island have since developed emergency release mechanisms. The Act usually provides that inmate eligibility for parole be advanced when overcrowding reaches a predetermined level. The parole board then selects inmates for early release from this new pool of eligibles. In other states, boards have adjusted their guidelines to more nearly reflect the prison bed space available (National Institute of Corrections, 1995, pp. 3–9). The Oregon board, for example, was reported to use a flexible term-setting matrix that moved time up or down based on the level of new prison intake. Several states reinstated discretionary release or the functional equivalent. For example, Florida has now reconstituted its board. In some states, such as Texas, boards were informally instructed to establish a parole quota system so that releases would approximate admissions. Until recently when new construction was completed, North Carolina had gradually revested the board with release authority for certain offenders. Even Maine, the first state to abolish parole, has expanded the role of the clemency advisory board to process the greater number of reviews in response to overcrowding (Burke, 1988).

Apart from formal procedures, board members are well aware of the desperate need for beds and court injunctions lurking just around the corner. But "backdoor management" is not an easy task, or one that boards always relish. As gubernatorial appointees, members are part of and empowered by the same political process that causes the overcrowding in the first place.

Parole Violators Add to the Overcrowding Problem   The hope of parole as the backdoor population manager has another, darker side, however. Agents recommend and boards decide whether to return parolees to prison for violating the conditions of their release. Ironically, boards help create the same overcrowded conditions they are supposed to cure. Table 2 shows that the percent of prison admissions that were parole violators increased from 19.6 to 30.2 in ten years. Technical violators alone accounted for about 17 percent of all prison admissions in 1993—the great majority of these people would not be in prison had they not been on parole. Yet boards are even more vulnerable to criticisms for continuing a violator on parole than for releasing an inmate before the term expires. In the public's view, the parolee has already had one break by being paroled. Every serious felony committed by a continued parole violator will be viewed as a crime that would have been prevented if the board had just done its job. Never mind that the same

TABLE 2
Inmates Received in State and Federal Prisons by Admission Type and Year

Admission type*	1983	1987	1993
Total number received	232,976	324,846	489,434
Percent new court commitments	80.4	74.5	69.8
Percent parole violators	19.6	25.5	30.2
Total violators returned	45,568	82,959	147,712
Percent technical violations	47.8	61.3	56.0
Percent with new felony convictions	52.2	38.7	44.0

Excludes returning escapees and transfers.
Source: Bureau of Justice Statistics, 1984, 1988, 1994.

parolee would have committed the same or similar crime after a six-month $12,000 return to prison.

Unrealistic Parole Conditions   Unfortunately, parole conditions serve as much to comfort agencies and parole boards and help the release decision withstand public scrutiny as to establish realistic expectations for the parolee. In a 1982 survey, 135 different conditions of parole were recorded with an average number of "standard" conditions of 14.8 (Rhine et al., 1991, p. 120). Boards were asked in 1988 to indicate from a list of fourteen items which were standard conditions in their state. The most common, of course, was "obey all laws." However, 78 percent required "gainful employment" as a standard condition, 61 percent "no association with persons of criminal records," 53 percent "pay all fines and restitution," and 47 percent "support family and all dependents," none of which can consistently be met by most parolees (Rhine et al., 1991, pp. 102–107). Thus, we design systems so that almost all parolees are likely to fail at some point.

Conditions that Might Work   Realistic standard conditions would be limited to "report to your parole agent," "obey laws," and "receive permission to leave the county or state." But even realistic conditions are commonly violated. Should violators go to prison for missing a drug test, an appointment with their agent, or visiting a girl friend across the county line?

Need for Intermediate Sanctions   The second obstacle to successful guidelines is that most jurisdictions have few program or procedural options between reprimand and return to prison. Whether intermediate sanctions will reduce crime in the long run is doubtful, but they are important in legitimating the agent's recommendation and the board's decision to leave the violator in the community. Sanctions demonstrate that parole conditions are taken seriously and violations have consequences for the offender, consequences that are at least inconvenient if not painful. Since 1990, sixteen states have formulated new responses to parole violations (National Institute of Corrections, 1995, pp. 8–9). Several jurisdictions, including California and the U.S. Parole Commission, have established standards for the revocation time parolees should serve for different types of violations (Burke et al., 1990, p. 19). Others have developed guidelines for revocation and alternative dispositions. More successful attempts, such as in Washington, have used a formal decision matrix for violation dispositions or, as in Oregon, extraordinary program moneys are made available or agents have access to county jail beds for short-term incarceration. But more often, the resources to operate progressive discipline and intermediate sanctions successfully aren't there. Many jurisdictions have such limited resources that they control little more than the conditions of parole. Several states allow agents to restructure parole conditions and impose local sanctions for minor violations without board review. While it may meet a need to demonstrate that "something" was done, it's hard to see how increasing the number or stringency of conditions will prevent future violations by parolees who fail to meet the previous conditions.

Response of Parole Field Supervision

While many legislatures may have been happy to see discretionary parole release disappear, the same cannot be said for parole supervision, which has actually increased. After twenty years of sentence "reform," almost all states have retained or reinstated post-release supervision (called conditional release when it follows a fixed prison term). We see in Table 1 that the dramatic drop in parole releases was not matched by a decline in supervision. The total percent of releases under parole-type supervision in 1993 was 83.4 percent, about 1 percent above the highest point for discretionary releases in 1977. Illinois, California, and Minnesota are examples of states that adopted determinate sentences but retained post-release supervision. Several states that originally abolished supervision reintroduced a supervision component. These include Florida, Connecticut, and Washington, where supervision returned four years later after heavy lobbying by local law enforcement. (Ringel et al., 1993, p. 15). Maine developed an interesting twist on supervision. When supervision was eliminated in 1976, judges began giving "split sentences." Offenders are sentenced to a prison term, part of which is suspended, followed by a probation period. Violators are returned by the court for the suspended part of the sentence.

New Supervision Models

The first response of the parole field agencies was to improve their accountability by adopting new models of supervision. These models were intended to

1. provide an objective way of evaluating the offender's public risk and personal needs.
2. allocate resources based on need.
3. direct the agent's time by prioritizing cases.
4. provide a management information system to evaluate the process.

The models are described as "management tools," not as devices to reduce recidivism directly. Almost all states now classify parolees and almost all of these systems include an assessment of the risk posed to the public and the parolee's needs. The risk assessment devices are based on research predicting the likelihood of failure, which usually means re-arrest or revocation, supplemented by nonpredictive policy items. Most are additive checklist systems. Case factors are assigned point values. The total points determine the classification level. The majority of systems in use were adapted from the State of Wisconsin model (Baird et al., 1989).

Problems Applying Risk Assessment Scales

The new supervision models and their risk assessment instruments pose several problems for operations staff. Most scales are not purely predictive, largely because violent crimes do not predict recidivism. Even the Wisconsin model includes points for a violent commitment offense, although not supported by research (Burke, 1989). As Gottfredson and Gottfredson (1986) remarked, "Severity of the instant offense has rarely been found to be a useful predictor of danger to the public, but has been consistently used for that purpose anyway." The dilemma for risk assessment is that property and drug offenders have higher re-arrest rates (Burke et al., 1990, p. 17). Thus, predictions are not focused on those offenders of most concern to the public.

However, scholars who study "career criminals" generally conclude that recidivists are opportunists for illegal gain or advantage, jacks of all trades, and the crimes they commit are more a product of circumstance than of specialized criminal skills. Using this paradigm, the likelihood of violent recidivism is greatest for those parolees involved in the most criminal activity of any type. The more they are out and about and illegally engaged with people and their property, the greater the chances they will run into vulnerable victims without protectors or circumstances where weapons are present, threats are made, and guns go off. The findings of Holland, et al (1982) support this view. Violent recidivism was weakly predictable by extensive criminal histories but not by prior violence. Instruments have reliability problems because they are completed at the field level, usually by agents, and some items require interpretation.

Scores can also be manipulated to modify work loads. Agents can use other case factors to predetermine their preferred supervision level and then "cook the numbers" to "back into" the matching classification.

Although there is some evidence of generalizability, too many jurisdictions have adopted instruments from other states or NIC without cross validating the scales on their own offenders (Wright et al., 1984). Revalidation of existing systems is also needed. The value of revalidation was demonstrated in 1994 in the Oregon parole and probation system, where a thorough review resulted in important improvements (DeComo et al., 1995). This suggests that many instruments could profit by a similar "major tune-up" using the type of procedures outlined by Baird (1991). Yet not much revalidation work had been done until recently (Baird et al., 1989; South Carolina, 1990; Hoffman, 1994; Bonta et al., 1996).

The usefulness of recidivism scales is also limited by low correlations, although these are not particularly worse than actuarial predictions of other types of behavior. Baird has estimated that the better risk scales explain from 8 percent to 15 percent of the variance in recidivism outcomes (1991, p. 9). Klein and Caggiano (1986, p. 31) applied six well-known risk assessment models to parole outcome data from Texas, California, and Michigan. A variety of recidivism measures were used. The best overall predictive items were prior criminality, young age, drug abuse, and poor employment history. They concluded, however, that "When all the variables were used together they (six models) did not predict more than 10 percent of the variance on any measure of recidivism." Despite their low level of prediction, scales are still useful for rationally allocating resources where resources dictate that some parolees be selected for minimal supervision.

Responding to the Attack with New Programs

The second response to the attack on parole was to create new programs to reduce overcrowding and position field supervision closer to the retribution and deterrence philosophy. In keeping with these changes, agencies began allowing agents to carry concealed firearms in the 1980s. Firearms are now provided by thirty-three jurisdictions and represent a major investment of training resources, agent time, and administrative oversight. The programming innovations likewise represent a theme of control and supervision rather than service and assistance. Parolees are held more accountable and for a broader range of behavior, including alcohol and substance abuse, restitution, curfews, and service fees. Parole aims to earn its way by providing a tough legitimate alternative to continued or renewed incarceration and by enhancing public safety through rigorous rule enforcement and deterrence. Innovations include home confinement and electronic monitoring, day reporting centers, intensive supervision, boot camps, and specialized case loads. Unfortunately none of the innovations has proved very successful.

CONCLUDING REMARKS

If the last twenty years has been a period of new models and program innovations, it has also been a period lacking in focus or direction. Agencies scrambled to force old organizations into new philosophies, creating disjunctive values, goals, and activity. Many are still struggling to contribute without a coherent conceptual basis of operation or a clear sense of purpose. In one sense, these innovations are attempts to solve serious social structural problems with simple technologies and thus avoid the deep divisive issues that plague criminal justice. While much emphasis is placed on decision rules, classifications, and numbering systems, it's by no means certain that the answer lies in better numbers. Indeed, better numbers may serve only to cloud the real issues. Some managers, for example, have mistaken parolee classification for parole work itself, as if the work is done once the proper category is determined (Clear and Gallagher, 1985). At the same time, while we are creating elegant categories, many agents are not sure what to do after they ring the doorbell. Counting contacts becomes a substitute for good casework and avoids the larger issue of whether the process itself contributes anything to the social good.

REFERENCES

Baird, Christopher. 1991. "Validating Risk Assessment Instruments Used in Community Corrections." San Francisco: National Council on Crime and Delinquency.

Baird, Christopher, Richard Prewstine, and Brian Klockziem. 1989. "Revalidation of the Wisconsin Probation/Parole Classification System." San Francisco: National Council on Crime and Delinquency.

Bonta, James, William Harman, Robert Hann, and Robert Cormier. 1996. "The Prediction of Recidivism Among Federally Sentenced Offenders: A Revalidation of the SIR Scale." *Canadian Journal of Corrections* 38(1).

Burke, Peggy. 1988. "Current Issues in Parole Decisionmaking: Understanding the Past; Shaping the Future." Justice Institute COSMOS Corp., Washington, D.C.

Burke, Peggy. 1995. *Abolishing Parole: Why the Emperor Has No Clothes.* Lexington, Ky: American Probation and Parole Association.

Burke, Peggy, Linda Adams, and Becki Ney. 1990. "Policy for Parole Release and Revocation: The National Institute of Corrections 1988–89 Technical Assistance Project." Longmont, Colo.: National Institute of Corrections.

Burke, Peggy, Chris Hayes, Helen Connelly, Linda Adams, and Becki Ney. 1989. "The Institute of Corrections Model Case Management and Classification Project: A Case Study in Dissemination." Longmont, Colo.: National Institute of Corrections.

Bureau of Justice Statistics. 1984, 1988, 1994. *Sourcebook of Criminal Justice Statistics.* Washington, D.C.: U.S. Department of Justice.

Champion, Dean. 1994. *Measuring Offender Risk: A Criminal Justice Sourcebook.* Westport, Ct.: Greenwood Press.

Clear, Todd, and Kenneth Gallagher. 1985. "Parole and Probation Supervision: A Review of Current Classification Practices." *Crime and Delinquency* 31:423–43.

DeComo, Robert, Dennis Wagner, and Christ Baird. 1995. "A Course Correction in Community Corrections Using Research to Improve Policies and Programs." *Perspectives* 19(4).

Glaser, Daniel. 1962. "Prediction Tables as Accounting Devices for Judges and Parole Boards." *Crime and Delinquency* 8:239–58.

Gottfredson Stephen, and Don Gottfredson. 1986. "The Accuracy of Prediction Models." In *Criminal Careers and Career Criminals*, Vol. 2, edited by Alfred Blumstein et al. Washington D.C.: National Academy Press.

Hoffman, Peter. 1994. "Twenty Years of Operational Use of a Risk Prediction Instrument: The US Parole Commission's Salient Factor Score." *Journal of Criminal Justice*, 22(6).

Hoffman, Peter, and Sheldon Adelberg. 1980. "The Salient Factor Score: A Non Technical Overview." *Federal Probation* 44(1).

Holland, Terrill R., Norman Holt, and Gerald Beckett. 1982. "Prediction of Violent Versus Non-violent Recidivism from Prior Violent and Non-Violent Criminality." *Journal of Adnormal Psychology* 91(3).

Holt, Norman. 1995. "California's Determinate Sentencing: What Went Wrong?" *Perspectives* 19(3).

Holt, Norman, and Daniel Glaser. 1985. "Statistical Guidelines for Custodial Classification." In *Correctional Institutions*, edited by Robert Carter, Daniel Glaser, and Leslie Wilkins. 3d ed. New York: Harper and Row.

Kassebaum, Gene, David Ward, and Daniel Wilner. 1971. *Prison Treatment and Parole Survival.* New York: John Wiley.

Klein, Stephen, and Michael Caggiano. 1986. *The Prevalence, Predictability and Policy Implications of Recidivism.* Santa Monica, Calif.: Rand Corp.

Martinson, Robert. 1974. "What Works? Questions About Prison Reforms." *Public Interest,* 35:22–54.

Martinson, Robert. 1979. "New Findings, New Views: A Note of Caution Regarding Sentencing Reform." *Hofstra Law Review* 7:243–58.

Martinson, Robert, and Judith Wilks. 1977. "Save Parole Supervision." *Federal Probation* 41(3).

McCleary, Richard. 1978. *Dangerous Men: The Sociology of Parole.* Beverly Hills, Calif.: Sage.

National Institute of Corrections. 1995. "Status Report on Parole, 1995: Results of an NIC Survey." Longmont, Colo.: National Institute of Corrections.

Rhine, Edward, William Smith, and Ronald Jackson. 1991. *Paroling Authorities: Recent History and Current Practices.* Laurel, Md.: American Correctional Association.

Ringel, Cheryl, Ernest Cowles, and Thomas Castellano. 1993. "The Recasting of Parole Supervision: The Causes and Responses of Systems Under Stress." Southern Illinois University, Paper presented at the Academy of Criminal Justice Science Conference, Kansas City, Mo. Also in *Critical Issues in Crime and Justice*, edited by A.R. Roberts. Newbury Park, Calif.: Sage, 1994.

Robison, James, and Gerald Smith. 1971. "The Effectiveness of Correctional Programs." *Crime and Delinquency.* 17(1).

Rothman, David. 1980. *Conscience and Convenience: The Asylum and its Alternatives in Progressive America.* Boston: Little, Brown.

Simon, Jonathon. 1993. *Poor Discipline: Parole and the Social Control of the Underclass, 1890–1990.* Chicago: University of Chicago Press.

South Carolina Reorganization Committee. 1990. "Evaluation and Validation of the South Carolina Parole Risk Assessment Instrument."

von Hirsch, Andrew. 1976. *Doing Justice: The Choice of Punishments.* New York: Hill and Wang.

Wiggins, Jerry. 1973. *Personality and Prediction.* Reading, Mass.: Addison Wesley.

Wright, K., Todd Clear, and P. Dickinson. 1984. "Universal Application of Probation Risk-Assessment Instruments: A Critique." *Criminology,* 22(2).

Between Prision and Probation: Intermediate Sanctions

PATRICK A. LANGAN

Latest state court figures indicate that nationwide the most severe sentence, prison, was given to 46% of convicted felons, and the least severe, probation, was given to 47% (*1*). Hence, more than 90% of all convicted felons received either the most or the least severe of the widely permissible penalties. Some observers recommend replacing current sentencing practices with a more graduated punishment system. Between prison and probation would exist a range of highly used and rigorously enforced intermediate sanctions. A felon receiving an intermediate sanction would be placed under the supervision of a probation officer but, unlike routine probation, would be closely supervised through electronically monitored house arrest, weekly contacts with the probation officer, and drug testing, and would be subjected to such additional penalties as a split sentence (a jail stay as part of the probation), a heavy fine, and community service.

Under proposed schemes, candidates for intermediate sanctions would include some of the felons now receiving minimal probation supervision (*2*) and some of those currently receiving prison. Regarding the latter, proponents argue that 15 to 25% of felons today receiving a prison sentence could be safely diverted and given an intermediate sanction in the community (*2, 3*).

Expanded use of intermediate sanctions has a variety of overlapping aims, including cutting government spending by reducing reliance on costly prisons, satisfying the public's desire for punishment through penalties other than imprisonment, and making probation a more credible penalty to the public by making prison a real possibility for any breach of sanction requirements (*2*).

To learn more about the current use of intermediate sanctions in the justice system, I analyzed results from a follow-up survey of convicted adult felons placed on state probation in 1986. The survey tracked 12,370 probationers for 3 years, from 1986 to 1989. Statistically weighted, the 12,370 represented 79,000 probationers.

State courts in 1986 sentenced 268,000 adult felons to probation (*4*). The estimate is based on samples of cases drawn from court and prosecutor records of 100 counties in 37 states selected to be nationally representative.

The author is with the Bureau of Justice Statistics, U.S. Department of Justice, 633 Indiana Avenue, NW, Washington, DC 20531, USA.

Samples from 32 of the counties in 17 states, consisting of 12,370 adult probationers altogether, formed the subjects for the follow-up. In all, 79,000 felons were given probation in the 32 counties in 1986, approximately one-fourth of the national total. The follow-up survey is based on information contained in state criminal history repositories and probation agency files.

NONCOMPLIANCE AND LAX ENFORCEMENT

The follow-up investigated the prevalence of 12 intermediate sanctions. In all, 91% of the follow-up subjects had at least 1 of the 12 (Table 1), revealing that a graduated punishment system already exists. Whether probationers actually complied with sanction requirements was also investigated with survey data available on 10 of the 12 sanctions. I focused my analysis on sanctioned probationers who completed their probation term by the time of the follow-up in 1989 (22% of follow-up subjects). Results indicated that sizable numbers were discharged from probation before having fully complied, including 24% of those ordered to participate in alcohol treatment, 20% ordered for mental health counseling, 32% ordered for drug treatment, 25% ordered placed in a residential facility, 33% ordered for drug testing, 31% ordered for house arrest, 35% ordered for day reporting, 21% ordered to

TABLE 1

Intermediate Sanctions Among Probation Follow-Up Subjects: Their Frequency of Use and Relationship to Rearrest Rates. S, Sanctioned; U, Unsanctioned.

Intermediate sanction	Sanctioned (%)	Rearrested for felony (%)	
		S	U
Any sanction	91	45	37*
Treatment			
Alcohol treatment	14	38	43*
Counseling	10	35	43*
Drug treatment	23	50	50
Surveillance			
Residential placement	5	44	42
Drug testing	31	52	48
House arrest	1	42	43
Day reporting	1	27	43*
Intensive supervision	10	56	39*
Retribution			
Split sentence	50	50	37*
Community service	12	35	43*
Supervision fees	32	42	42
Victim restitution	29	40	43

Significant difference (P < 0.05) between sanctioned and unsanctioned.

perform community service, 69% ordered to pay supervision fees, and 40% ordered to make restitution.

Altogether, 49% of sanctioned subjects had not fully complied by the time of their probation discharge. Of the noncompliant probationers, only a minority of them (21%) had been punished with jail confinement for their noncompliance. One reason more were not punished is that disciplinary hearings were not held in most of the noncompliance cases (52%).

These results suggest that, at present, intermediate sanctions are not rigorously enforced. One reason may be inadequate resources for enforcing and monitoring drug tests, house arrests, community service, payment of fines, treatment participation, and the like. From 1977 (the first year of national probation expenditure data) to 1990 (the latest year), prison, jail, parole, and probation populations all about tripled in size. Yet only spending for prisons and jails had accelerated growth in overall government expenditures. In 1990, prison and jail spending accounted for two cents of every state and local dollar spent, twice the amount spent in 1977. Spending for probation and parole accounted for two-tenths of one cent of every dollar spent in 1990, unchanged from what it was in 1977.

Inadequate funding may not be the sole reason for lax enforcement. To some extent, financial penalties are not enforced because collecting fines is not a priority of many probation agencies, and neither is it something that the agencies generally do well, according to Morris and Tonry (2). They recommend that this activity be privatized (2). Regarding intermediate sanctions more generally, Petersilia (3) discussed the possibility of having probation surveillance performed by police rather than probation agencies, explaining that police are better structured, manned, and trained for that activity than probation agencies.

Whether or not such reforms are adopted, given current indications of widespread noncompliance with intermediate sanctions, the likely net impact of a policy making prison a real possibility for any breach of requirements would actually be to raise, not reduce, prison population. To explain, prison diversion would reduce prison population, but the reduction might be more than offset were offenders currently receiving probation routinely sent to prison for sanction violations.

PRISON DIVERSION

One of the proposed ways of expanding intermediate sanctions usage is through prison diversion. Felons who would otherwise receive a prison sentence would instead be placed on probation, where they would be subject to rigorously enforced intermediate sanctions. The proposal raises two policy issues: (i) How well at safeguarding the public does probation do compared to prison? (ii) Does probation with intermediate sanctions provide greater safety than routine probation?

Regarding the first question, I compared rates of rearrest for serious crime (felonies or serious misdemeanors) between the probation follow-up and a follow-up survey of felons released from prison in 1983 (5). In all, about 63% of 109,000 released prisoners were rearrested within 3 years; whereas, 43% of 79,000 probationers were rearrested within 3 years. But these data do not warrant a conclusion about whether probation is better than prison. Naturally probationers did better than prisoners. In large part they were selected for probation precisely because they did not have an extensive prior criminal record and therefore posed a lesser threat of continued criminality. Comparison of the subjects from the two follow-ups matched on a measure of prior record (prior arrests) (Table 2) illustrates the impact of the selection process in producing widely different overall rearrest rates between probation and prison. Probationers had a rearrest rate 20 percentage points below prisoners. However, after matching on prior arrests, this difference disappeared. That is, had the probation follow-up had the same mix of first offenders and repeaters as the prison follow-up, the overall rearrest rate of probationers would have differed little from that of prisoners. Thus, neither prison nor probation is clearly superior to the other in deterring future crime among those punished. These results agree with numerous past recidivism studies involving comparisons of probationers and prisoners matched on prior record. When a difference was found, sometimes it favored probation, other times it favored prison, but the difference usually amounted to no more than a few percent, hardly compelling evidence of the advantage of one sentence over the other given the uncertainty about the adequacy of matching that invariably exists in studies of this kind.

TABLE 2
Probation (Prob.) and Prison Follow-Up Subjects Compared on (i) Percentage Rearrested, by Prior Arrests, and (ii) Prior Arrest Percentage Distribution. The 43% Rearrest Rate for Probation Includes Cases Missing Information on Prior Arrests.

Number of Prior Arrests	Rearrested Within 3 Years (%)		Follow-up (%)	
	Prob.	Prison	Prob.	Prison
Total	43.0	62.5	100.0	100.0
0	36.2	38.1	56.6	9.1
1	51.1	48.2	19.9	10.8
2	58.3	54.7	10.7	10.8
3	63.0	58.1	5.6	9.7
4	72.1	59.3	3.4	8.0
5	59.8	64.8	2.0	7.0
6–9	69.3	67.7	1.5	18.8
10 or more	86.2	78.8	0.3	25.9

To evaluate the second question, I compared recidivism rates between probation follow-up subjects who received a particular intermediate sanction and those not receiving that sanction. Results were mixed (Table 1). Certain sanctions were associated with reduced rearrest rates during the 3-year follow-up period (alcohol treatment, psychological counseling, day reporting, community service), some with increased rates (intensive supervision, split sentences). Other sanctions were unrelated to rearrest rates (drug treatment, residential placement, drug testing, house arrest, supervision fees, victim restitution). However, these results are ambiguous because sanctioned and unsanctioned probationers differed in terms of risk of continued criminality. Consequently, the pre-existing risk difference rather than the effect of a sanction could possibly account for any rearrest rate difference observed between sanctioned and unsanctioned probationers. To illustrate, intensive supervision was generally for high-risk offenders, such as persons with prior arrests and convictions, frequent drug abusers, males, and the unemployed. Intensively supervised probationers had a higher rearrest rate than others, not necessarily because intensive supervision made them worse but in large part because they were high-risk offenders and high-risk offenders had high rearrest rates. Similarly, probationers ordered to receive alcohol treatment had a lower rearrest rate than others, not necessarily because treatment helped but in part because offenders with alcohol problems tended to be older than others and age was inversely related to recidivism.

Randomized experiments with intermediate sanctions overcome these interpretational difficulties. To date only intensive supervision has been subjected to such tests. But because intensive supervision is actually a combination of intermediate sanctions (for example, frequent drug testing combined with house arrest and weekly contacts with a probation officer), their results have significance beyond the question of whether one sanction alone is effective. Unfortunately, experimental results have been disappointing. No difference has been found in recidivism rates between probationers randomly assigned to intensive supervision and those assigned to routine probation (6). Petersilia and Turner interpreted results as challenging the basic premise of intensive supervision: "that increased surveillance will act as a constraint on the probationer and the likelihood of detection will act as a deterrent to crime."

If Petersilia and Turner are correct, whatever public safety risks are associated with prison diversion would apparently be undiminished by imposing intermediate sanctions on diverted offenders. Relative to public safety, the best that can be said for diversion is that probation does as well as prison at deterring future crime among those punished. Still, one crime reduction benefit of prison over probation is clearly sacrificed by diversion: prison's capacity to protect the public by physically restraining, or incapacitating, the offender.

How many crimes will be committed that would have been averted through incapacitation depends on the target of the diversion policy. A policy of diverting first offenders (those with no prior arrest) would reduce prison use by 9% but add to probation caseloads some number of first of-fenders with an overall 3-year rearrest rate of 38% (Table 2). Some, but not all, of the 38% would have been averted. Diverting both first-time and sec-ond-time offenders would reduce prison use by about 20% (9.1 + 10.8%) but the rearrest rate of the added caseload members would then climb to 44% (the weighted average of 38% and 48%).

Unless prisons make offenders profounding worse (and there is no evi-dence of that), and unless removing an offender from society merely creates an enticing job opening for an otherwise law-abiding person to fill (and there is no persuasive evidence of that either, certainly not for most offenses), such prison diversion policies would increase the level of crime above what it oth-erwise would be (7).

It is not obvious, however, that the increase would be large enough to detect in either of the nation's two crime indicators: the Federal Bureau of Investigation's measure of crimes reported to police, and the Bureau of Jus-tice Statistics' (U.S. Department of Justice) measure of both reported and unreported crimes. Separate studies found that the potential incapacitative impact of, first doubling, and then tripling the size of the U.S. prison popu-lation, was nontrivial: doubling the prison population from 1973 to 1982 po-tentially reduced reported crime by 10 to 20% below what it otherwise would have been, thereby potentially preventing from 66,000 to 190,000 robberies and from 350,000 to 900,000 burglaries in 1982 alone (8); tripling the prison population from 1975 to 1989 potentially reduced reported and unreported violent crime by 10 to 15% below what it would have been, thereby poten-tially preventing a conservatively estimated 390,000 murders, rapes, rob-beries, and aggravated assaults in 1989 alone (9). Fewer than 390,000 would have been prevented had prison diversion proponents succeeded in at least slowing prison population growth from 1975 to 1989. How many fewer is dif-ficult to say, but the number could have been substantial even under a mod-est diversion policy. For example, the cost, in terms of violent crimes not prevented, of a 15% diversion policy would have been about 90,000 victims in 1989 if diversion were not done selectively. The cost, if done selectively, remains for prison diversion proponents to say.

REFERENCES AND NOTES

1. P. Langan and R. Solari, *National Judicial Reporting Program, 1990* (Bureau of Justice Statistics, U.S. Department of Justice, Washington, DC, 1993), tables 1.2 and 3.2.

2. N. Morris and M. Tonry, *Between Prison and Probation: Intermediate Punish-ments in a Rational Sentencing System* (Oxford Univ. Press, New York, 1990). See especially pp. 3, 13, 19, and 136.

3. J. Petersilia, *Expanding Options for Criminal Sentencing* (Rand Corp., Santa Monica, CA, 1987). See especially pp. 79 and 86.

4. P. Langan and M. Cunniff, *Recidivism of Felons on Probation, 1986–89* (Bureau of Justice Statistics, U.S. Department of Justice, Washington, DC, 1992), p. 3.

5. A. Beck and B. Shipley, *Recidivism of Prisoners Released in 1983* (Bureau of Justice Statistics, U.S. Department of Justice, Washington, DC, 1989), table 11.

6. J. Petersilia and S. Turner, *J. Crim. Law Crimin.* 82, 3 (1992), p. 651; C. Lichtman and S. Smock, *J. Res. Crime Delinq.* 18, 1 (1981), p. 81; M. Folkard, D. Smith, D. Smith, *IMPACT. Intensive Matched Probation and After-Care Treatment: Vol. II. The Results of the Experiment* (Home Office, London, 1976), p. 14.

7. M. Tonry, *Crime Delinq.* 36 1 (1990), p. 183.

8. A. Blumstein, J. Cohen, J. Roth, C. Visher, Eds., *Criminal Careers and Career Criminals* (National Academy Press, Washington, DC, 1986), vol. 1, p. 5. I derived estimates of the number of crimes prevented from data in table 5-1.

9. J. Cohen and J. Canela-Cacho, untitled paper cited in A. Reiss Jr. and J. Roth, Eds., *Understanding and Preventing Violence* (National Academy Press, Washington, DC, 1993), p. 293.

CHAPTER **3**

The Impact of Community Corrections on Offender Recidivism and Community Safety

INTRODUCTION

The most common question asked about community corrections is "Does it work?" And by "work," most mean whether the person granted probation or parole has refrained from further crime, or reduced his or her "recidivism." Recidivism is currently the primary outcome measure for community corrections, as it is for all corrections programs.

There are two stories to be told in terms of probation recidivism rates. On the one hand, most persons who are granted probation after being convicted of a lower level misdemeanor offense successfully complete their terms of probation. Of course, most of these probationers received few services and little supervision, so in essence, they were "rehabilitated" either as a result of their own efforts or simply because being placed on probation served some deterrent function and encouraged them to refrain from further crime.

The other story is one that is captured in the two articles in this chapter. These articles show that for *felons* (i.e., offenders convicted of felony, not misdemeanor, crimes), the recidivism rates are high, particularly in jurisdictions that use probation extensively, where offenders are serious to begin with, and where supervision is minimal. Michael Geerken and Hennessey Hayes summarize previous probation studies and show that felon rearrest rates vary from a low of 12 percent to a high of 65 percent. They show that felony probation recidivism rates seem to vary greatly from place to place, depending on the seriousness of the underlying population characteristics, length of follow-up, and the surveillance provided (higher surveillance ususally means higher recidivism rates). Parolee recidivism rates are even higher than probationer rates in many locations, as revealed in Norm Holt's

article contribution in Chapter 2. Of course, parolees are more serious offenders as a group than probationers, so higher recidivism rates are to be
expected.

But the Geerken and Hayes article makes an important contribution besides simply providing a good overview of felony probationer recidivism
rates. They examine the risk posed by felony probationers and parolees in
a unique and different way. They ask, what is the contribution of those on
probation and parole to the overall crime problem in a given community?
Their analysis shows that in New Orleans from 1973 to 1986, 8 percent of
all adult arrests for burglary or armed robbery involved offenders on probation and about 2 percent of all adult arrests for these crimes involved offenders on parole. They note that it is one thing to say that over half of probationers and parolees recidivate. It is quite another to conclude that
probationers and parolees are principally responsible for the level of crime
in a given community.

The Petersilia and Turner article compares the recidivism rates of felony
probationers with those of a matched sample of offenders who were sentenced to prison in California. After all, the courts currently use two major
options for criminal offenders: probation and prison. It is not particularly
useful to look at probation in a vacuum, but rather it is more instructive to
compare these two major sentencing options in terms of costs, public safety,
and offender recidivism.

After controlling for the known factors associated with both prison sentencing and recidivism, Petersilia and Turner found that across offender
types and recidivism measures, imprisonment was associated with a *higher*
probability of recidivism than was probation. For example, property offenders who were sentenced to prison were 17 percent more likely than the
matched probationers to have a new filed charge, and were 14 percent more
likely to have a new conviction. Of course, these results must be viewed as
suggestive rather than definitive since the prison versus probation sentence
was not imposed randomly at conviction, and it may have been related to
factors other than those controlled for in the statistical analysis. Nonetheless, the results suggest that prison certainly does not *reduce* offender recidivism and may well increase it.

The recidivism data presented for both prisoners and probationers are
high enough to argue for both increasing the incapacitation period for prisoners and finding some better means for incapacitating probationers.
Clearly, options other than routine probation and prison are sorely needed
for less serious felony offenders.

Hence the interest in intermediate sanctions. The hope is that intermediate sanctions may be feasible and cost-effective alternatives to prison for
the offenders not yet committed to serious criminality. These alternatives
could extend the incapacitation effect to some of the felony offenders who
are presently only nominally supervised on traditional probation. They could
also ease prison crowding by supervising less serious offenders in the com-

munity and avoiding any negative effects that imprisonment or having a prison record may have. Finally, such programs may cost less than the present total system costs for these offenders. Whether these lofty goals can be realized in practice is the subject of the next section.

Probation and Parole: Public Risk and the Future of Incarceration Alternatives

MICHAEL R. GEERKEN AND HENNESSEY D. HAYES
The Orleans Parish Criminal Sheriff's Office and Tulane University

The use of alternatives to incarceration has become very controversial in recent years. Rapidly increasing jail and prison populations have led to calls for increasing the use of alternatives, while continued high crime rates have led to demands for reductions in their use through mandatory sentencing and tough sentencing guidelines.

The contradictory pressures of jail and prison overcrowding and high crime rates have resulted in a heated debate over the continued use of alternatives to incarceration. Proponents of alternatives believe that diversion from incarceration serves the interests of the criminal justice system and the offender. Alternatives help to lessen the administrative pressures of increasing jail and prison populations and they facilitate the reform efforts of offenders. On the other hand, those who are skeptical about the effectiveness of alternatives argue that offenders rarely reform on release from custody, and that a significant percentage of all offenders released through some form of incarceration alternative continue to commit crimes. Those offenders are responsible, they argue, for a significant amount of all reported crime. For example, Petersilia reported that approximately two-thirds of a sample of felony probationers in California were rearrested during a 40-month follow-up period. The results of this study received a great

This research was supported by the National Institute of Justice, U.S. Department of Justice, grants 86-IJ-CX-0021 and 90-IJ-CX-0019.

Michael R. Geerken is Chief Administrative Officer for the Orleans Paris Criminal Sheriff's Office and Adjunct Associate Professor of Sociology at Tulane University. He has published in the areas of deterrence theory, incapacitation, geographical mobility, the psychological effects of sex and marital roles, drug use, survey methodology, and the uses of official crime statistics.

Hennessey D. Hayes is a research analyst at the Orleans Parish Criminal Sheriff's Office and a Ph.D. candidate, Department of Sociology, Tulane University. He has recently published work on federal civil procedure. His current research areas are juvenile justice policy, inmate classification, and juvenile delinquency causation.

"Probation and Parole: Public Risk and the Future of Incarceration Alternatives" by Michael R. Geerken and Hennessey D. Hayes, from *Criminology*, Vol. 31, No. 4, 1993, pp. 549–564. Reprinted by permission of the authors and the American Society of Criminology.

deal of attention, and the effectiveness of felony probation was seriously questioned.

Other research on probation, however, has shown that the results of Petersilia's 1985 study may be unique to felons in California. Vito, who followed a sample of felony probationers in Kentucky for 36 months, found that only 22% were rearrested. Likewise, McGaha followed a sample of felony probationers in Missouri for 40 months and found that only 22% were rearrested. These authors concluded that probation for felony offenders is relatively effective and that failure rates of 22% do not warrant abolishment of probation as a sentencing alternative.

In addition to these studies, Petersilia et al. reevaluated their sample in 1986 of felony probationers. In the second study probationers were matched with a sample of prison releasees, and the recidivism rates of both groups were compared. The authors found that those released from prison recidivated at higher rates than did the probationers.

Yet there remains a degree of skepticism among some criminal justice professionals and researchers about the effectiveness of alternatives to incarceration for felony offenders. In fact, our own informal discussions with a number of criminologists convince us that it is commonly believed that probationers and parolees, in particular, are responsible for a significant percentage of crime. In this paper we examine the evidence on which this belief is based.

We begin by summarizing the literature on probation and parole effectiveness and then we add results from our study of a sample of probated and paroled offenders arrested for burglary or armed robbery in New Orleans, Louisiana. While these results are indicative of the effectiveness of specific incarceration alternatives for the offender, they offer little information about the impact these alternatives have on the incapacitative effect of the criminal justice system.

In this paper we argue that measures of crimes committed while under alternative forms of supervision do not provide an appropriate basis for making policy recommendations about the use of such alternatives. Instead, the *contribution* of these crimes to the overall crime rate is the proper framework within which to formulate policy and provides an upper limit to the impact any restriction in the use of alternatives can have. Thus, we estimate the percentage of crime committed by persons on probation or parole to obtain a more valid estimate of the loss of incapacitative effect caused by continued use of these alternatives.

RESEARCH ON PROBATION AND PAROLE EFFECTIVENESS

A relatively recent review of research on probation prior to the 1980s shows that the percentage of probationers who "fail" (defined in various ways across studies) ranges anywhere from 16% to 55% (Allen et al., 1985; see

Table 1). Studies that defined failure as a reconviction yielded the lowest failure rates because probationers are more likely to avoid reconviction than rearrest (Sutherland et al., 1992:460).

A more recent study conducted by the Rand Corporation examined the success or failure rates of a sample of 1,672 offenders convicted of felonies in Los Angeles and Alameda counties, California (Petersilia, 1985a, 1985b; Petersilia et al., 1985). They found that approximately two-thirds (65%) of the offenders were arrested before their probation period expired. In addition, 51% of the sample members were reconvicted and 34% were reincarcerated. The authors concluded that use of probation as a sentencing alternative should perhaps be reduced for felony offenders and that perhaps one viable alternative sentence for felony offenders would be the increased use of intensive supervision (ISP), a form of probation requiring several contact visits and, in most cases, ongoing drug testing. They cautioned however, that ISP programs should be sufficiently evaluated before their use is promoted for all felony offenders.

In a study released by the Bureau of Justice Statistics in 1992 on the recidivism rates of probated felons, the authors reported that, of approximately 79,000 felons sentenced to probation in state courts in 32 U.S. counties, 43% were rearrested for a felony within three years of sentencing.

Whitehead examined the effectiveness of probation for a sample of New Jersey probationers. Unlike the studies reviewed by Allen et al., Whitehead varied his measure of recidivism and noted the effects on failure rates. When the measure was rearrest, 36% of probationers failed. However, when the measure was incarceration, the failure rate dropped to 15%. These rates were observed after three years of follow-up. After four years of follow-up, 40% were rearrested, but only 17% were reincarcerated.

The use of parole for the serious offender raises similar concerns about recidivism and public safety. Based on figures provided in the Uniform Parole Reports, Allen et al. reported that for 1979 approximately 25% of all felons released on parole were rearrested before the expiration of their term. They noted, however, that some of the failures were due to violations of the conditions of parole. In a more recent study, conducted by the Attorney General's Office for the state of Hawaii, researchers found that, of 366 offenders (approximately 68% of whom were arrested for an index offense) released on parole, approximately 46% were rearrested before their term expired. In an even more recent study, Gould et al. followed a sample of 102 nonviolent offenders released on parole from the Louisiana Department of Public Safety and Corrections for 12 months. They found that, when failure was defined as "revocation of the parole status" (p. 11), the failure rate observed was approximately 25%.

We have calculated failure rates, for probation and parole, for a group of burglary and armed robbery offenders whose 1974–1986 criminal justice records were assembled for the New Orleans Offender Study (Geerken et al., 1993, see Table 2). We selected the 4,160 terms of probation and the 327 terms

TABLE 1
Studies Reporting Recidivism Rates for Probationers

Study	Instant offense	Follow-up period	Failure criterion	Failure rate (%)
Caldwell (1951)	Internal Revenue Laws (72%)	Postprobation: $5^1/_2$–$11^1/_2$ years	Conviction	16.4
Davis (1964)	Burglary; forgery and checks	To termination: 4–7 years	2 or more violations/ revocations (technical and new offenses)	30.2
England (1955)	Bootlegging (48%) and forgery	Postprobation: 6–12 years	Conviction	17.7
Frease (1964)		On probation: 18–30 months	Inactive letter, bench warrant, revocation	20.2
Landis (1969)	Auto theft, forgery, and checks	To termination	Revocation (technical and new offenses)	52.5
Irish (1972)	Larceny and burglary	Postprobation: minimum of 4 years	Arrest or conviction	41.5
Comptroller General (1976)		Postprobation: 20-month average	Revocation and post-release conviction	55.0
Kusuda (1976)	Property	To termination: 1–2 years	Revocation	18.3
Missouri Division of Probation and Parole (1976)	Burglary, larceny, and vehicle theft	Postprobation: 6 months– 7 years	Arrest and conviction	30.0
Irish (1979)	Property	Postprobation: 3–4 years	Arrest	29.6
Petersilia (1985a)[a]	Felonies	40 months from term initiation	Re-arrest	65
Vito (1986)[a]	Felonies	36 months from term initiation	Re-arrest	22
McGaha et al. (1987)[a]	Felonies	40 months from term initiation	Re-arrest	22
Clarke et al. (1988)[a]	Felonies	3 years from term initiation	Re-arrest	33
Irish (1989)[a]	Felonies	5 years from term initiation	Re-arrest	12
			Violations	6
			Re-arrests and Violations	26
Jones (1991)[a]	Felonies and misdemeanors	From term initiation to 5-1-87 (median 3.4 years at risk)	Re-arrest	39

Whitehead (1991)[a]	Felonies	3 and 4 years from term initiation		3 & 4 yrs.
			Re-arrest	36, 40
			Reconvicted	31, 35
			Incarcerated	15, 17
			Imprisoned	9, 11
Langan and Cunniff (1992)[a]	Felonies	3 years from term initiation	Re-arrest	43
Geerken and Hayes (1993)[b]	Index offenses	To term expiration	Re-arrest	50

Source: Harry E. Allen et al. (1979:35).
[a] These studies do not appear in the original table but are included here to provide more recent information on probation effectiveness.
[b] Result extracted from Table 2 of this paper.

of parole that began for sample members between January 1, 1974 and December 31, 1981. Fifty percent of the probationers and 46% of the parolees were rearrested for an index offense during their period of supervision.

The results of the studies we reviewed along with the results from our sample indicate that there is a great deal of inconsistency in the degree of failure observed across samples and jurisdictions. Including more recent studies of probation effectiveness and the probation effectiveness observed for our sample with those reviewed by Allen et al. (1985; see Table 1), the range of failure rates is 12% to 65%. The failure rates reported in Table 1

TABLE 2
Probation and Parole Failure Rates, by Failure Criterion, for Persons Placed on Probation, 1974 through 1986

Failure criterion	Probation (N = 4,160)			Parole (N = 327)		
	Percent failed	Number failed	Mean days to failure	Percent failed	Number failed	Mean days to failure
Reincarceration in penitentiary	31.0	1,291	617	20.8	68	579
Violent index arrest	38.7	1,611	395	34.3	112	409
Any index arrest	50.0	2,081	356	45.6	149	362
Any index or drug arrest	55.5	2,309	343	49.9	163	338
Any arrest except alcohol-related and traffic	65.6	2,731	315	60.9	199	319
Any arrest except traffic	69.8	2,902	300	63.3	207	301
Any nontraffic arrest including technical violations	70.5	2,932	299	64.5	211	299

are inconsistent for a variety of reasons. First, researchers still have not arrived at a consensus on what the definition of probation failure should be. Second, the follow-up periods are markedly dissimilar across studies. Third, offender populations and data collection and recordkeeping methods vary significantly across jurisdictions.

Regardless of the degree of inconsistency in reported success or failure of probation and parole across studies, one general conclusion emerges: if the criterion for failure is rearrest, a significant proportion of offenders placed on probation or parole will recidivate before their term expires. Including results obtained from our own data, from one-third to two-thirds of all probationers were rearrested, and from one-quarter to one-half of all parolees were rearrested.

These failure rates are substantial enough to warrant concern over the future use of probation and parole. Given the high failure rates and large number of offenders under probation or parole supervision, it can be argued that the elimination of these alternatives would result in a significant decrease in crime. Indeed, the potential effect on the crime rate of reducing the use of probation and parole—and substituting imprisonment—is important for policy. But the proper measure of this effect is not the probation or parole failure rate, regardless of the criterion one uses to measure failure. Instead, the percentage of all crimes committed by persons on probation or parole provides an estimate of the potential effect on the crime rate of replacing these forms of supervision with imprisonment and, therefore, of the incapacitative effect lost through these alternatives. To our knowledge, such a calculation has not been made.

Below, we attempt to answer the following question: What reduction in crime might be achieved through a reduction in the use of probation and parole? This question has not been addressed by researchers on alternatives to incarceration. The answer to the question is both relevant and important if informed decisions are to be made about the future of sentencing alternatives for serious offenders.

DATA

The official record data base of the New Orleans Offender Study contains the 1974–1986 arrest, incarceration, and probation and parole supervision histories of the 22,497 individuals who were arrested for burglary or armed robbery in New Orleans from 1973 through 1986.

METHOD

To determine the impact that probated or paroled offenders have on the burglary and armed robbery rate, we examined the percentage of all burglary and armed robbery arrests between 1974 and 1986 that involved persons on probation or parole at the time. The New Orleans Offender Study data base is uniquely suited to making this calculation because it includes every arrest for burglary and every arrest for armed robbery in New Orleans during the study period and the supervision status of the arrestee.

Note that we can determine the probation and parole status of the offender only for arrests rather than crimes. In this analysis we assume, therefore, that the probability of arrest after commission of a crime is no different for probationers/parolees than for nonprobationers/nonparolees. Evidence suggests, however, that probationers' offenses are more likely to be detected (MacKenzie, 1991; Turner et al., 1992).

RESULTS

Table 3 indicates that only about 8% of adult arrests for burglary or armed robbery involved offenders on probation. Between 1% and 2% of all adult arrests for these crimes involved offenders on parole.

These percentages are contrary to expectation and surprisingly low. They suggest that even the complete elimination of probation and parole would have a very negligible effect on the burglary and armed robbery rates since more than 90 percent of all burglaries and armed robberies were committed by persons *not* on probation or parole at the time of their arrest. We draw no conclusion about the frequency of criminal activity of probationers or parolees compared with other groups of offenders. We argue only that since a low percentage of all burglary and armed robbery arrests are of persons on probation or parole at the time, policy changes tightening or eliminating these forms of supervision can affect only a small percentage of these crimes. Specifically, we argue that even complete abolishment of probation and parole would not affect the crime rate by more than 10 percent for either burglary or armed robbery. Note that these results measure the percentage of *adult* arrests involving persons under probation or parole supervision. The percentage of *all* arrests that could be affected by adult probation/parole policy is about 6%.

The percentage of all index charges for the study population while on adult probation is 6.3%; on adult parole, 0.9%. Since we do not have a complete count of all index arrests—only those for this population—the results

TABLE 3
Percentage of Burglary and Armed Robbery Arrests Between 1974 and 1986 for Persons on Probation and Parole

Index offense	Percent arrests of persons on probation (*N*)	Percent arrests of persons on parole (*N*)	Total arrests
Burglary	8.1 (1,981)	1.3 (320)	24,520
Armed robbery	8.4 (1,100)	1.8 (233)	13,020

for index crimes other than burglary and armed robbery must be interpreted with caution. Nevertheless, it is likely that policy changes tightening probation and parole would have a minimal effect on other index offenses as well.

THE LIMITS OF "GET TOUGH" POLICY

We acknowledge that caution must be exercised whenever one considers the results of a study limited in offender type and jurisdiction. Our purpose here has not been a complete evaluation of probation and parole policies in New Orleans, but rather a determination of the impact that elimination of these alternatives would have on the incapacitative effect of the criminal justice system. While the failure rates for the New Orleans Offender Study sample add to the body of literature on probation and parole effectiveness, our focus is primarily on the finding that these high failure rates for burglary and armed robbery are coupled with a minimal loss of incapacitative effect for these offenses.

This finding, that the incapacitative effects of probation and parole elimination are minimal, is both surprising and important. These results do not provide the means to make precise estimates of the effect of changes in probation and parole policy. They do, however, provide an upper limit of the effect any *tightening* of probation and parole policies would have on the crime rate through an increase in incapacitation—almost certainly less than 10%. This is true both for a serious property crime—burglary—and the most frequent violent crime—armed robbery.

In summary, the results of this study cannot be construed either as support for the abolishment of probation or parole or the increased use of these alternatives. The results do, however, dispel a commonly held belief among many criminal justice professionals and some researchers, that is, that probationers and parolees are responsible for a large percentage of crime.

REFERENCES

Allen, H.E., E.W. Carlson, and E.C. Parks

1979   Critical Issues in Adult Probation. Washington, D.C.: Law Enforcement Assistance Administration.

Allen, Harry E., Chris W. Eskridge, Edward J. Latessa, and Gennaro F. Vito

1985   Probation and parole effectiveness. In Harry E. Allen, Chris W. Eskridge, Edward J. Latessa, and Gennaro F. Vito (eds.) Probation and Parole in America. New York: Free Press.

Attorney General's Office, State of Hawaii

1989   Parole and Recidivism. Honolulu: Hawaii Criminal Justice Data Center.

Caldwell, Morris G.

1951   Review of a new type of probation study made in Alabama. Federal Probation 15:3–11.

Clarke, Stevens H., Yuan-Huei W. Lin, and W. LeAnn Wallace

1988   Probationer recidivism in North Carolina: Measurement and classification of risk. Institute of Government, University of North Carolina at Chapel Hill.

Comptroller General of the United States

1976   State and County Probation: Systems in Crisis, Report to the Congress of the United States. Government Printing Office, Washington, D.C.

Davis, George F.

1964   A study of adult probation violation rates by means of the cohort approach. Journal of Criminal Law, Criminology and Police Science 55:70–85.

England, Ralph W.

1955   A study of postprobation recidivism among five hundred federal offenders. Federal Probation 19:10–16.

Frease, Dean E.

1964   Factors Related To Probation Outcome. Olympia, Washington: Department of Institutions, Board of Prison Terms and Paroles, Section on Research and Program Analysis.

Geerken, Michael and Hennessey D. Hayes

1992   The New Orleans Offender Study: Codebook for official criminal history datasets. National Institute of Justice, Washington, D.C.

Geerken, Michael, Alfred Miranne, and Mary Baldwin Kennedy

1993   The New Orleans Offender Study: Development of official record databases. Report to the National Institute of Justice. Washington, D.C.

Gould, Larry A., Doris Layton MacKenzie, and William Bankston

1991   A comparison of models of parole outcome. Paper presented at the Annual Meeting of the American Society of Criminology, San Francisco.

Irish, James F.

1972   Probation and its Effect on Recidivism: An Evaluative Research Study of Probation in Nassau County, New York. Nassau County Probation Department, Mineola, New York.

1979   Probation and Recidivism. Nassau County Probation Department, Mineola, New York.

1989   Probation and recidivism: A study of probation adjustment and its relationship to post-probation outcome for adult criminal offenders. Nassau County Probation Department, Mineola, New York.

Jones, Peter R.

1991   The risk of recidivism: Evaluating the public-safety of a community corrections program. Journal of Criminal Justice 19:49–66.

Kusuda, Paul H.

1976   1974 Probation and Parole Terminations. Division of Corrections, Madison, Wisconsin.

Landis, Judson R., James K. Mercer, and Carole E. Wolff

1969   Success and failure of adult probationers in California. Journal of Research in Crime and Delinquency 6:34–40.

Langan, Patrick A. and Mark A. Cunniff

1992   Recidivism of Felons on Probation, 1986–1989. Bureau of Justice Statistics Special Report. Washington, D.C.: U.S. Department of Justice.

MacKenzie, Doris Layton

1991   The parole performance of offenders released from shock incarceration (boot camp prisons): A survival time analysis. Journal of Quantitative Criminology 7:213–236.

McGaha, Johnny, Michael Fichter, and Peter Hirschburg

1987   Felony probation: A re-examination of public risk. American Journal of Criminal Justice 11:1–9.

Missouri Division of Probation and Parole

1976   Probation in Missouri, July 1, 1968 to June 30, 1970: Characteristics, Performance, and Criminal Reinvolvement. Division of Probation and Parole, Jefferson City, Missouri.

Petersilia, Joan

1985a   Community supervision: Trends and Critical Issues. Crime and Delinquency 31:339–347.

1985b   Probation and felony offenders. Federal Probation 49:4–9.

Petersilia, Joan, Susan Turner, James Kahan, and Joyce Peterson

1985   Executive summary of Rand's study, "Granting Felons Probation: Public Risks and Alternatives." Crime and Delinquency 31:379–392.

Petersilia, Joan and Susan Turner, with Joyce Peterson

1986   Prison versus Probation in California: Implications for Crime and Offender Recidivism. R-3323-NIJ. Santa Monica, Calif.: Rand Corporation.

Sutherland, Edwin H., Donald R. Cressey, and David F. Luckenbill

1992   Principles of Criminology. 11th ed. New York: General Hall.

Turner, Susan, Joan Petersilia, and Elizabeth Piper Deschenes

1992   Evaluating intensive supervision probation/parole (ISP) for drug offenders. Crime and Delinquency 38:539–556.

U.S. Department of Justice

1992   Criminal Victimization in the United States, 1990. Washington, D.C.: U.S. Department of Justice.

Vito, Gennaro F.

1986   Felony probation and recidivism: Replication and response. Federal Probation 50:17–25.

Whitehead, John T.

1991   The effectiveness of felony probation: Results from an eastern state. Justice Quarterly 8:525–543.

Prison Versus Probation in California: Implications for Crime and Offender Recidivism

JOAN PETERSILIA AND SUSAN TURNER

All but eight states in the United States are under federal court orders to do something to alleviate overcrowding in prisons—overcrowding so severe that it constitutes "cruel and unusual punishment." In their efforts, many states have had to reduce the time offenders spend in prison, and some states have placed an increasing percentage of felons on probation. This may mean that convicted felons are spending more post-conviction time on the streets than ever before, a situation that not only severely strains the resources of probation and parole agencies, but also jeopardizes public safety.

PROBATION, IMPRISONMENT, AND CRIMINAL BEHAVIOR

In 1985, we completed a study which found that during the 40 months a group of felony probationers in two California counties were on probation, 65 percent were arrested and 34 percent were sentenced to jail or prison for new crimes.[1] Seventy-five percent of the official charges filed against the probationers involved burglary/theft, robbery, or other violent crimes.

These findings led us to believe that the majority of felons who are placed on probation in California constitute a serious threat to the public and that the increasing use of probation as a sentence for felons is a high-risk gamble. Our findings also showed that with the information currently available to (or legally usable by) the courts, it was not possible to improve the prediction of recidivism to more than 20 percent above chance.

Many would use those findings to support demands for adding prison space or for sending more felons to prison. Obviously, criminals cannot commit crimes in the community while they are in prison. However, it is not clear how felons will behave when they return to the community after imprisonment. To help policymakers and legislators explore the relative costs and effectiveness of imprisonment and probation as sentencing alternatives for selected felons, we have attempted to compare criminal behavior of pris-

Prepared for the National Institute of Justice, U.S. Department of Justice.

"Prison Versus Probation in California: Implications for Crime and Offender Recidivism" by Joan Petersilia and Susan Turner, R-3323-NIJ, 1986, The RAND Corporation. Reprinted with permission from RAND.

[1]Joan Petersilia et al., *Granting Felons Probation: Public Risks and Alternatives*, The Rand Corporation, R-3186-NIJ, January 1985.

oners and probationers after those sentences, the relative amounts of crime prevented through imprisonment (i.e., the incapacitation effect) during the period of the study, and the costs to the criminal justice system of that prevention.

DATA AND METHODS

There are basic differences between probationers and prisoners, many of them correlated with receiving a prison sentence and many also correlated with recidivism. To determine the association between the type of sanction and recidivism, we must somehow control for the effects of those differences. Otherwise, they, rather than the sanction, are likely to "explain" the variation in recidivism rates between the two groups. Past research on this subject has generally failed to introduce stringent controls for such differences. Considering that prisoners generally are more serious criminals and have more of the characteristics associated with recidivism, it is not surprising that they have higher recidivism rates. However, that does not justify the conclusion, which most studies have drawn, that prison "makes offenders worse"—that is, more likely to return to crime.

Only an experimental research design can establish definitively the relative effects of imprisonment and probation on recidivism. Without random assignment of offenders to one or the other sentencing condition, we cannot conclude that the sanction itself made the critical difference in an offender's subsequent behavior. We had neither the funding nor the jurisdiction to perform such an experiment. However, the research design we used does allow us to measure the *association* between prison or probation and recidivism for a sample of prisoners and probationers, and our results suggest the need for an actual experiment and further research in this critical area of criminal justice administration.

We attempted to overcome some of the methodological difficulties by using samples of prisoners and probationers who were as nearly "matched" as possible in background and criminal characteristics and other factors known to correlate with recidivism. Using information supplied by the California Youth and Adult Corrections Agency (YACA) and data from our earlier study of felony probation, we attempted to construct comparable groups of prisoners and probationers. We selected 511 probationers from the original study and identified 511 imprisoned offenders who matched the probationers on the following factors:

- Year of sentencing (1980).
- Gender (male).
- County of conviction (Los Angeles or Alameda).
- Conviction crime (assault, robbery, burglary, theft, or drug sale/possession).

- A summary score reflecting factors shown to be associated with the prison/probation decision in California.

To reliably estimate how strongly going to prison is associated with recidivism, we applied even more stringent controls in the analytic strategy than we used in the initial matching. Using logistic regression techniques, we controlled for (1) other remaining differences between our selected prisoners and probationers on factors shown to be associated with the prison/probation decision; (2) the offender's age at conviction (research has consistently found a relationship between age and recidivism); and (3) additional offender background characteristics that were correlated with recidivism *in our sample*.

Despite this matching effort, we must caution that our results do not establish any *causal* relationship between imprisonment and recidivism. Although we matched our samples on, and controlled for, factors that research and experience have found related to recidivism, there are undoubtedly other factors that influence both the sentencing decision and recidivism. We have no way of knowing or establishing how our samples may have differed on such factors, and thus whether they were fully "matched." Only random assignment to sentence could guarantee that these factors were not systematically influencing prisoners' behavior. Consequently, our results are only suggestive and should not be used to support specific policy recommendations.

MAJOR FINDINGS AND CONCLUSIONS

The Relationship Between Imprisonment and Recidivism

The majority of both the prisoners and the probationers in our sample "failed" during the two years following their release into society. Collectively, the 1,022 felons in the sample had over 1,300 charges filed against them in that period. About 45 percent of the filed charges were for property crimes, about 28 percent were for violent crimes, about 12 percent were for drug offenses, and about 15 percent were for miscellaneous crimes.

The prisoners had higher recidivism rates than the probationers, both across crime types and in the aggregate. In the two-year follow-up period, 72 percent of the prisoners were rearrested, as compared with 63 percent of the probationers; 53 percent of the prisoners had new filed charges, compared with 38 percent of the probationers; and 47 percent of the prisoners were incarcerated in jail or prison, compared with 31 percent of the probationers. However, although the prisoners' recidivism rates were higher than the probationers', their new crimes were no more serious, nor was there a significant difference in the length of time before their first filed charge (the average was about six months for both groups).

These initial, descriptive findings were confirmed when we controlled for other factors related to differences in recidivism rates. Considering all offenders as a group, for the majority of recidivism measures (e.g., rearrest, new filed charges, new convictions), we found that imprisonment was associated with a higher probability of recidivism. When we examined different offender types, we found that the association was significant only for offenders convicted of property crimes, who were 17 percent more likely than other comparable probationers to have a new charge filed against them after imprisonment. Drug offenders who had been imprisoned were 11 percent more likely to have a new filed charge than those who were given probation; and violent offenders were 3 percent more likely.

The positive association between imprisonment and recidivism could be interpreted in several ways: Assuming the prisoners and probationers had the same potential for recidivism, imprisonment might have made offenders more likely to recidivate than they would have been without the prison experience. Alternatively, the offender may not have changed as a result of being in prison, but society's (and the criminal justice system's) *response* to him may have. For example, property offenders in our sample who served time in prison recidivated more often than property offenders placed on probation. If property offenders are motivated primarily by economic considerations, it may be that more of them quite the criminal lifestyle when they find jobs in the community. If being an ex-prisoner reduces their legitimate employment opportunities more than being a probationer does, the prisoner *label*, not the prison experience itself, may account for the greater recidivism. And, as discussed earlier, it could be that some factor or factors not accounted for in our data but known to the sentencing judges explain the differences in post-release behavior.

The Incapacitation Effect

Today, prison sentences are almost universally intended to incapacitate, rather than rehabilitate, offenders. Imprisonment keeps offenders from committing crimes in the community while they are incarcerated. We tried to estimate how much crime imprisonment prevented in our sample, and at what cost, absolutely and relative to probation.

We estimated the number of offenses the probationers and prisoners committed during the three-year period following their 1980 convictions (including the time they spent in jail or prison), using a technique derived from the incapacitation literature. The results indicate that, on average, each prisoner committed an estimated 20 crimes and each probationer committed 25 crimes during the three-year period following his 1980 conviction. On average, each probationer was arrested 2.5 times during that period, and each prisoner, 2 times. At an assumed ratio of 10 crime commissions per arrest (a conservative figure), we estimate that the prisoners committed 20 percent fewer crimes than the probationers during the three years.

The Relative Costs of Probation and Imprisonment

What did the incapacitation effect in our sample cost society, absolutely and relative to probation? Neither the costs nor the benefits to society of incapacitation can be measured simply in terms of public resources and/or the tradeoff between providing prison cells or other public services. Being on the street an average of nine months longer than the prisoners during the three-year period, the probationers committed an estimated 25 percent more crime. Although our study could not quantify the effects, the additional crimes no doubt imposed other critical costs in victim injury and property loss.[2]

In terms of the costs to the criminal justice system, probation is commonly assumed to be considerably less expensive than prison. In policy discussions, probation supervision is generally assumed to cost about $1,500 per year for each probationer; prison (operational) costs are taken to be about $15,000 per prisoner. But these costs do not reflect the secondary costs of either sanction—which are considerable—nor do they reflect the real difference between prison and probation costs. Capturing the full effects of these sanctions requires, at a minimum, consideration of:

- Correction costs of the initial confinement (prison or jail).
- Costs of post-release probation or parole supervision.
- Police and court costs associated with processing post-release arrests.
- Costs of any post-release incarcerations resulting from new crimes.

We summed these four components for the probationers and prisoners in our sample. Our results suggest that felony probation sentences are more expensive than is commonly assumed, both absolutely and relative to imprisonment, and that prison sentences also cost the system more than is commonly assumed.

We estimate that each of the felony probationers in our sample cost the California criminal justice system about $12,000 in the three-year period following his 1980 conviction—about half of which was used by police and court agencies to process new arrests while the offender was on probation. Each prisoner was estimated to cost the system about $23,000 over the same three-year period, about 70 percent of which was used to pay for his initial year in prison. Thus, the system spent about twice as much on supervising and reprocessing prisoners as it did on probationers over the three-year period.

As with the recidivism results, we caution against overgeneralizing these cost estimates. The figures represent the costs to two urban counties in California, and the offenders in our sample had high recidivism rates, which drove up their reprocessing costs considerably. The costs of super-

---

[2]See Edwin W. Zedlewski, "When Have We Been Punished Enough?" *Public Administration Review*, November 1985.

vising lower-risk probationers (e.g., juveniles or misdemeanants) or adult probationers with higher success rates might be quite different. Also, other costs related to recidivistic crimes, such as the costs imposed on victims, are not included.

CONSIDERATIONS FOR CRIMINAL JUSTICE POLICY

Our findings suggest that imprisonment did not deter most of the offenders in the sample from further crime but *did* achieve its incapacitation objective. However, this objective was achieved at very high costs to the criminal justice system, both absolutely and relative to probation. Given current resources, only a fraction (currently about 10 percent) of arrestees can be imprisoned in existing facilities.

Our major conclusion is that public safety would clearly benefit from somehow incapacitating a larger proportion of the felony offenders represented in this study, and for a longer time. However, building more prisons can accomplish only part of this goal—even if the system can find less costly and less time-consuming prison-building methods.

The U.S. Department of Justice recently introduced a federal initiative aimed at reducing the time and cost of constructing new correction facilities. In connection with this initiative, a new prison has just been completed in Florida, using prefabricated concrete components. The prison took only 8 months to build and cost $16,000 per cell. Past prison construction has often taken as long as 5 years and has cost an average of $50,000 per cell. If states with different climates, construction and land costs, etc., can duplicate Florida's experience, construction of correctional institutions could become more economical in the future.

These findings are encouraging in view of the widespread interest in reducing the costs of imprisonment. However, even at one-third of the current cost of conventional construction, the price to increase the present prison population by only 1 percent (5,000 beds) is about $75 million (using a conservative $15,000 per-bed cost). Moreover, even if national prison capacity could be increased by that number of cells and at the lower cost, the prison system would still hold less than 25 percent of the felony convicts society wishes to monitor. Therefore, our results also lead us to suggest the need for more effective control of felons outside of prison.

We believe that the U.S. criminal justice system might be able to get additional return on the resources that are actually or potentially available by examining the benefits and costs of various intermediate-level sanctions for felony offenders, such as community-based programs that provide more intensive supervision than routine probation but are less restrictive than prison.

A number of counties are experimenting with intermediate sanctions such as intensive probation supervision, electronic monitoring, house arrest, and community service sentencing. Early results suggest that there may be feasible, cost-effective alternatives to prison for some of the offenders we studied. These alternatives may extend the incapacitation effect to some of the felony offenders who are presently only nominally supervised on traditional probation. They may also ease prison overcrowding by having less serious offenders supervised in the community and by avoiding any negative effects that might result from being in prison or being labeled an ex-prisoner. Consideration might also be given to increasing the time spent in prison by selected prisoners.

Many counties question the costs of intensified probation programs. However, our results show that when current police and court costs are added to the expenses of probation supervision, felony probationers cost the system a great deal. If intensive supervision programs actually reduce recidivism, they could ultimately be less costly than the present system, because they could recapture a significant portion of the present post-release processing and incarceration costs associated with recidivism. And, more important, they would reduce the pain and loss suffered by new victims.

CHAPTER 4

Experience with Intermediate Sanctions: Rationale and Program Effectiveness

INTRODUCTION

Sentencing practices in this country suggest that offenses can be divided into two categories. When the crime is relatively serious, offenders are put behind bars; when it is less so, they are put on probation, often with only perfunctory supervision. This twofold division disregards the range of severity in crime, and as a result, sentencing can err in one direction or another: either it is too harsh, incarcerating people whose crimes are not serious enough to warrant a sanction this severe, or too lenient, putting on probation people whose crimes call for more severe punishment.

This need for more flexible alternatives—punishments that in harshness fall between prison and probation—led many states to experiment with intermediate sanctions, such as intensive supervision probation and parole, house arrest, electronic monitoring, day reporting centers, and so on. Intermediate sanctions are probation and parole programs that emphasize closer monitoring and surveillance. These programs are also variously referred to as graduated sanctions, alternative sanctions, or intermediate punishments.

The stated, or public, purposes of intermediate sanctions are to:

- save taxpayers money by providing cost-effective alternatives to incarceration for prison and jail-bound offenders;
- deter offenders (specifically) and the public (generally) from crime;
- protect the community by exerting more control than traditional probation over offender behavior;

- rehabilitate offenders by using mandatory treatment requirements, which are then reinforced by mandatory drug testing and the swift revocations of violators.

Between 1980 and 1997 every state adopted some form of intermediate sanctions for adult and juvenile offenders. Today, a wide variety of intermediate sanctions exists in every major jurisdiction in the country.

Thanks to federal funding, we now have a rather significant body of literature on intermediate sanctions, including information on policy development, program design, and evaluation evidence. The three articles chosen for this chapter summarize this important body of community corrections literature.

The first article comes from *The Intermediate Sanctions Handbook*, edited by McGarry and Carter at the Center for Effective Public Policy. This publication is a must-read for any practitioner setting out to develop intermediate sanction programs. Alan Harland, who has worked with many jurisdictions to develop intermediate sanctions, takes the reader through the policy process of deciding which types of sanctions, for which offenders, make most sense, and how individual programs can be considered jointly so that the full continuum of sanctions is put in place, rather than simply isolated and disconnected programs.

The next two articles summarize what we know about the performance to date of the most popular intermediate sanction programs, including intensive supervision, house arrest, electronic monitoring, day fines, and boot camps. Michael Tonry's article is taken from his excellent book, *Sentencing Matters*. He summarizes the evaluation evidence on adult intermediate sanctions. Barry Krisberg and his colleagues, all leading juvenile justice authorities, summarize similar evidence regarding the costs and benefits of intermediate sanctions for juveniles.

The Tonry and Krisberg et al. articles report surprisingly consistent findings, both across both populations and program types. The bottom line from all of the evidence is that promoters of intermediate sanctions promised too much and delivered too little. Programs originally designed for incarceration-bound offenders ended up being used mostly for high-risk probationers. Programs, particularly for adults, delivered mostly surveillance and monitoring and little treatment, and hence officers ended up uncovering more of the offender's misdeeds, necessitating a return to custody, which drove up corrections costs. The juvenile program results are similar, although planned treatment was more consistently delivered. Hence, neither overall recidivism rates nor corrections costs have been reduced. Yet, when surveillance was coupled with treatment, slight (10 to 20 percent) reductions in recidivism were produced—across programs, populations, and jurisdictions.

To some degree, the failure of intermediate sanctions to reduce recidivism reflects the fact that most programs are more punitive than routine probation and parole. Stepped up surveillance and frequent drug tests lead in turn to increasing violations and incarceration rates, which drives up program and court costs. Intermediate sanctions' two objectives are, under present conditions, largely in conflict: The more stringently such programs impose their punitive conditions, the more likely they are to exacerbate prison crowding and to approach the costs of imprisonment—exactly the opposite of what proponents had hoped for.

The three articles reach similar conclusions. That is, the future viability of intermediate sanctions depends upon a realistic reappraisal of what they can be expected to accomplish. Proponents had suggested that intermediate sanctions could relieve prison crowding, enhance public safety, and rehabilitate offenders—all at a cost savings. The evaluations show unequivocally that current programs cannot accomplish such far-reaching and lofty goals. If community sanctions are made more effective through an emphasis on public safety and offender accountability, then an increase in program costs is likely. As Mike Tonry put it: "There is no free lunch." On the other hand, developing an array of sentencing options is an important and necessary first step toward a more comprehensive and graduated sentencing structure, where the punishment more closely matches the crime. To many observers, the goal of restoring the principle of just deserts to the criminal justice system is justification enough for the continued development of intermediate sanctions.

Defining a Continuum of Sanctions: Some Research and Policy Development Implications

ALAN T. HARLAND
Temple University

PRESSURE TO EXPAND THE RANGE OF INTERMEDIATE SANCTIONS

In an era in which alarm over public safety and the fiscal constraints upon government's capacity to respond both seem to be worsening, the criminal justice system's heavy reliance on the polar extremes of routine probation

Alan Harland is Professor of Criminal Justice at Temple University in Philadelphia, Pennsylvania.

"Defining a Continuum of Sanctions: Some Research and Policy Development Implications" by Alan T. Harland is from *The Intermediate Sanctions Handbook: Experiences and Tools for Policymakers*, edited by Peggy McGarry and Madaline M. Carter, Chap. 6, 1993, National Institute of Corrections, U.S. Department of Justice. Reprinted with permission.

and traditional forms of incarceration has come under extensive scrutiny and criticism. Fears about inadequate control and punishment of high-risk probationers on the one hand and concern about the ineffectiveness, unconstitutional crowding, and soaring construction and maintenance costs of penal institutions on the other have prompted widespread calls for more extensive development and use of mid-range, "intermediate" sanctions. This is usually understood to mean doing something between sentencing or revoking offenders to prison or jail and releasing them into the community under negligible probationary constraints.

Advocacy for expanding the range of intermediate sanctions has emerged from a broad alliance of critics from all shades of the professional, political, and academic spectrum. It has been met by rapid proliferation of a "new generation of alternatives," such as boot camps, day treatment and day-reporting centers, intensive supervision probation and parole programs, day fines, and home arrest/electronic monitoring, as well as by expansion and consolidation of earlier approaches such as community service, restitution, and traditional therapeutic and other treatment interventions.

NEED FOR STRUCTURED EXPANSION

Expansion of options without clear definition and a corresponding set of principles and standards to guide in their selection, application, and evaluation raises the threat of faddish adoption and unstructured discretionary use (and abuse) of intermediate sanctions. This, in turn, escalates the risk of applying the sanctions to inappropriate target populations and the corollary dangers of weakening their public safety impact and threatening their integrity and credibility through net-widening, cost overruns, breaches of desert principles, inequity, and undue disparity. These dangers are of more concern, as the types of intermediate sanctions being introduced become more and more onerous in striving to approximate the punitiveness and control associated with the terms of incarceration with which they are being designed to compete.

The challenge, therefore, is not simply to meet a need for more sanctioning options, but to develop options that will have clear relevance and credibility in the eyes of the practitioners and policymakers on whose understanding and support their long-term survival and success depends. This suggests a need to expand options in a comprehensive, principled, and highly goal-centered way, being wary of repeating the frustrations and failures so widely documented in earlier alternatives efforts. This requires an awareness and high level of systematic attention to well-conceived and articulated development, implementation, monitoring, and evaluation strategies. In short, we must approach the task as an information-driven process of planned change, rather than the crisis-oriented, bandaid fashion in which sanctioning options have so often and so unsuccessfully been introduced in the past.

EMERGENCE OF THE CONCEPT OF A CONTINUUM OF SANCTIONS

Recognition of the potential dangers of haphazard development and use of an increasingly diverse array of intermediate sanctions has lead to calls for development efforts that go beyond simply creating more options. Emphasis is placed instead upon the far more complex undertaking of establishing a **continuum of sanctions**. The importance of considering sentencing and revocation decisions in terms of a continuum of choices is a theme that has been emphasized recently in both the professional and academic literature on sentencing and intermediate sanctions, and it has attracted the highest levels of political attention. As is the case with so many other popular concepts in the criminal justice business, the ease with which an idea slips into common parlance bears no relation to a consensus on its essential meaning and significance. The expression "continuum of sanctions" is no exception: it is frequently used and misunderstood to mean simply a list or menu of criminal penalties or, more typically, correctional programs, such as the boot camps and others already mentioned.

The balance of this discussion will be concerned with the important difference between developing a wide-ranging **list or menu** of options and the far more difficult but potentially more vital task of constructing and applying a **continuum of sanctions**. More specifically, the focus here will be on what the idea of a continuum of sanctions means, and why the concept is potentially important and helpful to those interested in improving sentencing and correctional policy and practice, especially to those faced with difficult choices about recommending or imposing sanctions in an individual case or adopting or implementing them at a program or policy level.

DEFINING BASIC TERMS

The dictionary definition of "sanctions" is: "Coercive measures or interventions taken to enforce societal standards." The dictionary definition of the term "continuum" identifies its basic characteristic as an ordering or grading on the basis of some **fundamental common feature**. Combining the two, the result is as follows:

> A continuum of sanctions is a variety of coercive measures taken to enforce societal standards, ordered on the basis of a fundamental common feature.

An obvious aim behind the grading and scaling of sanctions, implicit in the continuum idea of providing some sense of order or sequence for their use, is to make it easier for judges and others to compare and make more rational decisions about the different options. Clarity on the basis for ordering sanctions will make it more likely that those selected will achieve expected goals and will facilitate decisions about interchangeability or equivalence of intermediate sanctions with terms of incarceration and with each other. Understanding the continuum concept, therefore, suggests the need for clarification in at least three areas.

- First, what is the precise nature and scope of the coercive measures embraced by the term "sanctions"?
- Second, by which essential common features (dimensions) might judges and other key decisionmakers find it most helpful to order the various sanctions on the list?
- Third, what techniques or methods might best be employed to scale and grade sanctions according to each of the dimensions identified?

The first question addresses the range and complexity of sanctioning options available. The other two questions, one conceptual and one methodological, further frame the tasks required to move beyond an undifferentiated list of sanctions to a continuum.

CLARIFYING ITEMS ON THE SANCTIONS MENU

Figure 1 summarizes the typical range of coercive measures or intervention possibilities in most jurisdictions and illustrates the sizable number of alternatives that may compete for the decisionmaker's attention in any given case. Fleshed out to reflect the actual legal and practical circumstances of an individual jurisdiction, this kind of list could serve as a checklist in a bench book for judges, for probation presentence investigators preparing recommendations, or for defense-based advocates preparing client-specific sentencing plans. It could also stand as a summary table of contents for the more detailed descriptive accounts of sentencing options that such a reference work would provide.

An essential starting point in the development of a continuum of sanctions and the pursuit of a more rational approach to their use is that the options outlined in Figure 1 be defined and understood as thoroughly as possible. This suggests the need for extended discussion among key decisionmakers, aimed at establishing a shared vocabulary and thorough baseline understanding of precisely what options are in use or potentially available and exactly what each one entails. Before it is possible to move from an unstructured array to a more organized continuum of sequenced and scaled alternatives, we must first develop a detailed grasp of what is on the current menu. Judges and legislators are often woefully unfamiliar with the specifics of many of the options available in their own courts and communities. By fully identifying and defining the range of options available to sentencing authorities, judgments can be made about whether and to what extent they are equivalent or interchangeable in any significant way, and how likely they are to satisfy any or all of the major goals of the decisionmakers involved.

Warning Measures (Notice of consequences of subsequent wrongdoing)	Admonishment/cautioning (administrative; judicial) Suspended execution or imposition of sentence	
Injunctive Measures (Banning legal conduct)	Travel (e.g., from jurisdiction; to specific criminogenic spots) Association (e.g., with other offenders) Driving Possession of weapons Use of alcohol Professional activity (e.g., disbarment)	
Economic Measures	Restitution Costs Fees Forfeitures Support payments Fines (standard; day fines)	
Work-related Measures	Community service (individual placement; work crew) Paid employment requirements	
Education-related Measures	Academic (e.g., basic literacy, GED) Vocational training Life skills training	
Physical and Mental Health Treatment Measures	Psychological/psychiatric Chemical (e.g., methadone; psychoactive drugs) Surgical (e.g., acupuncture drug treatment)	
Physical Confinement Measures	Partial or intermittent confinement	Home curfew Day treatment center Halfway house Restitution center Weekend detention facility/jail Outpatient treatment facility (e.g., drug/mental health)

Figure 1.   Summary listing of coercive measures and sanctioning options.

MOVING FROM A LIST TO A CONTINUUM: GOALS OF SANCTIONING AUTHORITIES

Clarity of purposes/goals is an obvious precursor to any meaningful assessment, comparison, and evaluation of the strengths and weaknesses of different sanctions. Selection and application of any of the listed options will be driven by a belief that it is reasonably compatible with the decision-maker's dominant **values and goals**.

Consequently, in addition to being well informed about the operational aspects of sanctions available to them, practitioners and policymakers must also be clear about the essential fears and concerns to which their decisions about sanctioning choices are intended to respond. If one believes, along with

	Full/continuous confinement	Full home/house arrest Mental hospital Other residential treatment facility (e.g., drug/alcohol) Boot camp Detention facility Jail Prison
Monitoring/ Compliance Measures (May be attached to all other sanctions)	Required of the offender	Mail reporting Electronic monitoring (telephone check-in; active electronic monitoring device) Face-to-face reporting Urine analysis (random; routine)
	Required of the monitoring agent	Criminal records checks Sentence compliance checks (e.g., on payment of monetary sanctions; attendance/performance at treatment, work, or educational sites) Third-party checks (family, employer, surety, service/treatment provider; via mail, telephone, in person) Direct surveillance/observation (random/routine visits and possibly search; at home, work, institution, or elsewhere) Electronic monitoring (regular phone checks and/or passive monitoring device—currently used with home curfew or house arrest, but could track movement more widely as technology develops)

Figure 1. *(Continued)*

Morris and Tonry, (Norval Morris and Michael Tonry, *Between Prison and Probation: Intermediate Punishments in a Rational Sentencing System*, Oxford: Oxford University Press, 1990) that sentences can be devised that are equivalent to imprisonment (or to each other), the question becomes, on what measures of equivalence or interchangeability might the various sanctioning options best be scaled and graded to help decisionmakers (such as judges) choose rationally among and between them?

Surprisingly little attention has been paid to the issue of scaling criminal penalties in such a way as to aid decisionmakers in judging how well they are likely to work at all and in relation to each other. Recent efforts to respond to the need for guidance with respect to intermediate sanctions have focused heavily on ways to grade them in terms of their weight or value on a scale of **severity** or **onerousness**. Among the most frequently applied attempts along these lines have been the efforts of day fines advocates to assign "units of punishment" to offenses rather than fixing dollar amounts, so that offenders of different financial means would be assessed the same number of punishment units for similar offenses but would satisfy them in terms of their individual payment abilities (each might be required, for example, to pay a day's income for each unit assessed).

Some have challenged the notion that scaling and fixing exchange rates for different sanctions to assure **equality of severity or suffering** is of primary importance. It has been suggested that sanctions might be more usefully and realistically scaled, and equivalencies gauged, in terms of their value (or perceived value) in satisfying broader, more functional system goals, rather than on their ability to satisfy purely retributive demands for assuring that comparable levels of pain be inflicted on offenders committing similar offenses. The decisionmakers instead might call for an ordering that allows ready comparison of the different options in Figure 1, not only in terms of how much pain and suffering each represents, but also on the basis of their perceived or demonstrated value as techniques for controlling the rate of crime (value as a general deterrent measure) or recidivism (value as a rehabilitative, incapacitative, or specific deterrent measure).

In addition to traditional **retributive** and utilitarian **preventive** aims, scaling and comparison could also proceed along a **restorative** dimension, based on the value of different sanctions in terms of their ability to address goals such as **reparation** to the victim, community, or society. The term "**accountability**"—in the sense of holding offenders accountable for their crimes—is also used widely, especially in juvenile justice restitution circles, as if it were an independent goal of criminal sanctions. In my view, this term is often only a code word for retribution or a rephrasing of the desire to make offenders "pay" for their crimes, which can mean either pay in the sense of suffer (retribution) or pay in the sense of compensate (reparation). In either case, conceptual clarity and intellectual integrity are better served by using the more specific underlying terms.

As well as comparing sanctions in terms of their value in satisfying the primary goals **of** sentencing (restorative, preventive, and retributive), other dimensions of a continuum of sanctions might involve scaling and grading in terms of various limiting principles or goals **at** sentencing. At the program or policy level, for example, decisionmakers from budget and oversight agencies may want to see sanctions graded and assessed according to the **economic costs** that each represents. A further possibility is to grade them in terms of their political implications, including their value on a scale of **public satisfaction** or approval by different criminal justice professionals, victim groups, or other important constituencies.

In sum, the various intervention options might be scaled according to their relative value in relation to a number of important goals of sanctioning authorities. A simplified graphic illustration of the type of decision tool to which such an undertaking might lead is presented in Figure 2. Collectively, the resulting ratings would inform judges and other decisionmakers

Type of Sanction	Scaling Dimensions						
	Retributive Severity	Crime Reduction[a]	Recidivism Reduction[b]	Reparation	Economic Cost	Public Satisfaction	Etc.
Sanction A Sanction B Sanction C Sanction D Etc.	Value in terms of pain and suffering[c]	Value in terms of impact on crime rate	Value in terms of impact on reoffense rate	Value in terms of compensating aggrieved parties[d]	Value in terms of cost efficiency	Value in terms of public approval ratings	Etc.

[a]General deterrence effects
[b]Specific deterrence, incapacitation, rehabilitation effects
[c]Or in terms of units of onerousness, intrusiveness, or deprivation of autonomy/liberty
[d]Direct victims and possibly indirectly affected individuals, groups, or entities (e.g., family members, insurers, taxpayers, community, society)

Figure 2. Illustration of scaling possibilities for criminal sanctions: type of sanction, by scaling dimensions and units of measurement.

involved in the sanctioning process as to how well each option is considered to "fit" or to "work" on the different dimensions or measures of effectiveness, efficiency, and fairness represented by the goals being measured. Assuming that a decisionmaking tool of this general nature would be of assistance to guide and structure discretion in the comparison and use of criminal sanctions, it remains to be considered how feasible it would be to construct.

THE MECHANICS OF SCALING AND GRADING SANCTIONS

Methodological and statistical techniques have been developed for classifying and multidimensional scaling in fields as far removed from criminal justice as numerical taxonomy in biology and zoology. These techniques have been applied by economists and marketing researchers investigating consumer reaction to a wide variety of product classes. They have also been used in criminal justice, although the emphasis has been on attempts to bring numerical precision to assessments of crime seriousness. Efforts to create "seriousness-index scores" for various offenses have demonstrated the complexity of the task and the multidimensionality of the concept, varying as it does according to the extent of harm sustained, characteristics of the victim and the offender, and situational factors such as, for example, whether a burglary was committed by day or night, in occupied or empty premises, by an armed or unarmed person, and so on.

The problem of fixing units of value to different sanctions, whether in terms of severity or some other scale, is no less challenging an undertaking than grading the seriousness of offenses. Opinions and facts about the relative merit, equivalence, or interchangeability of different sanctions on almost any of the dimensions in Figure 2 will likely vary depending upon the rater's understanding of the precise nature (**quality of the sanction**) and the duration and intensity (**quantity of sanction**) of the options under consideration. Raters may also be influenced by different **aspects of the case** as a whole, including judgments about degrees of **culpability** and the probability (risk) and consequences (stakes) of subsequent offending, as indicated by the **characteristics of the offense and the offender** being targeted to receive the sanction. If we are considering, for example, how many hours of community service work to assign or how high a fine might be in order to be equivalent to six months of incarceration, the answer is likely to be somewhat different depending on whether the time is to be served in an overcrowded, physically inadequate, and understaffed jail or in a state-of-the-art correctional facility. Likewise, the calculation might vary depending upon whether the type of community service to be performed is of the individual placement or the supervised work crew variety, or if the fine is assessed in traditional form or on a day fine basis.

Finally, assuming numerical scores could be inserted in the cells for every sanction and scaling dimension in Figure 2, selection and interchangeability decisions must further be guided by policies and rules determining the relative weight and priority to be given to each dimension when conflicts (e.g., between punishment and treatment) arise. Assuming adequate specification and description of the options, the next question that arises is; given such a range of choices, is there a consistent, principled order or sequence in which the various measures should be factored into the construction of an appropriate sanctioning response? In any given case or class of cases, how does the sanctioning decisionmaker know where to start the selection process, where to stop, and how to resolve conflicts that may arise between competing possibilities on the list? All things being equal, for example, should a comprehensive sanctioning scheme be primarily concerned with compensating victims and other interests of restorative justice or must those goals be subordinate to the public safety concerns of prevention advocates? Where does either rank in relation to retributive demands that offenders are made to suffer some appropriate degree of pain and suffering for their crimes, regardless of considerations of social utility? And how should costs (direct costs and opportunity costs) and public satisfaction be factored into the final analysis?

CONCLUSION

The research and policy development agenda is a substantial one before the notion of a continuum of sanctions can be translated into a practical application for guiding decisions about the development of sanctioning options. The task is essential, however, if we are to reduce a potentially bewildering mass of choices to an organized, meaningful, and readily comparable format within which judges and others can have some clear sense of expected outcomes and of how different intermediate sanctions fit in relation to imprisonment and to each other. The importance of the task is emphasized by the realization that we are almost completely lacking in information to fill in any of the cells in Figure 2 with any degree of confidence. Yet judges and other sanctioning authorities are obviously doing such scaling and grading implicitly, at least on the dimensions they consider salient, when they make sanctioning decisions.

The development of a continuum of sanctions is a conceptually and methodologically complex undertaking. It is an easy expression to use but a difficult one to understand and an even more difficult one to operationalize. Methodologists can supply the skills and tools for the job, but practitioners and policymakers, who are the key decisionmakers in sentencing, must supply the raw materials. They must specify clearly and thoroughly the sanctioning options to be scaled and, most importantly, the dimensions or goals on which the grading and sequencing of sanctions should be based.

Evaluating Intermediate Sanction Programs

MICHAEL TONRY
University of Minnesota

Three major developments in the 1960s and 1970s led to the perceived need in the 1980s and 1990s to develop intermediate sanctions that fall between prison and probation in their severity and intrusiveness. First, initially on the basis of doubts about the ethical justification of rehabilitative correctional programs, and later on the basis of doubts about their effectiveness, rehabilitation lost credibility as a basis for sentencing. With it went the primary rationale for individualized sentences.

Second, initially in academic circles (e.g., Morris 1974; von Hirsch 1976) and later in the minds of many practitioners and policymakers, just "deserts" entered the penal lexicon, filled the void left by rehabilitation, and became seen as the primary rationale for sentencing. With it came a logic of punishments scaled in their severity so as to be proportionate to the seriousness of crimes committed and a movement to narrow officials' discretion by eliminating parole release, eliminating or limiting time-off-for-good-behavior, and constraining judges' discretion by use of sentencing guidelines and mandatory penalties.

Third, beginning in the 1960s and continuing into the 1990s, crime control policy became a staple issue in election campaigns and proponents of "law and order" persistently called for harsher penalties. With this came a widespread belief that most sentences to ordinary probation are insuffi-

"Evaluating Intermediate Sanction Programs" by Michael Tonry, excerpts from *Sentencing Matters*, Chap. 4, pp. 100–133, © 1996 by Michael Tonry. Reprinted by permission of Oxford University Press, Inc.

ciently punitive and substantial political pressure for increases in the severity of punishments. Because, however, most states lack sanctions other than prison that are widely seen as meaningful, credible, and punitive, pressure for increased severity has been satisfied mostly by increases in the use of imprisonment.

These developments resulted in a quadrupling in the number of state and federal prisoners between 1975 (240,593) and midyear 1994 (1,012,851) and in substantial overcrowding of American prisons. At year-end 1993, the federal prisons were operating at 136 percent of rated capacity and thirty-nine state systems were operating above rated capacity. An additional 51,000 state prisoners in twenty-two jurisdictions were being held in county jails because prison space was unavailable (Bureau of Justice Statistics 1994a, 1994b).

Whatever the political and policy goals that vastly increased numbers of prisoners may have satisfied, they have also posed substantial problems for state officials. Prisons cost a great deal to build and to operate and these costs have not been lightly borne by hard-pressed state budgets in the recessionary years of the early 1990s. In 1994, corrections budgets were the fastest rising component of state spending (National Conference of State Legislatures 1993). However, failure to deal with overcrowding attracts the attention of the federal courts and throughout the 1990s as many as forty states have been subject to federal court orders related to overcrowding.

Intermediate sanctions have been seen as a way both to reduce the need for prison beds and to provide a continuum of sanctions that satisfies the just deserts concern for proportionality in punishment. During the mid-1980s, intermediate sanctions such as intensive supervision, house arrest, and electronic monitoring were oversold as being able simultaneously to divert offenders from incarceration, reduce recidivism rates, and save money while providing credible punishments that could be scaled in intensity to be proportionate to the severity of the offender's crime. Like most propositions that seem too good to be true, that one wasn't.

During the past decade's experimentation, we have learned that some well-run programs can achieve some of their goals, that some conventional goals are incompatible, and that the availability of new sanctions presents almost irresistible temptations to judges and corrections officials to use them for offenders other than those for whom the program was created.

A REVIEW OF THE EVIDENCE ON INTERMEDIATE SANCTIONS

The literature for the most part raises doubts about the effectiveness of intermediate sanctions at achieving the goals their promoters have commonly set. This does not mean that there are no effective programs. Only a handful have been carefully evaluated. Many of those have in the aftermath been altered. Many sophisticated and experienced practitioners believe that their programs are effective and some no doubt are. The evaluation literature does not "prove" that programs cannot succeed but that many have not and that managers can learn from that past experience. Sometimes that learning may be expressed as program adaptations intended to make achievement of existing goals more likely. Sometimes, it may lead to a reconceptualization of goals.

The literature consists of a handful of fairly sophisticated evaluations funded by the National Institute of Justice, a larger number of smaller, typically less sophisticated studies of local projects, and a large number of uncritical descriptions of innovative programs. There have been a number of efforts to synthesize the evaluation literature on intermediate sanctions, sometimes in edited collections (McCarthy 1987; Byrne, Lurigio, and Petersilia 1992; Tonry and Hamilton 1995), sometimes in unified books (Tonry and Will 1988; Morris and Tonry 1990). Given the time consumed in writing and publishing books, the collections and syntheses are current as of a year or two before their publication dates.

Boot Camps

The emerging consensus from assessments of boot camps (also sometimes called shock incarceration) must be discouraging to their founders and supporters. Although promoted as a means to reduce recidivism rates, corrections costs, and prison crowding, most boot camps have no discernible effect on subsequent offending and increase costs and crowding (Parent 1994; MacKenzie 1994). Most have been front-end programs that have drawn many of their participants from among offenders who otherwise would not have been sent to prison. In many programs, a third to half of participants fail to complete the program and are sent to prison as a result. In most programs, close surveillance of offenders after completion and release produces rates of violations of technical conditions and of revocations that are higher than for comparable offenders in less intensive programs.

The news is not all bad. Back-end programs to which imprisoned offenders are transferred by corrections officials for service of a 90- or 180-day boot camp sentence in lieu of a longer conventional sentence do apparently save money and prison space, although they too often experience high failure rates and higher than normal technical violation and revocation rates.

Boot camp prisons have spread rapidly since the first two were established in Georgia and Oklahoma in 1983. By April 1993, according to a National Institute of Justice report (MacKenzie 1993), thirty states and the U.S. Bureau of Prisons were operating boot camps. According to the results of a survey of local jurisdictions in May 1992, ten jail boot camps were then in operation and 13 other jurisdictions were planning to open jail boot camps in 1992 or 1993 (Austin, Jones, and Bolyard 1993). The earliest were opened in 1986 in New Orleans and in 1988 in Travis County, Texas.

Boot camps vary widely in their details (MacKenzie and Parent 1992; MacKenzie and Piquero 1994). Some last 90 days, some 180. Admission in some states is controlled by judges, in others by corrections officials. Some primarily emphasize discipline and self-control; others incorporate extensive drug and other rehabilitation elements. Some eject a third to half of participants, others less than ten percent. Most admit only males, usually under age twenty-five, and often subject to crime of conviction and criminal history limits, though there are exceptions to each of these generalizations.

The reasons for boot camps' popularity are self-evident. Many Americans have experienced life in military boot camps and remember the experience as not necessarily pleasant but as an effective way to learn self-discipline and to learn to work as part of a team. Images of offenders participating in military drill and hard physical labor make boot camps look demanding and unpleasant, characteristics that crime-conscious officials and voters find satisfying.

Most of what we know about the effects of boot camps on participants comes from a series of studies by Doris MacKenzie and colleagues at the University of Maryland (e.g., MacKenzie and Shaw 1990, 1993; Mackenzie, 1993, 1994; MacKenzie and Souryal 1994), from a General Accounting Office survey of research and experience (1993), and from an early descriptive overview of boot camps commissioned by the National Institute of Justice (Parent 1989).

The conclusions with which this subsection began are drawn from MacKenzie's work and later analyses by Dale Parent. In addition to findings on completion rates, recidivism rates, and cost and prison bed savings, MacKenzie and her colleagues looked closely in Louisiana at effects on prisoners' self-esteem (MacKenzie and Shaw 1990). One early hypothesis concerning boot camps was that successful completion would increase participants' self-esteem which would in turn lead to more effective participation in the free community and reduced recidivism. The first half of the hypothesis was found to be correct; using psychometric measures, MacKenzie and Shaw found that successful participants' self-esteem was enhanced compared with comparable prisoners in conventional prisons. Unfortunately, later assessments of successful participants after release found that their enhanced self-esteem soon disappeared (a plausible explanation for why the second half of the hypothesis concerning recidivism was not confirmed).

One tentative finding concerning possible positive effects of rehabilitative programs on recidivism merits emphasis. Although MacKenzie and her colleagues concluded overall that boot camps do not by themselves result in reduced recidivism rates, they found evidence in Illinois, New York, and Louisiana of "lower rates of recidivism on some measures" that they associated with strong rehabilitative emphases in those states' boot camps (MacKenzie 1994, p. 16). An earlier article describes a "somewhat more positive" finding that graduates under intensive supervision after release "appear to be involved in more positive social activities (e.g., work, attending drug treatment) than similar offenders on parole or probation" (MacKenzie and Shaw 1993, p. 465).

If a primary goal of boot camps is to reduce prison use, the policy implications of research on boot camps are straightforward. Parent (1994, p. 10) sees at least three: " First, boot camps should recruit offenders who have a very high probability of imprisonment." This means that participants should be selected by corrections officials from among prisoners rather than by judges from among sentenced offenders. Second, boot camps should minimize failure rates by reducing in-program failures and post-release failures. This means that misconduct within the boot camp should be punished within the boot camp whenever possible rather than by transfer to a regular prison and that misconduct after release should be dealt with within the supervision program whenever possible rather than by revocation and reincarceration. Third, participants in boot camps should be selected from among prisoners who otherwise would serve a substantial term of imprisonment. Transfer of prisoners serving nine-month terms to a 180-day boot camp is unlikely to reduce costs and system crowding. Transfer of prisoners serving two- or three-year mandatory minimum terms is likely to reduce both.

Intensive Supervision

Intensive supervision for probationers and parolees (ISP) was initially the most popular intermediate sanction, has the longest history, and has been the most extensively and ambitiously evaluated. ISP has been the subject of the only multi-site experimental evaluation involving random allocation of eligible offenders to ISP and to whatever the otherwise appropriate sentence would have been (Petersilia and Turner 1993).

Evaluation findings parallel those for boot camps. Front-end programs in which judges control placement tend to draw more heavily from offenders who would otherwise receive less restrictive sentences than from offenders who would otherwise have gone to prison or jail. The multi-site ISP evaluation by the RAND Corporation, in which jurisdictions agreed in advance to cooperate with a random assignment system for allocating offenders to sanctions, was unable to evaluate front-end ISP programs when judges refused to accept the outcomes of the randomization system (Petersilia and Turner 1993). Back-end programs draw from prison populations, but even for some of these programs, suggestions have been made that their creation may lead judges to sentence more minor offenders to "a taste of prison" in the belief that they will quickly be released into ISP (Clear 1987).

Like the boot camp evaluations, the ISP evaluations have concluded that offenders sentenced to ISP do not have lower recidivism rates for new crimes than do comparable offenders receiving different sentences, but typically (because of closer surveillance) experience higher rates of violation of technical conditions and higher rates of revocation. Also like boot camps, early proponents argued that ISP while reducing recidivism rates and rehabilitating offenders would save money and prison resources (Petersilia, Lurigio, and Byrne 1992, pp. ix–x); evaluations suggest that the combination of net widening, high revocation rates, and related case processing costs makes the cost savings claims improbable for most programs.

There is one tantalizing positive finding from the ISP evaluation literature, that parallels a boot camp finding (MacKenzie and Shaw 1993): ISP did succeed in some sites in increasing participants' involvement in counseling and other treatment programs (Petersilia and Turner 1993). The drug treatment literature demonstrates that participation, whether voluntary or coerced, can reduce both drug use and crime by drug-using offenders (Anglin and Hser 1990; President's Commission on Model State Drug Laws 1993). Because Drug Use Forecasting data (e.g., National Institute of Justice 1993) indicate that half to three-fourths of arrested felons in many cities test positive for drug abuse, ISP may hold promise as a device for getting addicted offenders into treatment and keeping them there (Gendreau, Cullen, and Bonta 1994).

Contemporary programs, with caseloads ranging from two officers to twenty-five probationers to one officer to forty probationers, are typically based on surveillance, cost, and punishment rationales. More frequent contacts between officer and offender (in some programs, as many as twenty or thirty per month) lead to closer surveillance which in turn enhances public safety by making it likelier that misconduct will be discovered and punished. Because of closer surveillance, low- to mid-risk offenders can be diverted from prison to less-costly ISP without jeopardizing public safety. Because of the frequency of contacts, subjection to unannounced urinalysis tests for drugs, and rigorous enforcement of restitution, community service, and other conditions, ISP will be much more punitive than conventional probation.

Contemporary ISP programs are of three types, each with an exemplar that was the subject of a major National Institute of Justice-funded evaluation. Georgia established the most noted "prison diversion" program to which convicted offenders were sentenced by judges under criteria that directed the judge to use ISP only for offenders who otherwise would have been sent to prison. An in-house evaluation concluded that most ISP participants had been diverted from prison and, on the basis of comparisons with a matched group of offenders who were imprisoned, that the program had achieved lower recidivism rates and had reduced prison use (Erwin 1987). Subsequent analyses by others concluded that most participants had not been diverted from prison, that the comparison group was not comparable, that low rates of new crimes resulted not from the program but from the low-risk nature of the offenders, and that prison beds had not been saved (Morris and Tonry 1990, chap. 7; Clear and Byrne 1992).

The second form, "prison release ISP," had as its evaluated exemplar a New Jersey program to which low-risk prisoners were released after a careful seven-step screening process and then placed in low caseloads with frequent contacts and urinalyses and rigorously enforced conditions. A major evaluation, based on a post hoc comparison group, concluded that the program was effectively implemented, reduced recidivism rates, and saved public moneys (Pearson 1987, 1988). Subsequent analyses by others accepted the implementation finding but challenged the recidivism findings (because the comparison group appeared to consist of higher-risk offenders and thus was not comparable) and the cost findings (nearly half of the initial participants were sent back to prison following revocation for breach of conditions which, given the short sentences they would otherwise have served and the costs of processing the revocations, made cost-savings claims suspect) (Morris and Tonry 1990, chap. 7). Todd Clear hypothesized that judges might sentence low-risk minor offenders to prison in the belief that they would be released to ISP and that if under two percent of the eligible defendants were sentenced to prison on that basis, any possible cost savings from ISP would be lost (Clear 1987).

The third form, "case management ISP," had as its evaluated exemplar a Massachusetts program designed by the state probation department in which probationers were classified on the basis of risk of offending (using a validated risk-classification instrument). The evaluation documented significant implementation problems, and concluded that offenders given intense supervision were no likelier than other comparable offenders to commit new crimes but were likelier to have their probation revoked because of technical condition violations (Byrne and Kelly 1989).

Notwithstanding the nonconfirmatory evaluation findings, ISP was adopted in most states. A General Accounting Office survey in 1989 identified programs in forty states and the District of Columbia (U.S. General Accounting Office 1990b; Byrne and Pattavina 1992). Probably they exist in every state; programs can be organized by state or county correctional agencies, can be located in parole, probation, and prison departments, and as a result are easy to miss in national mail and phone surveys.

Two exhaustive syntheses of the American ISP literature have been published (U.S. General Accounting Office 1990b; Petersilia and Turner 1993) and do not differ significantly in their conclusions from those offered here. One question that naturally arises is why ISP programs have survived and continue to be created? Unlike boot camps, for which evaluation findings casting doubts on effectiveness are recent, the ISP findings have been well-known and accepted since at least 1990. The answers appear to be that ISP's surveillant and punitive properties satisfy a public preference that sanctions be demanding and burdensome and that ISP is becoming seen as an appropriate mid-level punishment. Petersilia, Lurigio, and Byrne (1992, p. xiv) note, "to many observers, the goal of restoring the principle of just deserts to the criminal justice system is justification enough for the continued development of intermediate sanctions."

Here too, the policy implications are straightforward. Because recidivism rates for new crimes are no higher for ISP participants than for comparable imprisoned offenders, ISP is a cost-effective prison alternative for offenders who do not present unacceptable risks of violence. ISP may offer a promising tool for facilitating treatment for drug-using offenders and can by itself and linked with other sanctions provide credible mid-level punishments as part of a continuum of sanctions.

House Arrest and Electronic Monitoring

The lines that distinguish community penalties begin to blur after ISP. House arrest, often called home confinement, has as a precursor the curfew condition traditionally attached to many probation sentences, and may be ordered as a sanction in its own right or as a condition of ISP (Ball, Huff, and Lilly 1988). Most affected offenders, however, do not remain in their homes but instead are authorized to work or participate in treatment, education, or training programs. Finally, house arrest is sometimes, but not necessarily, backed up by electronic monitoring; Renzema (1992), for example, reports that 10,549 people were on house arrest in Florida in August 1990, of whom 873 were on electronic monitoring.

House arrest comes in front- and back-end forms. In an early Oklahoma program (Meachum 1986), for example, prison inmates were released early subject to participation in a home confinement program. In Florida, which operates the largest and most diverse home confinement programs, most are front-end programs in which otherwise prison-bound offenders are supposed to be placed. In some states, especially in connection with electronic monitoring, house arrest is used in place of pretrial detention (Maxfield and Baumer 1990).

House arrest programs expanded rapidly beginning in the mid-1980s. The earliest programs were typically small (from thirty to fifty offenders) and often were composed mostly of driving-while-intoxicated (DWI) and minor property offenders (this was also true of most of the early electronic monitoring programs) (Morris and Tonry 1990, chap. 7).

Programs have grown and proliferated. The largest program is in Florida where more than 13,000 offenders were on house arrest in 1993 (Blomberg, Bales, and Reed 1993). Programs coupled with electronic monitoring, a subset, existed nowhere in 1982, in seven states in 1986, and in all fifty states in October 1990 (Renzema 1992, p. 46).

Considered by itself, the use of electronic monitoring has grown even more from its beginnings in 1983 in the Mexico courtroom of Judge Michael Goss and the Florida courtroom of Judge J. Allison DeFoor II (Ford and Schmidt 1985). In 1986, only ninety-five offenders were subject to monitoring (Renzema 1992, p. 41), a number that rose to 12,000 in 1990 (Baumer and Mendelsohn 1992, p. 54) and to a daily count of 30,000 to 50,000 in 1992 and 1993 (Lilly 1993, p. 4).

No American evaluations of the scale or sophistication of the best on boot camps or ISP have been published. One analysis of agency data for

Florida's front-end house arrest program concluded that it draws more offenders from among the prison-bound than from the probation-bound (Baird and Wagner 1990). However, this conclusion is based on dubious analyses.

A case study of the development, implementation, and evolution of a back-end program in Arizona cautions that house arrest programs are likely to share the prospects and problems of intermediate sanctions generally. Originally conceived as a money-saving system for early release of low-risk offenders, the program—which combined house arrest with electronic monitoring—wound up costing money. One problem was that, in addition to satisfying stringent statutory criteria (no violent or sex crimes, no prior felony convictions), inmates had to be approved for release by the parole board, which proved highly risk averse and released very few eligible inmates. When the program became operational, the rate of revocation for technical violations (34 percent of participants) was twice that for ordinary parolees. Finally, many probation officers began to justify the program not as an early release system for low-risk offenders, but as a mechanism for establishing tighter controls and closer surveillance for parolees than would otherwise be possible (Palumbo, Clifford, and Snyder-Joy 1992).

There are no other large-scale evaluations. House arrest coupled with electronic monitoring has been the subject of many small studies and a linked set of three studies in Indianapolis (Baumer, Maxfield, and Mendelsohn 1993). Both of two recent literature reviews (Baumer and Mendelsohn 1992; Renzema 1992) stress the scantiness of the research evidence on prison diversion, recidivism, and cost-effectiveness. On recidivism, Renzema (1992, p. 49) notes that most of the "research is uninterpretable because of shoddy or weak research designs." Baumer and Mendelsohn (1992, pp. 64–65) stress that "the incapacitative and public safety potential of this sanction have probably been considerably overstated" because the technology cannot control offenders' movement. They predict that house arrest will continue primarily to be used for low-risk offenders and will play little role as a custody alternative.

Day Reporting Centers

Day reporting centers, like the remaining two sanctions discussed, community service and day fines, differ from those discussed so far in that they were developed earlier and much more extensively outside the United States than in. The earliest American day reporting centers—places in which offenders spend their days under surveillance and participating in treatment and training programs while sleeping elsewhere—date from the mid-1980s. The English precursors, originally called day centres and now probation centres, began operation in the early 1970s. Most of our knowledge of American day reporting centers comes from descriptive writing; no published literature as yet provides credible findings on the important empirical questions.

The English programs date from creation of four "day-training centres" established under the Criminal Justice Act 1972, charged to provide intensive training programs for persistent petty offenders whose criminality was believed rooted in general social inadequacy, and from creation of ad hoc day centers for serious offenders that were set up by a number of local probation agencies. The training centers for a number of reasons were adjudged unsuccessful and were soon canceled.

The probation-run day centers, however, thrived, becoming the "flavor of the month" after enabling legislation was enacted in 1982, numbering at least 80 by 1985, and serving thousands of offenders by the late 1980s (Mair 1993a, p. 6). Programs vary, with some emphasizing control and surveillance more than others, some operating as a therapeutic community, and most offering a wide range of (mostly compulsory) activities. The maximum term of involvement is sixty days and some programs have set thirty-day or forty-five-day limits.

A major Home Office study (Mair 1988) concluded that "most centres unequivocally saw their aim as diversion from custody" (Mair 1993a, p. 6), that more than half of the participating offenders had previously been imprisoned, and that 47 percent had six or more prior convictions. A later reconviction study (Mair and Nee 1992) found a two-year reconviction rate of 63 percent. However, George Mair writes, though "on the face of it this may look high . . . the offenders targeted by centres represent a very high-risk group in terms of probability of reconviction" (Mair 1993a, p. 6). In addition, the reconviction data did not distinguish between those who completed the program and those who failed. The results were seen as so promising that the Criminal Justice Act 1991 envisioned a substantial expansion in use of day reporting centers.

A 1989 survey for the National Institute of Justice identified twenty-two day-reporting centers in eight states (Parent 1990), though many others have since opened. Most American centers opened after 1985. The best known (at least the best documented) centers were established in Massachusetts—in Springfield (Hampton County Sheriff's Department) and in Boston (the Metropolitan Day Reporting Center)—and both were based in part on the model provided by the English day centres (Larivee 1991; McDevitt and Miliano, 1992).

As with the English centers, American programs vary widely. Many are back-end programs into which offenders are released early from jail or prison. Some, however, are front-end programs to which offenders are sentenced by judges and some are used as alternatives to pretrial detention (Parent 1991). Programs range in duration from forty days to nine months and program content varies widely (Parent 1991). Most require development of hour-by-hour schedules of each participant's activities, some are highly intensive with ten-or-more supervision contacts per day, and a few include twenty-four-hour-per-day electronic monitoring (McDevitt and Miliano 1992). Unfortunately, no substantial evaluations have been published (a number of small in-house evaluations are cited in Larivee [1991] and McDevitt and Miliano [1992]).

Community Service

Community service is the most underused intermediate sanction in the United States. Used in many countries as a mid-level penalty to replace short prison terms for moderately severe crimes, community service in the United States is used primarily as a probation condition or as a penalty for trifling crimes like motor vehicle offenses. This is a pity because community service is a burdensome penalty that meets with widespread public approval (e.g., Doble, Immerwahr, and Robinson 1991), that is inexpensive to administer, that produces public value, and that can to a degree be scaled to the seriousness of crimes.

Doing work to benefit the community as a substitute for other punishments for crime has a history that dates at least from Imperial Rome. Modern use, however, is conventionally dated from a 1960s effort by judges in Alameda County, California, to avoid having to impose fines for traffic violations on low-income women, when they knew that many would be unable to pay and would be in danger of being sent to jail as a result.

The California program attracted widespread interest and influenced the establishment of community service programs in the United States and elsewhere. In the United States, many millions of dollars were spent in the 1970s by the Law Enforcement Assistance Administration, for programs for adults, and by the Office for Juvenile Justice and Delinquency Prevention, for programs for children, but with little lasting effect (McDonald 1992).

Community service did not come into widespread use as a prison alternative in the United States (Pease [1985] and McDonald [1986] provide detailed accounts with many references). Largely as a result, there has been little substantial research on the effectiveness of community service as an intermediate punishment (Pease 1985; Morris and Tonry 1990, chap. 6; McDonald 1992).

The only well-documented American community service project, operated by the Vera Institute of Justice, was established in 1979 in the Bronx, one of the boroughs of New York, and eventually spread to Manhattan, Brooklyn, and Queens. The program was designed as a credible penalty for repetitive property offenders who had previously been sentenced to probation or jail and who faced a six-month or longer jail term for the current conviction. Offenders were sentenced to seventy hours community service under the supervision of Vera foremen. Participants were told that attendance would be closely monitored and that nonattendance and noncooperation would be punished. An agreement was struck with the judiciary that immediate arrest warrants would be issued and prompt revocation hearings held for noncompliant participants. The goal was to draw half of participants from the target prison-bound group and half from offenders with less extensive records; after initial judicial reluctance was overcome (when only a third were prison diversions), the 50/50 balance was achieved. An extensive and sophisticated evaluation concluded that recidivism rates were unaffected by the program, that prison diversion goals were being met, and that the program saved taxpayers' money (McDonald 1986, 1992).

For offenders who do not present unacceptable risks of future violent (including sexual) crimes, a punitive sanction that costs much less than prison to implement, that promises no higher reoffending rates, and that creates negligible risks of violence by those who would otherwise be confined, has much to commend it.

Both American and European research and experience show that community service can serve as a meaningful, cost-effective sanction for offenders who would otherwise have been imprisoned.

Monetary Penalties

Monetary penalties for nontrivial crimes have yet to catch on in the United States. That is not to deny that millions of fines are imposed every year. Studies conducted as part of a fifteen-year program of fines research coordinated by the Vera Institute of Justice showed that fines are nearly the sole penalty for traffic offenses and in many courts are often imposed for misdemeanors (Hillsman, Sichel, and Mahoney 1984; Cole, Mahoney, Thornton, and Hanson 1987). And in many courts, most fines are collected. Although ambiguous lines of authority and absence of institutional self-interest sometimes result in haphazard and ineffective collection, courts that wish to do so can be effective collectors (Cole 1992).

Nor is it to deny that convicted offenders in some jurisdictions are routinely ordered to pay restitution and in most jurisdictions are routinely ordered to pay growing lists of fees for probation supervision, for urinalyses, and for use of electronic monitoring equipment. A survey of monetary exactions from offenders carried out in the late 1980s identified more than thirty separate charges, penalties, and fees that were imposed by courts, administrative agencies, and legislatures (Mullaney 1988). These commonly included court costs, fines, restitution, and payments to victim compensation funds. They often included a variety of supervision and monitoring fees, and in some jurisdictions (including the federal system under the Sentencing Reform Act of 1984) extended to repayment to the government of the full costs of prosecution and of carrying out any sentence imposed.

The problem is neither that monetary penalties are not imposed nor that they cannot be collected, but that, as George Cole and his colleagues reported when summarizing the results of a national survey of judges' attitudes about fines, "At present, judges do not regard the fine alone as a meaningful alternative to incarceration or probation" (Cole, Mahoney, Thornton, and Hanson 1987).

This American inability to see fines as serious penalties stands in marked contrast to the legal systems of other countries. In the Netherlands, the fine is legally presumed to be the preferred penalty for every crime, and Section 359(6) of the Code of Criminal Procedure requires judges to provide a statement of reasons in every case in which a fine is not imposed. In Germany in

1986, for another example, 81 percent of all sentenced adult criminals were ordered to pay a fine, including 73 percent of those convicted of crimes of violence (Hillsman and Greene 1992, p. 125).

European monetary penalties for serious crimes take two forms. The first is the "day fine," in use in the Scandinavian countries since the turn of the century and in Germany since the 1970s, which scales fines both to the defendant's ability to pay (some measure of daily income) and to the seriousness of the crime (expressed as the number of daily income units assessed) (Grebing 1982). The second is the use of the fine as a prosecutorial diversion device; in exchange for paying the fine, often the amount that would have been imposed after conviction, the criminal charges are dismissed.

Only the day fine has attracted much American attention, and the results to date are at best mildly promising. The initial pilot project was conducted in Staten Island, New York, in 1988–89, again under the auspices of the Vera Institute of Justice. Judges, prosecutors, and other court personnel were included in the planning and implementation was remarkably successful. Most judges cooperated with the new voluntary scheme, the distribution of fines imposed changed in ways that showed that judges were following the system, the average fine imposed increased by 25 percent, the total amount ordered on all defendants increased by 14 percent, and 70 percent of defendants paid their fines in full (Hillsman and Greene 1992).

A second modest pilot project was conducted for twelve weeks in 1989 in Milwaukee (McDonald, Greene, and Worzella 1992) and four projects funded by the Bureau of Justice Assistance operated for various periods between 1992 and 1994 in Maricopa County (Phoenix), Arizona, Bridgeport, Connecticut, Polk County, Iowa, and Coos, Josephine, Malheur, and Marion Counties in Oregon (Turner 1992). The Milwaukee project applied only to noncriminal violations, resulted in reduced total collections, and was abandoned. The Phoenix project, known as FARE (for Financial Assessments Related to Employability), was conceived as a mid-level sanction between unsupervised and supervised probation. The Iowa pilot included only misdemeanants and the Oregon projects included misdemeanants and probationable felonies (excluding Marion County, the largest, which covered only misdemeanants). Only in the Connecticut did the pilot cover a range of felonies and misdemeanors.

SUMMARY AND CONCLUSIONS

Readers, I hope, will draw at least six conclusions from this chapter. First, for offenders who do not present unacceptable risk of violence, well-managed intermediate sanctions offer a cost-effective way to keep them in the community at less cost than imprisonment and with no worse later prospect for criminality.

Second, boot camps, house arrest, and intensive supervision are highly vulnerable to net-widening when entry is controlled by judges. For boot camps, the solution is easy: have corrections officials select participants from among admitted prisoners. For house arrest and ISP, the solution is less easy: corrections officials can control entry to back-end programs; sentencing guidelines may be able to structure judges' decisions about admission to front-end programs.

Third, community service and monetary penalties remain woefully underdeveloped in the United States and much could be learned from Europe. Day fines remain as yet a promising idea, but have yet to demonstrate that they can win acceptance as a penalty for nontrivial crimes. Conditional discharges, in which convictable defendants pay a substantial fine in exchange for conditional dismissal of charges, like those common in Sweden, the Netherlands, and Germany remain unexplored as a potentially useful European penal import.

Fourth, front-end intermediate sanctions are unlikely to come into widespread use as prison alternatives unless sentencing theories and policies become more expansive and move away from oversimplified ideas about proportionality in punishment.

Fifth, intermediate sanctions may offer promise as a way to get and keep offenders into drug and other treatment programs. With drug treatment programs, at least, there is evidence that coerced treatment programs can reduce both later drug use and later crimes, and there is evidence in the ISP and boot camp literatures that these programs can increase treatment participation.

Sixth, there is no free lunch. The failure of most intermediate sanctions to achieve promised reductions in recidivism, cost. and prison use were never realistic, though for the most part they were offered in good faith. Intermediate sanctions can reduce costs and divert offenders from imprisonment, but those results are not easy to obtain.

REFERENCES

Anglin, Douglas, and Yih-Ing Hser. 1990. "Treatment of Drug Abuse." In *Drugs and Crime*, edited by Michael Tonry and James Q. Wilson. Vol. 13 of *Crime and Justice: A Review of Research*, edited by Michael Tonry and Norval Morris. Chicago: University of Chicago Press.

Austin, James, Michael Jones, and Melissa Bolyard. 1993. *The Growing Use of Jail Boot Camps: The Current State of the Art.* Research in Brief. Washington, D.C.: National Institute of Justice.

Baird, S. C., and D. Wagner. 1990. "Measuring Diversion: The Florida Community Control Program." *Crime and Delinquency* 36:112–25.

Ball, R. A., C. R. Huff, and J. R. Lilly. 1988. *House Arrest and Correctional Policy.* Newbury Park, Calif.: Sage.

Baumer, Terry L., M. G. Maxfield, and R. I. Mendelsohn. 1993. "A Comparative Analysis of Three Electronically Monitored Home Detention Programs." *Justice Quarterly* 10:121–42.

Baumer, Terry L., and Robert I. Mendelsohn. 1992. "Electronically Monitored Home Confinement: Does It Work?" In *Smart Sentencing: The Emergence of Intermediate Sanctions*, edited by James M. Byrne, Arthur J. Lurigio, and Joan Petersilia. Newbury Park, Calif.: Sage.

Blomberg, Thomas G., William Bales, and Karen Reed. 1993. "Intermediate Punishment: Redistributing or Extending Social Control?" *Crime, Law, and Social Change* 19:187–201.

Bureau of Justice Statistics. 1992a. *Prisoners in 1991.* Washington, D.C.: Bureau of Justice Statistics, U.S. Department of Justice.

Bureau of Justice Statistics. 1994b. "State and Federal Prison Population Tops One Million." Press release dated October 27, 1994. Washington, D.C.: U.S. Department of Justice.

Byrne, James M., and Linda M. Kelly. 1989. *Restructuring Probation as an Intermediate Sanction: An Evaluation of the Massachusetts Intensive Probation Supervision Program.* Final report to the National Institute of Justice. Lowell, Mass.: University of Lowell, Department of Criminal Justice.

Byrne, James M., Arthur J. Lurigio, and Joan Petersilia. 1992. *Smart Sentencing: The Emergence of Intermediate Sanctions.* Newbury Park, Calif.: Sage.

Byrne, James M., and April Pattavina. 1992. "The Effectiveness Issue: Assessing What Works in the Adult Community Corrections System." In *Smart Sentencing: The Emergence of Intermediate Sanctions*, edited by James M. Byrne, Arthur J. Lurigio, and Joan Petersilia. Newbury Park, Calif.: Sage.

Clear, Todd. 1987. "The New Intensive Supervision Movement." Paper presented at the annual meeting of the American Society of Criminology, Montreal, November.

Clear, Todd R., and James M. Byrne. 1992. "The Future of Intermediate Sanctions: Questions to Consider." In *Smart Sentencing: The Emergence of Intermediate Sanctions*, edited by James M. Byrne, Arthur J. Lurigio, and Joan Petersilia. Newbury Park, Calif.: Sage.

Cole, George F. 1992. "Monetary Sanctions: The Problem of Compliance." In *Smart Sentencing: The Emergence of Intermediate Sanctions*, edited by James M. Byrne, Arthur J. Lurigio, and Joan Petersilia. Newbury Park, Calif.: Sage.

Cole, George F., Barry Mahoney, Marlene Thornton, and Roger A. Hanson. 1987. *The Practices and Attitudes of Trial Court Judges Regarding Fines as a Criminal Sanction.* Washington, D.C.: National Institute of Justice.

Doble, John, Stephen Immerwahr, and Amy Robinson. 1991. *Punishing Criminals: The People of Delaware Consider the Options.* New York: Edna McConnell Clark Foundation.

Erwin, Billie. 1987. *Evaluation of Intensive Probation Supervision in Georgia.* Atlanta: Georgia Department of Corrections.

Ford, Daniel, and Annesley K. Schmidt. 1985. *Electronically Monitored Home Confinement.* Research in Action. Washington, D.C.: National Institute of Justice.

Gendreau, Paul, Francis T. Cullen, and James Bonta. 1994. "Intensive Rehabilitation Supervision: The Next Generation in Community Corrections?" *Federal Probation* 58:72–78.

Grebing, Gerhardt. 1982. *The Fine in Comparative Law. A Survey of 21 Countries.* Occasional Paper no. 9. Cambridge: University of Cambridge, Institute of Criminology.

Hillsman, Sally, and Judith A. Greene. 1992. "The Use of Fines as an Intermediate Sanction." In *Smart Sentencing: The Emergence of Intermediate Sanctions,* edited by James M. Bryne, Arthur J. Lurigio, and Joan Petersilia. Newbury Park, Calif.: Sage.

Hillsman, Sally, Joyce Sichel, and Barry Mahoney. 1984. *Fines in Sentencing: A Study of the Use of the Fine as a Criminal Sanction.* Washington, D.C.: National Institute of Justice.

Larivee, John J. 1991. "Day Reporting in Massachusetts: Supervision, Sanction, and Treatment." *Overcrowded Times* 2(1):7–8.

Lilly, J. Robert. 1993. "Electronic Monitoring in the U.S.: An Update." *Overcrowded Times* 4(5): 4, 15.

McDevitt, Jack, and Robyn Miliano. 1992. "Day Reporting Centers: An Innovative Concept in Intermediate Sanctions." In *Smart Sentencing: The Emergence of Intermediate Sanctions,* edited by James M. Bryne, Arthur J. Lurigio, and Joan Petersilia. Newbury Park, Calif.: Sage.

McDonald, Douglas. 1986. *Punishment without Walls: Community Service Sentences in New York City.* New Brunswick, N.J.: Rutgers University Press.

McDonald, Douglas. 1992. "Punishing Labor: Unpaid Community Service as a Criminal Sentence." In *Smart Sentencing: The Emergence of Intermediate Sanctions,* edited by James M. Bryne, Arthur J. Lurigio, and Joan Petersilia. Newbury Park, Calif.: Sage.

McDonald, Douglas, Judith Greene, and Charles Worzella. 1992. *Day Fines in American Courts: The Staten Island and Milwaukee Experiments.* Issues and Practices. Washington, D.C.: National Institute of Justice.

MacKenzie, Doris Layton. 1993. "Boot Camp Prisons 1993." *National Institute of Justice Journal* 227:21–28.

MacKenzie, Doris Layton. 1994. "Boot Camps: A National Assessment." *Overcrowded Times* 5(4):1, 14–18.

MacKenzie, Doris Layton, and Dale Parent. 1992. "Boot Camp Prisons for Young Offenders." In *Smart Sentencing: The Emergence of Intermediate Sanctions,* edited by James M. Bryne, Arthur J. Lurigio, and Joan Petersilia. Newbury Park, Calif.: Sage.

MacKenzie, Doris Layton, and A. Piquero. 1994. "The Impact of Shock Incarceration Programs on Prison Crowding." *Crime and Delinquency* 40:222–49.

MacKenzie, Doris Layton, and J. W. Shaw. 1990. "Inmate Adjustment and Change during Shock Incarceration: The Impact of Correctional Boot Camp Programs." *Justice Quarterly* 7(1):125–50.

MacKenzie, Doris Layton, and J. W. Shaw. 1993. "The Impact of Shock Incarceration on Technical Violations and New Criminal Activities." *Justice Quarterly* 10:463–87.

MacKenzie, Doris Layton, and C. Souryal. 1994. *Multi-Site Evaluation of Shock Incarceration.* Report to the National Institute of Justice. College Park: University of Maryland, Department of Criminology and Criminal Justice.

Mair, George. 1988. *Probation Day Centres.* London: H.M. Stationery Office.

Mair, George. 1993. "Day Centres in England and Wales." *Overcrowded Times* 4(2):5–7.

Mair, George, and Claire Nee. 1992. "Day Centre Reconviction Rates." *British Journal of Criminology* 32:329–39.

Maxfield, M., and T. Baumer. 1990. "Home Detention with Electronic Monitoring: Comparing Pretrial and Postconviction Programs." *Crime and Delinquency* 36:521–36.

Meachum, Larry R. 1986. "House Arrest: Oklahoma Experience." *Corrections Today* 48(4):102ff.

Morris, Norval. 1974. *The Future of Imprisonment.* Chicago: University of Chicago Press.

Morris, Norval, and Michael Tonry. 1990. *Between Prison and Probation: Intermediate Punishments in a Rational Sentencing System.* New York: Oxford University Press.

Mullaney, Fahy G. 1988. *Economic Sanctions in Community Corrections.* Washington, D.C.: National Institute of Corrections.

National Conference of State Legislatures. 1993. *State Budget Actions—1993.* Denver: National Conference of State Legislatures.

National Institute of Justice. 1994. *Drug Use Forecasting (DUF)—1993 Annual Report.* Washington, D.C.: National Institute of Justice.

Palumbo, Dennis J., Mary Clifford, and Zoann K. Snyder-Joy. 1992. "From Net-Widening to Intermediate Sanctions: The Transformation of Alternatives to Incarceration from Benevolence to Malevolence." In *Smart Sentencing: The Emergence of Intermediate Sanctions,* edited by James M. Byrne, Arthur J. Lurigio, and Joan Petersilia. Newbury Park, Calif.: Sage.

Parent, Dale. 1989. *Shock Incarceration: An Overview of Existing Programs.* Washington, D.C.: National Institute of Justice.

Parent, Dale. 1990. *Day Reporting Centers for Criminal Offenders: A Description Analysis of Existing Programs.* Washington, D.C.: National Institute of Justice.

Parent, Dale. 1991. "Day Reporting Centers: An Emerging Intermediate Sanction." *Overcrowded Times* 2(1):6, 8.

Parent, Dale. 1994. "Boot Camps Failing to Achieve Goals." *Overcrowded Times* 5(4):8–11.

Pearson, Frank. 1987. *Final Report of Research on New Jersey's Intensive Supervision Program.* New Brunswick, N.J.: Rutgers University, Department of Sociology, Institute for Criminological Research.

Pearson, Frank. 1988. "Evaluation of New Jersey's Intensive Supervision Program." *Crime and Delinquency* 34:437–48.

Pease, Ken. 1985. "Community Service Orders." In *Crime and Justice: A Review of Research,* vol. 6, edited by Michael Tonry and Norval Morris. Chicago: University of Chicago Press.

Petersilia, Joan, Arthur J. Lurigio, and James M. Byrne. 1992. "Introduction: The Emergence of Intermediate Sanctions." In *Smart Sentencing: The Emergence of Intermediate Sanctions,* edited by James M. Byrne, Arthur J. Lurigio, and Joan Petersilia. Newbury Park, Calif.: Sage.

Petersilia, Joan, and Susan Turner. 1993. "Intensive Probation and Parole." In *Crime and Justice: A Review of Research*, vol. 17, edited by Michael Tonry. Chicago: University of Chicago Press.

President's Commission on Model State Drug Laws. 1993. *Final Report.* Washington, D.C.: U.S. Government Printing Office.

Renzema, Marc. 1992. "Home Confinement Programs: Development, Implementation, and Impact." In *Smart Sentencing: The Emergence of Intermediate Sanctions*, edited by James M. Byrne, Arthur J. Lurigio, and Joan Petersilia. Newbury Park, Calif.: Sage.

Tonry, Michael, and Kate Hamilton. 1995. *Intermediate Sanctions in Overcrowded Times.* Boston: Northeastern University Press.

Tonry, Michael, and Richard Will. 1988. *Intermediate Sanctions.* Final Report submitted to the National Institute of Justice. Castine, Maine: Castine Research Corporation.

Turner, Susan. 1992. "Day-Fine Projects Launched in Four Jurisdictions." *Overcrowded Times* 3(6):5–6.

U.S. General Accounting Office. 1990. *Intermediate Sanctions: Their Impacts on Prison Crowding, Costs, and Recidivism Are Still Unclear.* Gaithersburg, Md.: U.S. General Accounting Office.

U.S. General Accounting Office. 1993. *Prison Boot Camps: Short-Term Prison Costs Reduced, But Long-Term Impact Uncertain.* Washington, D.C.: U.S. General Accounting Office.

von Hirsch, Andrew. 1976. *Doing Justice: The Choice of Punishments.* New York: Hill & Wang.

What Works With Juvenile Offenders?
A Review of "Graduated Sanction" Programs

BARRY KRISBERG, ELLIOTT CURRIE, AND DAVID ONEK

These are tough times for juvenile offenders. Across the country, there have been repeated calls to "get tougher" on young people who break the law—and those calls have often been followed by increasingly draconian responses.

Dr. Barry Krisberg is president of the National Council on Crime and Delinquency, which is headquartered in San Francisco. **Dr. Elliott Currie** is a lecturer in the legal studies program at the University of California at Berkeley and director of the East Bay Corridor Project. **David Onek** is a research associate with the National Council on Crime and Delinquency.

"What Works with Juvenile Offenders? A Review of 'Graduated Sanction' Programs" by Barry Krisberg, Elliott Currie, and David Onek is from *Criminal Justice*, Summer 1995, pp. 20–29. Reprinted with permission of the American Bar Association.

Part of the rationale for these developments is the claim that nothing but incarceration "works" with serious juvenile offenders.

PUBLIC PERCEPTION NOT BORNE OUT BY RESEARCH

A careful consideration of the evidence for that popular view finds it wanting. Criminologists have suspected for many years that some kinds of intervention programs for juvenile offenders do indeed "work" to prevent recidivism and often do so far more cheaply than imprisonment.

Under a grant from the federal Office of Juvenile Justice and Delinquency Prevention, the National Council on Crime and Delinquency (NCCD) recently analyzed a vast array of materials on interventions with young offenders. Our research confirms a more optimistic view.

We found, unsurprisingly, that not *everything* works; not all programs to turn around young offenders makes a difference. But some programs *do* work—and, increasingly, we are coming to understand *why* they work. The overall finding is clear: The idea that rehabilitation is nothing more than useless "pork" is a myth. And it is a myth that dramatically hobbles our ability to cope with serious juvenile crime.

Graduated sanction programs for juvenile offenders are one type of solution being explored by states across the nation. Types of graduated sanctions include:

- immediate sanctions, which are appropriate for first-time, nonviolent offenders;
- intermediate sanctions, which target repeat minor offenders and first-time serious offenders; and
- secure care, which is reserved for repeat serious and violent offenders.

In a model graduated sanctions system, the majority of youths are placed in community-based immediate and intermediate sanction programs while secure care is reserved for the violent few.

Research has been conducted on individual programs and statewide systems, and there have been meta-analyses of large numbers of individual studies. Drawing from all of this research, it is possible to determine the common characteristics of *effective* graduated sanction programs.

STUDIES ON GRADUATED SANCTIONS

The research on graduated sanctions for juveniles is uneven. There are some areas with fairly strong results, but others in which research data are almost nonexistent.

One reason for the overall dearth of graduated sanctions research is that such studies are quite difficult to conduct. Large samples are rare because there are usually small numbers of serious juvenile offenders. Small sample sizes make it very difficult to find statistically significant results. This is particularly true of programs for the most serious offenders, where the numbers of offenders are especially small.

Another common problem in graduated sanctions research is finding comparable control groups. It is difficult to design a study with random assignment (where individuals are randomly assigned to different programs so the results can be compared without concern about selection bias) because practitioners often resist it. But without random assignment, researchers must find a control group that is comparable to the experimental group.

Such control groups often are not carefully selected or the differences between the two groups are not taken into account in the analysis. The result is that it is often impossible to tell if differences between the outcomes of the experimental and control groups were due to differences between the experimental and control *programs* or to the types of youths each program served.

This said, some types of graduated sanction programs have been adequately researched. There has been fairly extensive testing of highly structured alternative programs for youths who otherwise would be incarcerated. There are also some solid studies of intensive supervision programs.

Some conclusions can be drawn from the limited body of research that does exist. Community-based graduated sanction programs seem to be at least as successful as traditional incarceration programs in reducing recidivism. Studies of the best-structured graduated sanction programs have shown them to be *more* effective than incarceration. In addition, community-based programs often cost significantly less than their traditional counterparts.

INDIVIDUAL PROGRAMS

Nothing Works?   In the 1970s, Martinson's claim that "nothing works" with juvenile offenders was widely disseminated among criminal justice researchers. (Robert Martinson, *What Works? Questions and Answers about Prison Reform*, 36 Pub. Interest 22–45 (1974)) Martinson and his followers argued that it was fruitless to attempt to rehabilitate juvenile offenders; instead, they recommended a greater focus on deterrence and incapacitation.

In the late 1970s and afterward, however, Martinson's conclusion came under critical scrutiny. There is a substantial and growing body of evidence that some things do work with juvenile offenders. Indeed, Martinson himself renounced his earlier views in the late 1970s. (Robert Martinson, *New Findings, New Views: A Note of Caution Regarding Sentencing Reform*, 7 Hofstra L. Rev. 242–58 (1979))

California Youth Authority   Studies since the 1960s have shown community-based programs to be at least as effective as traditional correctional programs. In the 1960s the California Youth Authority, as part of the Community Treatment Project, randomly assigned youths to either an intensive community-treatment program, with caseloads no larger than twelve, or traditional training schools.

Early results showed that the community-based group did better than the traditional group. (Ted Palmer, *California's Community Treatment Program for Delinquent Adolescents*, 8 J. Res. in Crime & Delinq. 74–82 (1971))

After one year, the rate of parole failure for the community group was 18 percent, compared to a rate of 35 percent for the traditional group; after two years, the community group had a parole failure rate of 39 percent, compared to 60 percent for the traditional group.

A later study, though critical of claims for this level of success, concluded that the community group fared no worse than the traditional group. (Paul Lerman, *Community Treatment and Social Control* (Univ. of Chicago Press 1975))

Silverlake   The Silverlake experiment, conducted by Empey and Lubeck, studied juvenile offenders from Los Angeles County who were randomly assigned to either a county correctional facility (the control group) or a small, community-based program that emphasized daily school attendance and intensive group therapy (the experimental group). (Lamar Empey & Steven Lubeck, *The Silverlake Experiment* (Aldine 1971))

The rearrest rates for the two groups were virtually identical—60 percent for the experimental group versus 56 percent for the control group. Empey and Lubeck concluded that enhanced community-based programs were as effective as traditional correctional placements. Significantly, the community program cost $1,700 per youth per year while the traditional program cost $4,600.

Provo   A similar study was conducted by Empey and Erickson in Provo, Utah. (Lamar Empey & Maynard Erickson, *The Provo Experiment* (Lexington Books 1972)) Youths were randomly assigned to either traditional probation or to intensive probation, which included daily counseling sessions.

These two groups were compared to each other and also to a group of youths released from training schools across the state, although the training school youths were not randomly assigned. Both of the groups that remained in the community had lower recidivism rates than the training school group.

The probation groups averaged 2.4 new arrests over the four-year tracking period, while the training school group averaged 5.3 new arrests. The intensive probation group fared significantly better than the traditional probation group, although these differences leveled out after one year.

UDIS   A study by Murray and Cox of the Unified Delinquency Intervention Services (UDIS) programs in Chicago found something similar using a new outcome measure—the "suppression effect," or reductions in the frequency of reoffending. (Charles Murray & Louis Cox, *Beyond Probation* (Sage, 1979))

The study compared youths assigned to a UDIS alternative program with youths sent to traditional Department of Corrections facilities. The youths in both groups showed large reductions in the incidence of reoffending. The most intensive of the UDIS programs produced suppression effects comparable to institutionalization.

VisionQuest   Greenwood and Turner evaluated the San Diego VisionQuest program, which served as an alternative to incarceration for serious juvenile offenders. (Peter Greenwood & Susan Turner, *The VisionQuest Program: An Evaluation* (RAND 1987))

VisionQuest youths spent 12–15 months in various challenging outdoor "impact" programs, with a consistent education plan and individual treatment plan following them through each program stage. In the Greenwood and Turner study, the outcomes for VisionQuest graduates were compared to those of delinquent youths who had been placed in a traditional correctional institution operated by the county.

In spite of the fact that the experimental VisionQuest group consisted of more serious offenders than the control group, the VisionQuest group outperformed the controls. VisionQuest youths were substantially less likely to be rearrested in the first year after release than the traditional group (55% vs. 71%). When differences in group characteristics were statistically controlled, it was determined that first-year rearrest rates for VisionQuest youths were about half that of the controls.

FANS   Still more recently, Henggeler et al. completed an experimental study of South Carolina's Family and Neighborhood Services (FANS) program. This public program utilizes the principles of "multisystemic" therapy—a "highly individualized family- and home-based treatment" designed to deal with offenders in the context of their family and community problems. (Scott Henggeler et al., *Family Preservation Using Multisystemic Therapy: An Effective Alternative to Incarcerating Serious Juvenile Offenders*, 60(6) J. Consulting & Clinical Psychol. (1992))

FANS targeted serious and violent offenders at imminent risk of out-of-home placement. The program employed masters-level therapists who worked with very small caseloads (four families each) over an average of slightly more than four months. The caseworkers were available on a twenty-four-hour basis and saw the juvenile and/or the family as often as once daily, usually in the home.

Youths in the study were randomly assigned either to FANS or to normal probation treatment, in which few services were provided. The evaluation found that experimentals outperformed controls. At fifty-nine weeks after the initial referral, there were significant positive differences in rates of incarceration, arrests, and self-reported offenses between FANS youths and controls.

Youths in the FANS program acquired only about *half* as many arrests as the controls; 68 percent of controls experienced some incarceration versus 20 percent of the FANS group. These findings were reinforced by self-report measures and by favorable changes among the FANS group in family cohesion and reduced aggression with peers.

IPP Studies of intensive probation programs for youthful offenders come to similar conclusions. Barton and Butts, for example, completed an evaluation of the Wayne County Intensive Probation Program (IPP) in Detroit, Michigan. (William Barton & Jeffrey Butts, *The Metro County Intensive Supervision Experiment* (Inst. for Soc. Res. 1988))

Youths in IPP were placed into one of three alternative programs: an intensive supervision program run by the state, a family preservation program run by a private provider, or a day treatment program run by a private provider.

In the Barton and Butts evaluation, the experimental group consisted of youths assigned to one of these three programs, while the control group contained youths placed in a state institution. Youths were randomly assigned to one of the two groups.

The researchers found that the overall performances of the experimental and control groups were comparable over a two-year follow-up period. In addition, IPP programs cost less than one-third as much as incarceration—Barton and Butts estimated that the programs saved $8.8 million over three years.

ISU Wiebush evaluated the Lucas County, Ohio, Intensive Supervision Unit (ISU), a public program that targeted nonviolent felony offenders. (Richard G. Wiebush, *Juvenile Intensive Supervision: Impact on Felony Offenders Diverted From Institutional Placement*, 39 Crime & Delinq. 68–88 (1993))

ISU provided case-management and surveillance services to its youths. A comprehensive treatment plan was developed for each youth. ISU probation officers have average caseloads of only fifteen youths. Wiebush used a quasi-experimental design to compare the outcomes for ISU youths with a group of youths who were eligible for ISU but instead were incarcerated and then released to parole supervision.

Analysis of the youths' pre-program characteristics showed that there were few differences. Outcome measures included rearrest, readjudication, and incarceration. All youths were tracked for their first eighteen months in the community.

The results showed that there were no significant differences between the two groups in the extent or seriousness of recidivism, except that the ISU youth had more technical violations. It was concluded that ISU was as effective as incarceration for serious offenders. Moreover, ISU cost just $6,020 per year, compared to $32,320 for incarceration.

VJO Fagan conducted an in-depth study of the Violent Juvenile Offender (VJO) program, which provided a continuum of care for violent juvenile offenders in four urban sites. (Jeffrey Fagan, *Treatment and Reintegration of Violent Juvenile Offenders: Experimental Results*, 7 Just. Q. 233–63 (1990))

VJO youths were initially placed in small, secure facilities and were gradually reintegrated into the community through community-based residential programs followed by intensive supervision. There was continuous case management starting in secure care and extending through the reintegration phases. Eligible youths were randomly assigned to experimental VJO programs or traditional juvenile corrections programs.

In Boston and Detroit, the two sites (out of four total sites) with the strongest implementation of the program design, VJO youths had significantly fewer and less serious rearrests than the control group when time at risk was taken into account. In addition, youths in these two sites had significantly longer intervals until their first arrest, regardless of time at risk.

Fagan concluded that "the principles and theories built into [VJO] programs can reduce recidivism and serious crime among violent juvenile offenders." (*Id.* at 254) Further, Fagan stated that "reintegration and transition strategies should be the focus of correctional policy, rather than lengthy confinement in state training schools with minimal supervision upon release." (*Id.* at 233)

Skillman Not every study, to be sure, is as encouraging. Although the Fagan study seemed to reaffirm the importance of aftercare supervision, an evaluation by Greenwood et al. of experimental aftercare programs in Detroit and Pittsburgh found different results. (Peter Greenwood, Elizabeth Piper Deschenes & John Adams, *Chronic Juvenile Offenders: Final Results from the Skillman Aftercare Experiment* (RAND 1993))

The two experimental programs shared common core features, including prerelease planning involving the aftercare worker, youth, and family; an intensive level of supervision, including several daily contacts; efforts to resolve family problems; efforts to involve the youth in community activities; and highly motivated caseworkers.

Youths in the study, all of whom were returning home from residential placement, were randomly assigned either to one of the experimental aftercare programs or to traditional post-release supervision. There were no significant differences between the experimental and control groups in the number of rearrests, number of reconvictions, and severity of reoffenses. There were also no significant differences between the groups in self-reported offenses.

An explanation offered by the authors for these disappointing results is the difficulty, as discussed earlier, in finding significant differences when there are small sample sizes. Each site had a sample of approximately fifty experimental and fifty control youths.

Greenwood et al. concluded that "the levels of intensive aftercare supervision and services for chronic juvenile offenders, as provided in this demonstration project, appear to have had much less effect on subsequent behavior than many of the advocates of aftercare or intensive supervision had hoped." (*Id.* at xii)

Effective alternatives   Taken together, these studies of community-based graduated sanction programs show that such programs can serve as safe, cost-effective alternatives to incarceration for many youths. Even the less favorable studies we have discussed show community-based programs to be as effective as traditional training schools in reducing recidivism. And the more encouraging studies suggest that when alternative programs are carefully conceived and well-implemented, they can be *more* effective.

STATE SYSTEMS

In addition to studies of individual graduated sanction programs, studies have been conducted of state systems that emphasize graduated sanctions.

Massachusetts   The Massachusetts Department of Youth Services (DYS) places less emphasis on incarceration than perhaps any other state system in the nation. In 1972, Massachusetts closed down its traditional training schools.

Today, the state relies on a sophisticated network of small, secure programs for violent youths coupled with a broad range of highly structured community-based programs for the majority of committed youths. Most of these community-based programs are operated by private nonprofit agencies under contract with DYS. Secure facilities are reserved for only the most serious offenders (approximately 15% of all commitments). The largest of these secure programs houses just twenty offenders.

The impact of the Massachusetts system was initially studied by Coates et al. in the late 1970s. (Robert Coates, Alden Miller & Lloyd Ohlin, *Diversity in a Youth Correctional System* (Ballinger 1978)) Coates and his colleagues compared the outcomes of a sample of youths released from the newly established community-based programs in 1974 with a group released from Massachusetts training schools in 1968, before the state's reforms were enacted.

The researchers reported that the average recidivism rates for youths in the community-based programs sample were actually *higher* than for youths in the training school sample (74% vs. 66%). This finding may be partially explained by a decrease in less serious offenders being committed to DYS.

In any case, a closer analysis of the data revealed that in those parts of the state where community programs were properly implemented, recidivism rates were equal or slightly lower than the training school sample. The authors concluded that "regions that most adequately implemented the re-form measures with a diversity of programs did produce decreases in re-cidivism over time." (*Id.* at 177) In addition, community program youths throughout the state showed better attitudinal adjustment than institu-tionalized youths.

In 1989, NCCD completed a second study of the Massachusetts system. (Barry Krisberg, James Austin & Patricia A. Steele, *Unlocking Juvenile Cor-rections* (NCCD 1989))

NCCD's research on the Massachusetts community-based approach re-vealed recidivism rates that were as good as or better than most other ju-risdictions. DYS youths showed a significant decline in the incidence and severity in offending in the twelve months after entry into DYS community programs as compared to the pre-DYS period. These declines in offending were sustained over the next two years.

NCCD also found that the Massachusetts approach was cost effective: Massachusetts saved an estimated $11 million annually by relying on community-based care.

Utah   NCCD also studied the Utah juvenile justice system, which like Massachusetts, relies on community-based programs for most committed youths. (Barry Krisberg et al., *The Impact of Juvenile Court Sanctions* (NCCD 1988))

Using a pre/post test design, the study found that although a high pro-portion of youths were rearrested, there was a substantial "suppression ef-fect"—youths showed large declines in the frequency and severity of of-fending after correctional intervention.

Maryland   Gottfredson and Barton found different results in a study of the closing of the Montrose Training School in Maryland. (Denise C. Gottfred-son & William H. Barton, *Deinstitutionalization of Juvenile Offenders* (Univ. of Md. 1992))

The experimental group consisted of youths committed to the Maryland Division of Youth Services after Montrose had been closed. These youths were placed in community-based programs. The control group was youths who had been incarcerated in Montrose before it was closed.

The researchers found that the control group outperformed the exper-imental group on most recidivism measures. This result is similar to the orig-inal Massachusetts study completed by Coates et al., although those earlier researchers found positive results in the regions with strong program im-plementation.

The Maryland study, like the original Massachusetts study, was con-ducted immediately after the closing of a training school when community-based programs were at the earliest stage of implementation. It may be that these community-based programs need to operate and improve for several years before positive results will be found, as NCCD's later Massachusetts study suggests.

Resources Considered and Recidivism Reduced These studies suggest that states with well-implemented graduated sanction systems are as effective at reducing recidivism as states that rely on traditional approaches. In addition, states employing graduated sanction systems save significant resources, which can be shifted to delinquency prevention programs.

META-ANALYSES

Meta-analysis is an analytic technique that synthesizes results across multiple program evaluations. Several recent meta-analyses have again rebuked the claim that "nothing works" with juvenile offenders and supported the notion that rehabilitation can be effective, particularly when it is delivered in a community setting. The meta-analyses also point to specific strategies that appear more promising than others.

Lipsey Lipsey has provided the most comprehensive meta-analysis of delinquency studies to date. (Mark W. Lipsey, *Juvenile Delinquency Treatment: A Meta-Analytic Inquiry into the Variability of Effects*, in *Meta-Analysis for Explanation: A Casebook* (Thomas D. Cook et al. eds., Russell Sage Found. 1991))

His analysis incorporates 443 such studies, 373 of which were published between 1970 and 1987, including studies of both institutional and community-based programs. All of the studies had experimental designs.

Lipsey found that 64 percent of the study outcomes favored the treatment group, 30 percent favored the control group, and 6 percent favored neither group. The primary outcome measure in 85 percent of the studies was formal contact with the police or juvenile justice system (arrests, police contact, court contact, probation contact, parole contact, institutionalization, or institutional disciplinary contact).

Programs employing behaviorally oriented, skill-oriented, and multimodal treatment methods—methods employed by many of the graduated sanction programs discussed earlier—produced larger effects than other treatment approaches. Deterrence and "shock" approaches—methods employed by control-based incarceration programs—were associated with negative results.

In addition, Lipsey found that the successful treatment approaches produced larger positive effects in community rather than institutional settings, providing strong support for community-based graduated sanction programs.

Garrett Along similar lines, Garrett analyzed 111 quasi-experimental studies of adjudicated delinquents conducted between 1960 and 1983. (Carol Garrett, *Effects of Residential Treatment on Adjudicated Delinquents: A Meta-Analysis*, 22 J. Res. in Crime & Delinq. 287–308 (1985))

Most (81%) of the studies were from institutional treatment programs; the rest (19%) were from community residential treatment programs. Three-fourths of the studies involved a control group; the remaining one-fourth used a pre/post design with no comparison group. The outcome measures used varied from study to study and included recidivism, institutional adjustment, psychological adjustment, and academic performance.

Garrett found that the treatment groups, on average, outperformed the controls on these outcome measures. She concluded that the results "are encouraging in that adjudicated delinquents were found to respond positively to treatment on many criteria. The change was modest in some cases, substantial in others, but overwhelmingly in a positive direction." (*Id.* at 306)

Behavioral treatment showed larger positive effects than psychodynamic treatment or life skills treatment. The individual treatment approaches with the largest positive effects were contingency management, family therapy, and cognitive-behavioral. Garrett concluded that "the results of the meta-analysis suggest that treatment of adjudicated delinquents in an institutional or community residential setting does work." (*Id.* at 287)

Whitehead and Lab A less encouraging study was Whitehead and Lab's meta-analyses of fifty studies of institutional and community-based programs. (John T. Whitehead & Steven P. Lab, *A Meta-Analysis of Juvenile Correctional Treatment*, 26 J. Res. in Crime & Delinq. 276–95 (1989)) The researchers concluded that "correctional treatment has little effect on recidivism." (*Id.* at 291) This conclusion, however, was based on an extremely rigid definition of successful treatment.

Andrews et al. Whitehead and Lab's conclusion was challenged by Andrews et al. in a meta-analyses which included forty-five of the fifty studies used by Whitehead and Lab. (D.A. Andrews et al., *Does Correctional Treatment Work? A Clinically Relevant and Psychologically Informed Meta-Analysis*, 28 Criminology 369–404 (1990))

The researchers added thirty-five studies of both juvenile and adult programs to their analysis. The researchers coded the programs into four categories. Programs had either (1) "appropriate" correctional service; (2) "inappropriate" correctional service; (3) unspecified correctional service; or (4) nonservice criminal sanctioning.

The appropriate correctional service group included (1) service delivery to higher risk cases, (2) all behavioral programs (except those involving delivery of service to lower risk cases), (3) comparisons reflecting specific responsivity-treatment comparisons, and (4) nonbehavioral programs that clearly stated that criminogenic need was targeted and that structured intervention was employed. (*Id.* at 379)

The inappropriate correctional service included (1) service delivery to lower risk cases and/or mismatching according to a need/responsivity system, (2) nondirective relationship-dependent and/or unstructured psychodynamic counseling, (3) all milieu and group approaches with an emphasis on within-group communication and without a clear plan for gaining control over procriminal modeling and reinforcement, (4) nondirective or poorly targeted academic and vocational approaches, and (5) "Scared Straight." (*Id.*)

Andrews et al. found that programs with appropriate correctional service had the most positive outcomes, followed by unspecified correctional service. Inappropriate service and nonservice criminal sanctioning were both associated with negative outcomes.

The authors reaffirmed the importance of rehabilitation, concluding that "appropriate correctional service appears to work better than criminal sanctions not involving rehabilitative service and better than services less consistent with . . . principles of effective rehabilitation." (*Id.* at 384)

Palmer In a comprehensive review of the existing meta-analyses, Palmer summarized the findings into four main points (Ted Palmer, *The Re-Emergence of Correctional Interventions* (Sage 1992)):

1) When individual programs were grouped together and analyzed as a single, generic approach (e.g., counseling), many approaches did not seem to successfully reduce recidivism.

2) Despite the above finding in regard to groups of programs, there were many individual programs that seemed successful. The experimental group outperformed the controls in many or most individual programs. Specifically, experimentals significantly outperformed controls in at least 25 percent to 35 percent of all programs, while controls significantly outperformed experimentals in just under 10 percent. Statistically successful individual programs could be found in almost every generic program category, even if the category as a whole seemed unsuccessful.

3) Although generic approaches may not have been shown to have better outcomes, some were associated with equal outcomes. Such approaches seem to be as effective as traditional approaches, and often cost much less.

4) At the generic level, the interventions considered most successful were behavioral, cognitive-behavioral, skill-oriented or life skills, multimodal, and family intervention.

Palmer concluded that "the large number of positive outcomes that have been found in the past three decades with studies whose designs and analysis were at least adequate leaves little doubt that many programs work." (*Id.* at 76)

WHAT WORKS

Rehabilitation Important

These meta-analyses serve to rebuke the claim that nothing works with juvenile offenders and reaffirm the importance of rehabilitation. They suggest that rehabilitation is more successful in community rather than institutional settings. In addition, they point to specific interventions—such as behavioral, skill-oriented, and multimodel approaches—that seem more successful than others.

Research Literature on Critical Components

In the past, several researchers have identified what they believe are the critical components of successful programs for delinquent youths. Altschuler and Armstrong, for example, cited six key components:

- continuous case management;
- emphasis on reintegration and reentry services;
- opportunities for youth achievement and involvement in program decision making;
- clear and consistent consequences for misconduct;
- enriched educational and vocational programming; and
- a variety of forms of individual, group, and family counseling matched to youths' needs.

(David Altschuler & Troy Armstrong, *Intervening with Serious Juvenile Offenders*, in *Violent Juvenile Offenders* [Robert Mathias et al. eds., NCCD 1984])

Greenwood and Zimring also identified several features essential for program success. (Peter Greenwood & Frank Zimring, *One More Chance: The Pursuit of Promising Intervention Strategies*, Rand 1985). Their factors include:

- providing opportunities for success and development of positive self-image;
- bonding youths to prosocial adults and institutions;
- providing frequent, timely, and accurate feedback for both positive and negative behavior;
- reducing the influence of negative role models;
- requiring youths to recognize and understand thought processes that rationale negative behavior;
- creating opportunities for juveniles to discuss childhood problems; and
- adapting program components to meet the needs of each individual youth.

NCCD Findings on Critical Components

Our review of the research literature lends support to the factors identified by these researchers and also points to additional components critical to the effectiveness of graduated sanction programs. NCCD found that the programs that work most reliably are those that actually address key areas of risk in a youth's life and seek in a variety of ways to strengthen the factors, personal and institutional, that make for healthy adolescent development; provide adequate support and supervision; and offer a long-term stake in the community.

These principles apply to youths at all levels of a graduated sanction system. What is most important, the research suggests, is not so much the particular stage of intervention as the quality, intensity, direction, and appropriateness of the intervention itself. (*Cf.* Andrews et al. *supra.*)

It is important to sort out what the emerging literature tells us in order to provide a more coherent view of what seems clearly promising or just as clearly ineffective, and what seems potentially useful but about which we know too little, so far, to be definitive.

THEMES FOR SUCCESS

The programs that clearly do seem to make a difference are, by the same token, those that engage youths' problems and deficits, have an underlying developmental rationale (if often a broad one), and try to alter the institutional and ecological conditions that most affect youths' lives.

As earlier reviews of the evidence have repeatedly found, overall implementation factors such as the consistency and integrity of the intervention are generally more important than the specific "model" of intervention or its specific theoretical underpinning. (*See, e.g.,* W.E. Wright & M.C. Dixon, *Community Prevention and Treatment of Juvenile Delinquency: A Review of Evaluation Studies*, 14 J. Res. in Crime & Delinq. 35–67 (1977).)

But within that general picture there are some crucial themes that we believe appear again and again in the most successful and carefully evaluated programs. These themes apply at the substantive level.

- Programs are "holistic" (or "comprehensive" or "multisystemic"), dealing with many aspects of youths' lives simultaneously, as needed.
- Programs are intensive, often involving multiple contacts weekly or even daily with at-risk youth.
- Programs mostly—though not exclusively—operate outside the formal juvenile justice system under a variety of auspices: public, nonprofit, or university.
- Programs build on youths' strengths rather than focus on their deficiencies.
- Programs adopt a socially grounded approach to understanding a youth's situation and dealing with it, rather than a mainly individual or medical-therapeutic approach.

As is true of virtually every intervention into any kind of problematic behavior, the programs that work on the process or implementation level tend to be those that are continued over a reasonably long time, are reasonably "dose-intensive," are delivered by energetic and committed if not necessarily highly trained staff, and do what they set out to do—that is, possess "therapeutic integrity."

Another critical program component is systematic case management. Successful programs have a case-management system that begins at intake and follows youths through the different program phases until discharge. Individual treatment plans are developed to address the specific needs of each youth and are updated on a regular basis.

Successful programs provide frequent feedback, both positive and negative, to youths on their progress. Positive behavior is acknowledged and rewarded, while clear and consistent sanctions are given for negative behavior.

Education, vocational training, and counseling strategies can be effective if they are intensive and tied to the individual needs of juveniles. The most effective type of counseling seems to be that which employs a cognitive-behavioral approach. The counseling component should include family counseling in addition to individual and group counseling because many of the problems faced by youths are caused or exacerbated by family dysfunction.

Family issues are just one of several key areas in the lives of youths that must be addressed in treatment. Successful programs also typically deal with issues relating to community, peers, school, and work.

It is far more productive to work on these issues when youths remain living with their families, or at least remain in their own communities, while receiving treatment. Of course, for public safety reasons, community-based treatment is not always appropriate, and families, increasingly, may be dysfunctional or nonexistent. Nonetheless, the findings suggest that youths should always be treated in the least restrictive environment possible.

Intensity of service for youths who remain in the community is critical. Successful community programs have low caseloads, ensuring that youths receive constant and individualized attention. Frequent face-to-face contacts, telephone contacts, and contacts with parents, teachers, and employers are essential in order to provide close monitoring and consistent support for youths. This type of service is most successful if its intensity is gradually diminished over a long period of time.

Finally, successful programs gradually reintegrated youths into their homes and communities. Intensive aftercare services are crucial to program success, particularly for residential programs.

CHAPTER 5

Community Corrections for Drug-Abusing Offenders

INTRODUCTION

Drug-abuse research has established that there is a strong statistical association between crime and drugs: Criminal activity increases when offenders are using drugs, and drug abusers are at least as violent as, if not more violent than, their counterparts who don't use drugs. Nonetheless, because of severe overcrowding in the nation's prison system, 75 percent of all convicted drug offenders are granted probation (higher in some states), and nearly all parolees have drug problems. Their presence in the community clearly constitutes a potential threat to public safety.

Communities have adopted a number of responses to drug offenders in the community, and the three articles in this chapter summarize the most frequent and promising programs.

The most common community-based response has been to order offenders to submit to periodic urinalysis testing by probation and parole officers. The Bureau of Justice Assistance, beginning in 1987 and running through 1990, sponsored a national demonstration program to assess the costs and benefits of placing drug-involved offenders on special, intensive drug-testing case loads. Offenders who were eligible for the program were randomly assigned to drug-testing case loads or routine probation or parole, and all participants were tracked for one year.

The Turner, Petersilia, and Deschenes article summarizes the evaluation findings. Some of the results are similar to those reviewed by Michael Tonry in Chapter 4. Despite differences in drug-testing schedules, system responses, and offender characteristics, offender recidivism results were surprisingly similar: in no instance did the drug-testing programs reduce officially recorded recidivism. On the contrary, the impact of those drug-testing programs was to increase technical violations and their resulting pressure on jail and prison commitments. Clearly, drug testing *alone* (similar to simply increasing offender-to-officer contact levels) is insufficient to change offender behavior, particularly when the offender is already committed to a substance-abusing lifestyle.

The Prendergast, Anglin, and Wellisch, and Turner and Longshore articles identify more positive programming techniques with drug offenders. Prendergast and his UCLA colleagues, nationally recognized leaders in drug abuse research, identify the principles of effective treatment. These include correctly matching offenders to treatment services, monitoring outcomes, delivering treatments over lengthy time periods, including those where relapse has occurred, and in some cases, treating specific forms of substance dependence with pharmacological agents. Their experience and research suggests that when such principles are followed, offender relapse to both drugs and crime can be significantly reduced.

Turner and Longshore, two RAND researchers, report similarly encouraging findings about Treatment Alternatives to Street Crime (TASC), a program begun in the 1970s and the best developed model of the linkage between the criminal justice system and the treatment system. Unlike other criminal justice programs, it explicitly addresses the drugs-crime link by referring offenders to treatment and monitoring their progress. The RAND researchers recently completed the first randomized evaluation of TASC, and the results are promising. Offenders who participated fully in the TASC program had lower subsequent levels of drug use and criminality.

There now exists rather solid empirical evidence that ordering offenders into treatment, and getting them to participate, reduces recidivism. Thus, the first order of business must be to allocate sufficient resources so that the designed programs (incorporating both surveillance and treatment) can be implemented. Sufficient monetary resources are essential to obtaining and sustaining judicial support and achieving program success.

Preventing addicts from committing crimes must be a top priority in the nation's crime control arsenal. To date, most communities have relied primarily on arrest and imprisonment to achieve this result. But incarceration is not necessarily the best—or only—answer. Imprisoning addicts who rely on crime to support their habits is effective in eliminating their opportunity to commit crime while in prison—a period that is now about eight months long, on average. But once offenders are released, their criminality continues. Furthermore, only a small percentage of drug addicts will ever spend any time in prison for crimes they commit. Several studies have shown that fewer than 1 percent of crimes committed by heroin addicts result in arrest, much less jail time. Treatment also turns out to be less expensive than incarceration for certain drug abusers: a recent study by RAND found that drug treatment was the least expensive way to reduce the use of cocaine. With such a high price tag in dollars and human toll, the effectiveness of a solely punitive approach to drug offenders must be questioned.

Much more worthwhile is a strategy that eliminates or reduces the only motivation many addicts have to steal: their dependency on drugs. The best weapon we have against this type of recidivism is effective community-based treatment programs.

Treatment for Drug-Abusing Offenders Under Community Supervision

Michael L. Prendergast, M. Douglas Anglin, and Jean Wellisch

INTRODUCTION

A growing body of research indicates that treatment for drug-abusing offenders can reduce substance use, criminal behavior, and recidivism, whether the offender enters treatment voluntarily or under some form of coercion (Anglin & Hser, 1990a,b; Falkin, Lipton, & Wexler, 1992; Leukefeld & Tims, 1992). Such research support for the effectiveness of drug treatment within the criminal justice system is in line with other research on the effectiveness of correctional rehabilitation programs generally (Andrews et al., 1990; Gendreau & Ross, 1987; Whitehead & Lab, 1989). The following discussion of treatment for drug-abusing offenders under community supervision discusses research-based principles of effective treatment, described several specific practices that have been found to be effective, and concludes with recommendations for policy.

PRINCIPLES OF EFFECTIVE TREATMENT

If drug abuse treatment within the criminal justice system is to overcome the "nothing works" mentality and to result in effective applications, then community-based programs that treat offenders need to adhere to principles that are based on sound research findings and proven clinical practice. Although the principles to be discussed are by no means exhaustive, they are those that have particular importance for the treatment and recovery process of offenders or that require greater programmatic attention from treatment providers and policymakers.

The authors are all with the UCLA Drug Abuse Research Center. Dr. Prendergast is assistant historian, Dr. Anglin is director, and Dr. Wellisch is research associate.

"Treatment for Drug-abusing Offenders Under Community Supervision" by Michael L. Prendergast, M. Douglas Anglin, and Jean Wellisch, from *Federal Probation*, Vol. 59, No. 4, December 1995, pp. 66–75.

Accurate Assessment of Clients' Needs

A comprehensive treatment strategy requires that a range of approaches and services be provided at appropriate levels of intensity in order to promote recovery from drug abuse. Foremost in the process of determining appropriate treatment elements is assessment of clients' needs and their readiness to receive treatment services to meet those needs. Clients cannot fully benefit from services for which they are not prepared. A staged approach of service delivery based on repeated or dynamic assessments of clients' needs produces better outcomes and allows for more cost-effective use of services. The assessment should focus on dynamic risk factors that are amenable to therapeutic change.

Several instruments are available for assessing drug abuse and other problems of clients. The most widely used instrument for drug abuse is the Addiction Severity Index (ASI) (McLellan et al., 1985). It permits trained clinic staff to calculate severity scores in seven areas: medical status, employment/support, alcohol, drug, legal, family/social relationships, and psychiatric status. Although the ASI was originally developed for a general addict population, its creators have established norms for men and women within criminal justice populations. In addition, the ASI has been translated into 10 languages.

Matching Clients to Treatment Services

Comprehensive screening and assessment instruments are needed to support effective matching strategies. Clinically, the question is which type of treatment is appropriate for which type of client and in which settings. "Type of client" refers both to the drug or drugs with which a person is involved and to the severity of the involvement, which may range from experimentation to long-term addiction. "Type of treatment" refers to a variety of dimensions: residential versus outpatient, type of drug problem (single or polydrug), pharmacotherapy and nonpharmacotherapy, intensity and duration, and specific techniques. Other considerations in determining appropriate treatment include gender, ethnicity, age, needed services, social support network, language, and level of psychological and cognitive functioning. As the client progresses in treatment, treatment planning should involve additional assessment, evaluation, and referral, as appropriate, to new treatment components or new services.

Although theoretically grounded, clinically usable, and empirically tested technology for matching drug abuse clients to appropriate treatment has yet to be developed, there is general agreement among researchers and others that, in principle, matching would accelerate treatment and recovery of clients and would also make better use of resources. The obstacles facing the implementation of an effective matching system may be more practical than theoretical. Matching requires a range of treatment options to which clients can be referred following assessment. A sophisticated matching system that takes into account multiple factors (client characteristics, type and severity of substance problem, criminal risk classification, psychological, social, and medical needs, and client preference) requires a well-developed, coordinated, and stable system of treatment and service options, a diverse treatment staff, and an efficient communication network (preferably computer-based).

Adequate Duration of Treatment

Length of stay in treatment has been found to be an important factor in producing declines in drug use and criminal behavior across a variety of treatment modalities and settings (Anglin & Hser, 1990b; De Leon, 1991; Hubbard et al., 1989). Three months is generally thought to be the minimum length of stay required for any positive outcomes, and 12 to 24 months is required to produce substantial and sustained behavioral change. As the severity of the drug abuse problem increases, the minimum stay to produce positive outcome becomes longer.

For many clients, treatment of long duration may be more important than intensity of services. Clients often need considerable time to break through denial about their drug abuse problem and to develop the motivation (however ambivalent) to participate in program activities that help achieve sobriety and maintain recovery; time also is needed for the initiation and reinforcement of successive iterations of desired change. It is important to emphasize that positive outcomes are not dependent merely on the amount of time that the client spends in treatment. Something must happen during that time that addresses the needs of the client. Some evidence (McLellan, Arndt, Metzger, Woody, & Obrien, 1993) indicates that client improvement is dependent on the frequency and variety of services that appropriately address the clients multiple problems. The importance of duration should not be thought of merely within the context of a specific program; a person may need to undergo a number of treatment episodes, possibly of different types or different intensities, before achieving a consistent pattern of recovery.

Continuity of Care

The importance of aftercare in the treatment of drug abuse was recognized as early as 1979 (Brown, 1979), but the number of clients who are discharged from a treatment program and continue to receive support in a less intensive form of treatment or during the difficult transition to community reintegration continues to be small. Aftercare services remain few. Even with relapse prevention measures (discussed below), once the person leaves a program, additional support is usually needed in order to maintain the gains made in treatment, reinforce prosocial behaviors, and discourage relapse.

Such support can include self-help groups, alumni groups, monitoring by the person's counselor or case manager, and other mechanisms for formal and informal monitoring of the person's recovery. The various 12-step fellowship groups are helpful in providing a source of support for recovery since they are widely available and easily accessible. Since relapse is likely, an effective system of continuing care provides quick and easy reentry to a treatment program on a voluntary basis. For those still under supervision, mechanisms should be in place (e.g., urine testing, identification of potential relapse triggers) so that the person can be returned to a higher level of treatment such as increased urine testing, outpatient, or even residential treatment.

Behavioral Change Through Leverage

Individuals involved in the criminal justice system need to have both reinforcing and aversive conditions, or incentives, before they are likely to be amenable and responsive to treatment for drug abuse. That is, there must be suitable consequences for both negative behavior and positive behavior. At the program level, various forms of contingency contracting (which includes both positive and negative reinforcers) are examples of incentives that may be effective in producing behavioral change.

To enforce the contractual arrangement and sustain positive changes, frequent and random biological testing (urine, breath, hair) for alcohol or other drugs is a key element in providing close monitoring of clients' progress in treatment. Positive test results, because they are objective and can often be determined relatively quickly (using onsite portable equipment), help break through clients' denial and provide useful information on clients' progress for program staff, probation or parole officers, and judges. For less severe users, the knowledge that they will be tested may discourage use; for more severe users, testing enables program staff to adjust the intensity of treatment. Whether testing with sanctions alone (in the absence of treatment) is effective in reducing drug use and criminal behavior appears to depend upon the stage of the criminal justice system within which it is instituted. For example, in Washington, DC, offenders on pretrial release have been tested regularly since the early 1980s, and results of the program indicate reduced rates of rearrest on drug charges and other charges (Carver, 1993).

Treatment Integrity

The survival and success of programs may depend as much on how they are implemented and managed as on their content (Petersilia, 1990). Successful operation of a treatment program involves the selection of a theoretically based, empirically tested treatment model, delivered by a staff trained in its use. A treatment model may be based upon self-empowerment, social learning, cognitive functioning, or behavioral theories, but to be effective the model must be implemented and sustained over time with adequate resources and by a management and staff who have appropriate experience and training, participate in ongoing staff development, receive needed technical assistance, and monitor the expected performance of clients. Consistent implementation of the underlying treatment model depends on management and staff understanding and "buying into" the treatment model, coordination of treatment services and other services, staff control of program activities, documentation of program services and activities, and clients' perception that the program is relevant and sensitive to their needs.

Linkages with Other Services

Drug-abusing offenders tend to have a variety of problems and deficits in addition to their problems with drugs. Treatment programs represent an opportunity to identify and address problems or situations that have important public health and social implications. This array of problems includes medical problems, psychological and emotional problems, limited education, and poor job skills. In addition, women offenders often have to contend with other problems, including the legacies of physical and sexual abuse, need for gynecological and pregnancy care, and need for child care. Growing numbers of offenders need assistance with the physical, emotional, and financial problems associated with being HIV positive or having AIDS. The relationship of drug abuse to all these problems is complex and varies from one problem or person to another. For example, treatment clients who use drugs or alcohol as a form of self-medication are likely to have difficulty remaining abstinent during and after treatment if their mental or physical problems are not addressed with appropriate medication or other means. People who cannot find steady employment because they are illiterate or lack job skills will likely have difficulty staying away from drugs once they leave treatment. Although most of the problems are related to drug abuse, they are not necessarily caused by drug abuse; thus, they need to be addressed directly, rather than assuming that they will disappear spontaneously as the person enters recovery.

PRACTICES

Evaluation studies of treatment for drug dependence have generally concluded that none of the prominent treatment modalities (of those commonly studied: methadone, therapeutic community/residential, and outpatient drug-free) is superior to any other for all clients, although differential effectiveness has been found for users of different drugs and for different subpopulations (Anglin & Hser, 1990b; Gerstein & Harwood, 1990; Prendergast et al., in press). Specific treatment approaches that have reasonably strong research support are discussed below.

Cognitive- and Behavioral-Based Treatments

Research and clinical literature has increasingly focused on the effectiveness of cognitive and behavioral approaches to treating drug abuse problems including cognitive skills training, relapse prevention training, and contingency contracting.

Cognitive Skills   A considerable body of research literature supports the effectiveness of correctional interventions that include a cognitive skills component (e.g., Gendreau & Andrews, 1990). Cognitive skills treatment is a general term that covers several related approaches: problem solving, social skills training, and relapse prevention training. The problem-solving approach to treatment starts from the assumption that successful functioning requires the ability to make effective use of various problem-solving skills and that deficiencies in these skills lead to various types of dysfunctional behavior including crime and drug abuse. A second assumption is that it is possible to intervene actively with drug abusers in order to remedy these cognitive deficits and thus to help them learn more socially acceptable and productive ways to lead their lives. While training in problem solving focuses on how to think, social skills training is concerned more with specific social or behavioral skills. Again, the assumption is that teaching social skills will help the person learn more adaptive ways of functioning and relating to others. The elements of social skills programs include modeling appropriate behavior, role playing, rehearsal of target behaviors, instruction and coaching in the target behaviors, and feedback.

Training in Relapse Prevention   High relapse rates have been a common finding in drug treatment programs and the criminal justice system, and efforts to develop techniques to reduce relapse rates have been a major focus of treatment research. At the program level, probably the leading method has been relapse prevention training (Gorski, Kelley, Havens, & Peters, 1993). Such training programs are based on theoretically and empirically based models of recovery and relapse, embody specific cognitive and behavioral principles and procedures, and use manual-driven protocols; they have also been adapted to a variety of criminal justice settings. Relapse prevention has been found to be effective with a variety of drug-abusing populations, including incarcerated inmates, and clinical impressions indicate that they should be effective with offenders under community supervision, although a particular model may need to be adapted to local circumstances.

Contingency Contracting   Another behavioral approach to treatment for drug abuse is contingency contracting, in which contracts signed by counselors and clients spell out specific consequences for specific behaviors. Although contracts often focus on negative consequences (sanctions) for non-compliance, such contracts can and should also include positive reinforcement (rewards) for appropriate behavior or for achieving specific treatment goals. Examples of the use of contingency contracting and other behavioral approaches are found in the drug courts that have been established in recent years. In the drug court of Oakland, California, contingency contracts specify the expectations for clients and the responsibilities of treatment staff, define success and failure, indicate rewards for positive behaviors and penalties for negative behaviors, and provide a clear structure for judicial decisions regarding clients. Successes are evident in the county's decreased jail population (Tauber, 1994). The drug court in Washington, DC, includes a "graduated sanctions" track in its treatment program. The sanction for the first positive test is 3 days in the jury box observing the proceedings against other defendants; the second positive test results in 1 day in jail; the third, 6 days in a jail-based detoxification program; the fourth, 12 days in jail; and the fifth, 24 days in jail. Preliminary results suggest that this combination of drug testing and sanctions is having a positive effect on clients' drug use ("Positive effects," 1994).

Pharmacotherapy for Opiate Dependence

Treating specific forms of substance dependence with pharmacological agents has become a well-established practice, evidenced in particular by the use of methadone, LAAM, and naltrexone for opiate addiction. Although a number of medications to treat cocaine/crack dependence are under study, none has been established as generally effective.

Methadone A large body of literature supports the effectiveness of methadone treatment in reducing opiate use and criminal activity, in improving psychosocial functioning, and in reducing HIV-risk behaviors, particularly injection drug use (Ball & Ross, 1991; Powers & Anglin, 1993). (Although methadone is pharmacologically effective only with opiates, methadone treatment may have some indirect effects on the use of cocaine when it is taken with heroin in the form of "speedballs"). For instance, researchers at UCLA (Anglin & McGlothlin, 1984, 1985; Hser, Anglin, & Chou, 1988) have shown that the percentage of nonincarcerated time engaged in daily opiate use decreased from about 70 percent (averaging across several studies) when not in maintenance methadone (MM) treatment to about 12 percent when in MM. Property crime involvement decreased from about 18 percent when not in MM to about 11 percent when in MM. Even when addicts are discharged from treatment, sustained improvement is still observable, although to a lesser degree when compared with in-treatment effects.

LAAM LAAM is a long-acting opiate, similar to methadone, that is taken three times a week rather than every day as with methadone. It was approved by the Food and Drug Administration in July 1993 for use in the treatment of opiate addiction. Given the time it takes for states to give their approval, for clinics to apply for and receive a license to use LAAM, and for staff to be trained in its use, it will be some time before LAAM is generally available. Once it is, it will provide an alternative pharmacotherapy for opiate-addicted clients who do not do well on methadone, who prefer not taking methadone, or who would benefit from less frequent attendance at the clinic.

Naltrexone   Naltrexone is an opiate antagonist that nullifies the effects of opiates by binding to receptor sites in the brain, thereby blocking access to the receptor for opiates. Naltrexone does not produce euphoria, is not addictive, has minimal side effects for most people, and is not subject to abuse. Naltrexone administration can begin only after the patient has been completely detoxified from all opiates including methadone. Once on naltrexone, patients cease to crave opiates as a result of naltrexone's blockade of opiate euphoria. A disadvantage of naltrexone is the low rate of patient acceptance and compliance, especially by street addicts. It has had more success with recovering physicians and other professionals and with people of higher socioeconomic status. Treatment with naltrexone is likely to be more effective if it is administered under some type of close monitoring (Brahen & Brewer, 1993; Brewer, 1993).

Treatments for Cocaine Dependence

Efforts to develop treatments specifically designed for cocaine dependence have lagged behind treatments for opiate dependence, and these efforts have tended to be modeled on treatment regimens developed for other types of chemical dependence. Findings from studies evaluating the effectiveness of cocaine treatment have begun to appear in the scientific literature only in the last few years, and few of these evaluations focus on cocaine-abusing offenders in community-based programs. The principles and practices previously discussed apply to cocaine treatments, and research continues to seek a pharmacotherapy for treatment of cocaine addiction. A number of recent evaluation studies of cocaine treatment are briefly summarized below (for a convenient summary of various approaches, also see Tims & Leukefeld, 1993).

Differential Effectiveness of Basic Modalities   Khalsa, Anglin, and Paredes (1992) assessed the relative effectiveness of the common treatments for cocaine abuse (inpatient, outpatient, self-help groups), separately and in various combinations, as provided to 300 cocaine users at a Veterans Administration medical center. The best group in terms of outcome consisted of those patients whose treatment consisted of an initial 21-day inpatient period, an outpatient followup regimen (individual and group counseling), and continued involvement in self-help groups throughout most of the followup period; those patients whose treatment consisted solely of a single 21-day inpatient treatment episode had the worst outcomes. Of the inpatient-only group, 45 percent relapsed to severe cocaine use within a year, whereas only 12 percent of the group receiving more and longer treatment exposure did so. The latter group also showed more favorable outcomes in terms of total time abstinent from cocaine, lesser use of alcohol and other drugs, and decreases in drug dealing and other crimes. The findings confirm the importance of providing long-term treatment and continuity of care to bring about long-term positive outcomes.

IMPLICATIONS AND RECOMMENDATIONS FOR POLICY

Research on drug abuse treatment for offender populations has resulted in a sufficient body of knowledge to provide community corrections providers with a set of principles and practices that have proven effective with many offenders with drug abuse problems. The principles outlined in this column provide the basis for assessing whether a treatment approach, at the program level or the system level, is likely to be effective and at a reasonable cost. They also suggest a number of directions for policy.

Accept the Role of Treatment for Drug Abuse   Evaluation research on treatment for substance abuse has progressed to the point where it is no longer necessary to ask "Is drug abuse treatment effective?" Researchers and clinicians have come to realize that the appropriate question about substance abuse treatment is not "What works?" but "What works most cost effectively for which types of offender, under which conditions, and in which settings?"

Supervision Is not Enough   For offenders with serious drug problems, it is treatment, not merely supervision, however intensive, that is needed. Supervision alone, whether in jail or prison, in a shock incarceration program, or under probation or parole, is seldom sufficient to have an impact on the substance abuse problems of most offenders (Petersilia, Turner, & Deschenes, 1992). For offenders with severe dependence ("hardcore users"), low-intensity treatment, intervention efforts alone such as educational programs or 12-step groups, or intermediate sanctions such as community service, day fines, or electronic monitoring are also unlikely to have much lasting impact, although they may be important elements of a full program. Treatment for hardcore users needs to be intensive, long-term, and comprehensive.

Treatment Goals Should Be Realistic   The treatment of drug abuse, particularly of high-severity or hardcore abuse, has some similarities to treating the chronically mentally ill, in which "cure" is not a generally expected goal of treatment. Instead, reasonable goals for drug abuse treatment are to minimize the number of individuals who enter higher restriction supervision or higher intensity treatment, to minimize the need for the more serious and costly options of long-term incarceration or residential treatment, and to maximize time in the community with acceptable behaviors. For many drug-abusing offenders, this process may be accomplished in a few months or years; for others, very long-term intervention, with constant support and monitoring, may be necessary.

Creative and Flexible Policies Are Needed Changing problems and circumstances require new approaches and policies. For example, some of the public opposition to methadone programs has resulted from the federal policy of requiring all clients receiving methadone to attend stand-alone clinics, which encourages the loitering, illegal parking, dealing, and other problems. These activities could be reduced, if not eliminated, through changes in federal regulations and policy that would allow for greater flexibility in providing methadone treatment such as methadone buses, hospital-based methadone clinics, and physician dispensing to long-term well-functioning clients (medical maintenance).

Cooperation Among Agencies Is the Key to Efficiency Publicly funded treatment programs are not adequately funded to provide treatment of sufficient duration to bring about lasting behavioral changes in many of the clients with severe drug dependence and abuse problems. As long as the focus of treatment services remains at the level of specific programs, it is difficult to provide the types of intervention and supervision needed to deal with the chronic, relapsing nature of drug abuse. If, however, the focus shifts from the program to the system level, a greater range of options will become available and a greater likelihood of success becomes possible.

Although individual programs can implement principles and practices to improve outcomes for their clients, significant gains in the overall effectiveness of drug abuse treatment within the criminal justice system will require closer cooperation between criminal justice agencies and drug treatment providers, along with the participation of other service agencies. To be optimally effective, any approach to treating offenders needs to be more systems oriented—one that recognizes the importance of ongoing communication among drug treatment and criminal justice agencies, planning together, providing services jointly where appropriate and feasible, and generally supporting efforts to offer the range and continuity of services required by this population. TASC and drug courts are examples of this coordinated approach, and other examples can be found at the state and county levels throughout the country. But it is a trend that needs support from policymakers, providers, and researchers if it is to succeed in improving the delivery of services to drug-abusing offenders.

REFERENCES

Andrews, D. A., Zinger, I., Hoge, R. D., Bonta, J., Gendreau, P., & Cullen, F. T. 1990. Does correctional treatment work? A clinically relevant and psychologically informed meta-analysis. *Criminology*, 28(3), 369–404.

Anglin, M. D., & Hser, Y-I. 1990a. Legal coercion and drug abuse treatment: Research findings and social policy implications. In J. A. Inciardi (Ed.), *Handbook of drug control in the United States* (pp. 151–176). Westport, CT: Greenwood Press.

Anglin, M. D., & Hser, Y-I. 1990b. Treatment of drug abuse. In M. Tonry & J. Q. Wilson (Eds.), *Drugs and crime* (pp. 393–460). Chicago: University of Chicago Press.

Anglin, M. D., & McGlothlin, W. H. 1984. Outcome of narcotic addict treatment in California. In F. Tims & J. Ludford (Eds.), *Drug abuse treatment evaluation: Strategies, progress, and prospects* (NIDA Research Monograph 51, pp. 106–128). Rockville, MD: National Institute on Drug Abuse.

Anglin, M. D., & McGlothlin, W. H. 1985. Methadone maintenance in California: A decade's experience. In L. Brill & C. Winick (Eds.), *The yearbook of substance use and abuse*, 3, 219–280.

Ball, J. C., & Ross, A. 1991. *The effectiveness of methadone maintenance treatment.* New York: Springer-Verlag.

Brahen, L. S., & Brewer, C. 1993. Naltrexone in the criminal justice system. In C. Brewer (Ed.), *Treatment options in addiction: Medical management of alcohol and opiate abuse* (pp. 46–53). London: Gaskell.

Brewer, C. 1993. Naltrexone in the prevention of relapse and opiate detoxification. In C. Brewer (Ed.), *Treatment options in addiction: Medical management of alcohol and opiate abuse* (pp. 54–62). London: Gaskell.

Brown, B. S. (Ed.). 1979. *Addicts and aftercare: Community integration of the former drug abuser.* Beverly Hills: Sage Publications.

Carver, J. A. 1993. Using drug testing to reduce detention. *Federal Probation*, 57(1), 42–47.

De Leon, G. 1991. Retention in drug-free therapeutic communities. In R. W. Pickens, C. G. Leukefeld, & C. R. Schuster (Eds.), *Improving drug abuse treatment* (NIDA Research Monograph 106). Rockville, MD: National Institute on Drug Abuse.

Falkin, G. P., Lipton, D. S., & Wexler, H. K. 1992. Drug treatment in state prisons. In D. R. Gerstein & H. J. Harwood (Eds.), *Treating drug problems* (Vol. 2, pp. 89–131). Washington, DC: National Academy Press.

Gendreau, P., & Andrews, D. A. 1990. Tertiary prevention: What the meta-analysis of the offender treatment literature tells us about "what works." *Canadian Journal of Criminology*, 32, 173–184.

Gendreau, P., & Ross, R. R. 1987. Revivification of rehabilitation: Evidence from the 1980s. *Justice Quarterly*, 4(3), 349–407.

Gerstein, D. R., & Harwood, H. J. (Eds.). 1990. *Treating drug problems* (Vol. 1). Washington, DC: National Academy Press.

Gorski, T. T., Kelley, J. M., Havens, L., & Peters, R. H. 1993. *Relapse prevention and the substance-abusing criminal offenders* (Technical Assistance Publication Series 8). Rockville, MD: Center for Substance Abuse Treatment.

Hser, Y-I., Anglin, M. D., & Chou, C-P. 1988. Evaluation of drug abuse treatment: A repeated measures design assessing methadone maintenance. *Evaluation Review*, 12(5), 547–570.

Hubbard, R. L., Marsden, M. E., Rachal, J. V., Harwood, H. J., Cavanaugh, E. R., & Ginzburg, H. M. 1989. *Drug abuse treatment: A national study of effectiveness.* Chapel Hill: University of North Carolina Press.

Khalsa, H., Anglin, M. D., & Paredes, A. 1992. Cocaine abuse: Outcomes of therapeutic interventions. *Substance Abuse*, 13(4), 165–179.

Leukefeld, C. G., & Tims, F. M. 1992. *Drug abuse treatment in prisons and jails* (NIDA Research Monograph 118). Rockville, MD: National Institute on Drug Abuse.

McLellan, A. T., Arndt, I. O., Metzger, D. S., Woody, G. E., & OBrien, C. P. 1993. The effects of psychosocial services in substance abuse treatment. *Journal of the American Medical Association*, 269(15), 1953–1959.

McLellan, A. T., Luborsky, L., Cacciola, J., Griffith, J., McGahan, & OBrien, C. P. 1985. *Guide to the Addiction Severity Index: Background, administration, and field testing results* (DHHS Pub. No. (ADM) 85-1419). Rockville, MD: National Institute on Drug Abuse.

Petersilia, J. 1990. Conditions that permit intensive supervision programs to survive. *Crime and Delinquency*, 36(1), 126–145.

Petersilia, J., Turner, S., & Deschenes, E. 1992. Intensive supervision programs for drug offenders. In J. M. Byrne, A. J. Lurigio, & J. Petersilia (Eds.), *Smart sentencing: The emergence of intermediate sanctions* (pp. 18–37). Newbury Park, CA: Sage Publications.

"Positive effects are seen in D.C. court project." (1994, June), *CJN Newsletter*, 2(12).

Powers, K. I., & Anglin, M. D. 1993. Cumulative versus stabilizing effects of methadone maintenance: A quasi-experimental study using longitudinal self-report data. *Evaluation Review*, 17(3), 243–270.

Prendergast, M., Anglin, M. D., Maugh, T., & Hser, Y. (In press). *The effectiveness of treatment for drug abuse.* Rockville, MD: National Institute on Drug Abuse.

Tauber, J. S. (1994, Summer). Drug courts: A judicial manual. *CJER Journal* (Special Issue).

Tims, F. M., & Leukefeld, C. G. (Eds.), 1986. *Relapse and recovery in drug abuse* (NIDA Research Monograph 72). Rockville, MD: National Institute on Drug Abuse.

Tims, F. M., & Leukefeld, C. G. (Eds.). 1993. *Cocaine treatment: Research and clinical perspectives* (NIDA Research Monograph 135). Rockville, MD: National Institute on Drug Abuse.

Whitehead, J. T., & Lab, S. P. 1989. A meta-analysis of juvenile correctional treatment. *Journal of Research in Crime and Delinquency*, 26(3), 276–295.

Drug Testing in Community Corrections: Results of an Experimental Evaluation

SUSAN TURNER, JOAN PETERSILIA, AND ELIZABETH PIPER DESCHENES

INTRODUCTION

Drug-involved offenders have inundated the criminal justice system, particularly community corrections. Not only has the number of offenders on probation and parole reached record levels, but professionals in the field believe that the composition of caseloads has become more serious, particularly with respect to drug involvement. It is estimated that over half of the 3 million persons on probation or parole are drug-involved, either as users, sellers, or both (Nurco et al., 1990).

Performing probation/paroles' dual responsibilities—of controlling offenders in the community and facilitating their growth to crime-free lives—seems particularly challenging when applied to drug offenders. Research has shown that many probationers continue to use drugs while on probation and parole (Petersilia et al., 1985, 1990; Wish et al., 1986), and that drug use is associated with higher rates of committing crimes (Chaiken and Chaiken, 1982; Anglin, 1988).

On the other hand, research has shown that the effectiveness of drug abuse treatment can be enhanced with criminal justice involvement (Anglin and Hser, 1990; Gerstein and Harwood, 1990), and that probation/parole programs that combine treatment with strict surveillance can reduce recidivism by as much as 15 percent over surveillance-oriented probation alone (Petersilia and Turner, 1990).

Thus, the ultimate challenge is for probation/parole staff to manage drug offenders so that they receive the maximum exposure to rehabilitation programs, while at the same time closely monitoring their behavior so that violations are quickly detected and, if serious enough, result in the offender's removal from the community.

In many communities, officials have been meeting this challenge by implementing Intensive Supervision Probation/Parole (ISP) programs with periodic drug testing. Although there is no standard ISP program, these programs generally utilize smaller caseloads and more intensive contacts than traditional probation/parole programs. It is hoped that smaller case-

Susan Turner is a senior researcher in RAND's Criminal Justice Program in Santa Monica, California. Joan Petersilia is Professor of Criminology at University of California Irvine. Elizabeth Piper Deschenes is Associate Professor, California State University, Long Beach.

"Drug Testing in Community Corrections: Results of an Experimental Evaluation" by Susan Turner, Joan Petersilia, and Elizabeth Piper Deschenes, from *Journal of Probation and Parole*, No. 20, Spring 1993. Reprinted with permission.

loads will allow officers to maintain close surveillance of, and work more closely with, each offender. In addition to increased contact levels and drug testing, ISP programs often include a variety of other program features including job placement, electronic monitoring and house arrest, community service, and referrals for drug and alcohol treatment (Byrne et al., 1989, Petersilia, 1987).

The utility of drug testing while under supervision is based upon several premises. Knowledge that one may be tested for drugs may deter persons from use. The importance of this belief is underscored by the White House Office of National Drug Control Policy that asserts "drug tests should be a part of every stage of the criminal justice process—at the time of arrest and throughout the period of probation or incarceration—because they are the most effective way of keeping offenders off drugs both in and out of detention" (White House, 1989, p. 26).

In addition to deterrence, testing can be used to identify the drug-abusing offender for special handling by the criminal justice system. Identification may lead to treatment. And in this case, drug testing can provide a more reliable indicator of recent drug use than self-reports (Wish et al., 1986). Drug testing can also be used as a tool for identifying the most active of the predatory offenders—those offenders who commit offenses for material gain, such as robbery and burglary. Research has shown that predatory offenders who frequently and persistently use large amounts of multiple drugs commit crimes at higher rates than do less drug-involved offenders (Chaiken and Chaiken, 1982). Once identified, high-rate predatory offenders can be targeted for more intensive monitoring.

In summary, drug testing holds promise both as a deterrent and a diagnostic technique. However, very little empirical study has been done of its implementation and effectiveness for offenders on probation and parole, although this is undoubtedly its largest use in the criminal justice system. Anecdotal evidence suggests, however, that drug testing has not been unanimously applauded by community corrections staff. Probation and parole staff voice conflicting views on its usefulness. Many complain that the court orders too many drug tests, mandating testing schedules that are unreasonable and costly. Staff often note that when they do implement such testing orders, and return to the court requesting revocation on a dirty test, judges fail to revoke to custody, heeding pressures to use scarce prison and jail space for the truly dangerous. Equally frustrating is the lack of treatment beds in many communities, thus limiting further the usefulness of the test to coerce drug-using offenders into treatment.

Given the widespread use of testing in community supervision, it is important to begin to ask a number of key questions:

- How do probation/parole agencies implement drug testing orders?
- How many offenders are actually tested, with what frequency and results?
- How does the criminal justice system respond to positive drug tests?

- Do such tests result in added probation/parole referrals to treatment programs, or revocation?
- What impact does ISP with drug testing have on offender recidivism, as measured by official records of technical violations and new arrests?

STUDY DATA

This article uses information collected from five jurisdictions that participated in the Bureau of Justice Assistance's "Intensive Supervision Program for Drug Offenders." The BJA Demonstration program funded jurisdictions to implement intensive supervision programs for drug offenders, following a general model developed in Georgia. The Demonstration program ran from 1987 through 1990. The five sites used in the current analyses are: Contra Costa, California; Seattle, Washington; Des Moines, Iowa; Santa Fe, New Mexico; and Winchester, Virginia. These sites were similar in that each of them

- Designed an ISP program specifically for adult drug offenders.
- Incorporated urinalysis testing as one of the major ISP components (although the actual frequency of tests varied, from less than one to almost three per month).
- Implemented ISP as a probation/parole enhancement program (as opposed to prison diversion).
- Faithfully implemented an experimental design in which eligible offenders were randomly assigned to either the ISP program or routine probation/parole supervision, thus permitting a strong test of the effectiveness of ISP contrasted with routine supervision

RAND served as the evaluator of the ISP Demonstration, randomly assigning offenders, designing the data collection instruments, training the data coders, assembling the coded information and analyzing the data. The offender's presentence investigation (PSI) supplied most of the necessary information for offender background characteristics; program implementation and recidivism data were abstracted from officer chronological notes. In addition to the individual offender data, semistructured phone interviews were conducted with ISP staff on questions relating to the implementation of drug testing in ISP, goals for testing, and ISP staff perceptions of the impact of testing on offender drug use and criminal behavior.

INTENSIVE SUPERVISION WITH DRUG TESTING: SITE DESCRIPTIONS

All five sites were similar in that they included drug testing as a component of enhanced probation/parole targeted at drug offenders. However, each site tailored the ISP program to their local clients' needs and risks, their own financial resources, and internal and external political constraints. Thus, while the programs shared common characteristics, they often differed on other dimensions. (See Petersilia, Turner, and Deschenes, 1992 for more complete program descriptions and offender profiles.)

Individual sites were responsible for defining who would be eligible for ISP participation. The BJA initiative stated that the ISP programs were to target "drug offenders." The operationalization of "drug offender," however, was different across sites. ISP program protocol also varied in terms of the emphasis on surveillance and treatment, although all did encompass both surveillance and treatment activities in their programs. Sante Fe stressed a strong therapeutic approach, emphasizing counseling and job development. In contrast, the Seattle ISP program was the most highly surveillance-oriented, utilizing close cooperation with local law enforcement, and strict sanctions for positive urine tests. The Des Moines ISP program was also more surveillance—than treatment—oriented. ISP programs in Contra Costa and Winchester fell in between these two extremes.

Although sites evidenced differences in the basic demographics prior record characteristics of participants, the vast majority of study participants in all sites were males in their late twenties and early thirties, with lengthy prior records.

RESULTS

The Implementation of Drug Testing in ISP

Despite the different operationalization of "drug offender," the resulting samples were highly drug-dependent. Over ninety-five percent of offenders in Seattle, Des Moines, Sante Fe, and Winchester were dependent upon one or more types of drugs. Drugs had previously impacted offenders' lives in important ways. Over one-third of offenders in Des Moines and Sante Fe, and approximately half of the offenders in Winchester and Seattle had been involved in drug sales and dealing. In addition, substantial percentages of offenders had participated in prior drug treatment: about one-third of offenders in Seattle and Washington had previously been in treatment. Percentages were higher in Sante Fe and Des Moines where 43 and 65 percent (respectively) had previously been in treatment. Treatment episodes included not only outpatient, but residential placements as well. Between 42 and 93 percent of those offenders with prior drug treatment had been placed in a residential/therapeutic setting.

In designing their ISP programs, each site decided what contact and drug testing schedules would be implemented. Their decisions were driven mostly by local preferences and resources, as opposed to empirical data, since no empirical data currently exists as to the most effective testing schedules.

All sites used the Syva EMIT test. Reported costs ranged between $8 and $12 per full screen, and the results were obtained anywhere between 24 hours and two weeks. Sites generally requested a screen of drug tests for multiple drugs, as opposed to single substances. Not all sites requested the same drugs in the screens, but cocaine, amphetamines, barbiturates, marijuana, PCP, and opiates were generally included.

Most ISP supervisors had evaluated different types of testing technologies and chose the EMIT test because they believed in its accuracy. Gas chromatography/mass spectrometry (GC/MS) was available for confirmatory tests in Contra Costa, Sante Fe, and Winchester. However, the use of confirmatory tests varied across sites. In Sante Fe, ISP supervisors reported that all positive tests were confirmed by GC/MS. The ISP supervisor in Seattle reported that the court never required the use of confirmatory tests.

Each ISP program decided how to implement drug testing. In Contra Costa and Sante Fe, offenders were notified by phone the day before they were to be tested to come in and provide a urine sample. In the other programs, testing was conducted during regular office visits, although the offender was usually aware of whether he/she would be tested on any given visit.

Despite the difference in testing conditions, a high percentage of offenders in all sites were tested. With the exception of Seattle, over 90 percent of all ISP offenders were tested at least once during the one-year follow-up period. The average total number of tests taken during the year ranged from just under five in Seattle, to just under 35 in Sante Fe and Des Moines. Over half of all ISP offenders tested positive at least once during the one-year follow-up period. However, these percentages are based on *all* ISP offenders, not just those who were tested. If we consider only those offenders who were tested, these data suggest that about three quarters of tested offenders tested positive for drug use during the year on ISP probation/parole.

As we have seen, most ISP offenders tested positive for drugs during the follow-up years. But which drugs were they testing positive for? Across the different sites, positive tests most frequently occurred for cocaine and marijuana use. Over one third of all tested offenders in the ISP sites tested positive for cocaine; between 24 and 57 percent tested positive for marijuana. Opiate use (primarily heroin) was less frequent, although almost 20 percent of offenders in Des Moines tested positive for opiates. And as other studies have found (Carver, 1986; Toborg et al., 1989), many offenders are not users of a single drug type. Between 25 and 50 percent of the ISP offenders were poly-drug users, testing positive for two or more drugs during the follow-up period—the most common combination being cocaine and marijuana use.

An obvious question is whether the results from the drug ISP sites mirror drug use patterns that have been reported in other offender samples. Levels of use uncovered in the drug ISP sites were similar to that uncovered in other contexts. In a study of intensive supervision probationers in New York, 68 percent tested positive by urinalysis, primarily for cocaine and marijuana (Wish et al., 1986). Results from the National Institute of Justice's Drug Use Forecasting (DUF) Program have provided information on drug use on samples of arrestees in major cities across the United States since 1986. Recent results show that with few exceptions, between approximately 50 and 80 percent of male offenders test positive for any drug, with cocaine being the most prevalent drug in many sites (National Institute of Justice, 1991). Marijuana is also used by a large percentage of offenders.

What Was the System Response to Dirty Tests?

Urinalysis has generally been included in community supervision for the purposes of identifying and monitoring offender drug use and determining the need for treatment. The desirability of drug tests over self-reports has been demonstrated by a number of individuals (Wish et al., 1986) since offenders often underreport the extent of their drug use. In our conversations with the ISP staff, we found similar reasons for their use of urinalysis as well. In addition, many ISP staff felt that the drug testing would help deter drug use and reduce criminal behavior. How did system officials utilize positive drug test information? Were their responses mainly to refer to treatment, or to impose punitive sanctions?

ISP programs generally include guidelines for the response to dirty tests. However, the structure and formality of the guidelines differed across sites. Even with the guidelines, many ISP staff stressed that the specific response would often depend upon the individual offender and his/her progress in the program.

Our data provide the opportunity to examine system responses to positive drug tests while offenders were on ISP supervision. Our analyses examined the most serious response to a positive urine test for the ISP offenders during the follow-up period. We categorized the responses into four major types: (1) minimal (no action, warning, warrant issued); (2) added treatment conditions (referral to outpatient/inpatient treatment; (3) added control conditions (increased testing, new conditions added); and (4) custody (jail, prison).

This analysis revealed a great deal of variation among the sites. The most punitive response was in Seattle where 71% of the offenders who tested positive were placed in custody as a result. This finding is consistent with their local policy for which offenders were charged with a violation for each positive drug use test and taken to court, where a short jail term was often imposed. More than the other sites, Des Moines and Sante Fe used positive drug tests to refer offenders to treatment; about 25 percent of positive offenders received treatment referrals as the most serious system response. In Winchester, more than half of offenders who tested positive received no formal action against them.

We queried ISP staff concerning restrictions on their choice of responses, particularly treatment responses. ISP staff in Contra Costa and Sante Fe were often unable to obtain inpatient beds for the ISP offenders. ISP staff in Seattle, Des Moines, and Winchester, on the other hand, felt they were not greatly hampered by the availability of treatment slots. ISP staff acknowledged that treatment slots were less available than in the past; however, the three sites felt they could get their ISP offenders into inpatient treatment. This perception may have been the result of the latter sites' working with treatment "brokers" to find beds. In Seattle and Des Moines, ISP staff worked closely with TASC staff to locate treatment beds. In Winchester, ISP staff worked with a local mental health agency that performed drug evaluations for ISP offenders.

How Did Testing Impact Offender Recidivism?

We turn now to the question of impact. Is there evidence that ISP programs with drug testing—as implemented and responded to in these five sites—affects recidivism? We are interested in whether the ISP programs were associated with increased: (1) technical violations; (2) arrests for new offenses; and (3) return to custody (jail and prison). The hope of ISP programs is that more frequent testing and contacts will serve to deter offenders from new crimes.

Two important points should be kept in mind as we discuss impact. The ISP programs were actually "packages" including several components, one of which is urinalysis. In this respect, they do not provide us with a definitive answer about the impact of urinalysis testing on offender behavior. However, urinalysis testing was incorporated as part of the intensive supervision "package," and as a practical matter, the entire program is the "treatment." Second, this analysis draws upon the strength of the random assignment component of the evaluation. Because offenders were randomly assigned to ISP or routine supervision, in a clear sense, the outcomes we observed are the direct causal result of the ISP programs.

Our results revealed that:

- ISP significantly increased the level of technical violations, particularly drug technicals in Contra Costa, Seattle, and Winchester.
- ISP did not affect officially recorded arrests, generally, or for drug crimes in particular.
- ISP increased the percent of offenders going to jail for technical conditions in Contra Costa and Seattle, and in Des Moines increased the number of offenders going to prison.

In no instance did ISP reduce recidivism, as measured by officially recorded technical violations and arrests.

CONCLUSIONS AND POLICY RECOMMENDATIONS

Our analysis of the drug ISP programs has provided a number of important findings. True to their original design, the ISP programs were more intensive in terms of providing more face-to-face contacts, counseling, and drug testing than the routine supervision programs. Drug testing revealed high percentages of offenders using illegal drugs, primarily cocaine and marijuana. System responses to positive drug tests varied across sites. However, despite differences in drug testing schedules, system responses, and offender characteristics, offender recidivism results were surprisingly similar: in no instance did the drug ISP programs reduce officially recorded recidivism. On the contrary, the impact of those drug ISP programs was to increase technical violations and their resulting pressure on jail and prison commitments.

Given these findings, what can we say about the success of the drug testing ISP programs? The officially recorded measures suggest ISP, as structured in the programs studied, was not effective in reducing recidivism, but this is not the only measure of success. Most ISP staff considered it a valuable tool for monitoring drug use and most believed that drug testing itself reduced drug use and criminality for some of the offenders under ISP supervision. All five jurisdictions have plans to continue with drug testing and many have expanded it to other offender populations.

ISP programs that incorporate drug testing can also be evaluated in terms of their ability to provide an intermediate sanction. All five sites screened their current populations to identify those they felt most in need of additional services and supervision offered by a drug ISP program. These offenders were then provided with more intensive testing and monitoring than offenders on routine supervision. From this standpoint, all programs were successful in providing an intermediate sanction for serious drug-involved offenders.

However, it is also obvious from the current study that there is no clear sense of how best to use drug testing with serious offenders. We did not know which testing frequencies are the most effective, the relative advantages of testing alone versus testing combined with treatment, or which sanctions are best employed to reduce drug use and crime. Fortunately recent research is beginning to address these issues. With funding from the National Institute of Justice, RAND is collaborating with the Maricopa County Probation Department in an experimental evaluation designed to test the impact of the frequency of drug testing alone, and testing combined with treatment and sanctions. Results from this study should help us understand and better target services for drug-involved offenders under community supervision.

Although drug testing appears a popular tool in the supervision of drug offenders in the community, the technology appears to have moved faster than some agencies' ability to utilize the information effectively in the treatment and surveillance of offenders. However, as community corrections awaits the results of empirical studies, such as the ones noted above, useful and practical advice on how to implement drug testing is available from several fronts. In 1991, the Bureau of Justice Assistance released the "American Probation and Parole Association's Drug Testing Guidelines and Practices for Adult Probation and Parole Agencies." The guidelines, compiled from information from 125 state and local probation and parole agencies, provide the best practices available for agencies developing a new program or updating an already existing program. The guidelines address issues such as agency mission, purposes of testing, and offender selection to help clarify why drug testing is being conducted. Practical advice on the implementation of drug-testing policies and procedures, authority to test, selecting technologies, etc. provide concrete guidance for the operationalization of drug testing within a jurisdiction. However, as the APPA guidelines aptly point out, drug testing is not a panacea for resolving the drug problem in any particular jurisdiction; it is a tool that should complement other probation and parole operations.

In addition to these formal guidelines, research findings can inform drug-testing policies. Current drug-testing technologies allow for accurate and reliable detection of illegal drugs in an offender's system. Drug testing alone, however, may not be sufficient to deter offender drug use and crime; combining treatment and criminal justice sanctions in a coordinated fashion appears to be critical. Longer periods of treatment and treatment combined with legal sanctions are associated with more positive outcomes (Hubbard et al., 1989; Anglin and Hser, 1990). To accomplish these aims, close supervision of drug-involved offenders, including the use of strict monitoring and graduated sanctions for program violations, appear to be necessary. Lengthy treatment and close supervision, however, come at a high price. Individual jurisdictions need to balance the costs of such programs against their utility and effectiveness.

REFERENCES

Anglin, M. Douglas. 1988. "The Efficacy of Civil Commitment in Treating Narcotic Addiction." In *Compulsory Treatment of Drug Abuse: Research and Clinical Practice*, National Institute on Drug Abuse Research Monograph No. 86, edited by C. G. Luekefeld and F. M. Tims. Rockville, MD: U.S. Department of Health and Human Services.

Anglin, M. Douglas, and Y. I. Hser. 1990. "Treatment of Drug Abuse." Pp. 393–460 in *Drugs and Crime*, edited by M. Tonry and J. Q. Wilson. Vol. 13. Chicago: Chicago Press.

Ball et al. 1991. *American Probation and Parole Association's Drug Testing Guidelines and Practices for Adult Probation and Parole Agencies.* Washington, DC: Bureau of Justice Assistance.

Byrne, James, Arthur J. Lurigio, and Christopher Baird. 1989. "The Effectiveness of the New Intensive Supervision Programs." *Research in Corrections* 12:1–48.

Carver, J. A. 1986. "Drugs and Crimes: Controlling Use and Reducing Risk through Testing." *NIJ Reports.* Washington, DC: U.S. Department of Justice, National Institute of Justice.

Chaiken, Jan, and Marcia Chaiken. 1982. *Varieties of Criminal Behavior.* Santa Monica, CA: RAND

Gerstein, D. R., and H. J. Harwood, Editors. 1990. *Treating Drug Problems, Vol. 1, Institute of Medicine.* Washington, DC: National Academy Press.

Hubbard, Robert L., Mary Ellen Marsden, J. Valley Rachal, Henrick Harwood, Elizabeth Cavanaugh, and Harold M. Ginzburg. 1989. *Drug Abuse Treatment: A National Study of Effectiveness.* Chapel Hill, NC: The University of North Carolina Press.

National Institute of Justice 1991. "Drug Use Forecasting: Drugs and Crime Annual Report." *Research in Action.* Washington, D.C.: U.S. Department of Justice.

Petersilia, Joan. 1987. *Expanding Options for Criminal Sentencing.* R-3544-EMC. Santa Monica, CA: RAND.

Petersilia, Joan, et al. 1985. *Granting Felons Probation: Public Risks and Alternatives.* R 3186-NIJ. Santa Monica, CA: RAND.

Petersilia, Joan, and Susan Turner. 1990. *Intensive Supervision for High-Risk Probationers: Findings from Three California Experiments.* R-3936-NIJ/BJA. Santa Monica, CA: RAND.

Petersilia, Joan, Susan Turner, and Elizabeth P. Deschenes. 1992. *Intensive Supervision for Drug Offenders.* In *Smart Sentencing: The Emergence of Intermediate Sanctions*, edited by James M. Byrne, Arthur Lurigio, and Joan Petersilia. Newbury Park, CA: Sage Publications.

Toborg, M., J. P. Bellassai, A. M. J. Yezer, and R. P. Trost. 1989. *Assessment of Pretrial Urine Testing in the District of Columbia.* Summary Report. Washington, DC: U.S. Department of Justice, National Institute of Justice.

White House. 1989. *National Drug Control Strategy Office of National Drug Control Policy.* Washington, DC: U.S. Government Printing Office.

Wish, Eric D., M. Cuadrado, and J. Martorana. 1986. "Estimates of Drug Use in Intensive Supervision Probationers: Results from a Pilot Study." *Federal Probation* 50:4–16.

Evaluating the Treatment Alternatives to Street Crime (TASC) Program

SUSAN TURNER AND DOUGLAS LONGSHORE

BACKGROUND

More than twenty years ago, the federal government established a program known as Treatment Alternatives to Street Crime (TASC). TASC programs serve as brokers between the criminal justice system and community-based

Data collection, analysis, and reporting were funded by the National Institute on Drug Abuse (contract N01DA-1-8408) at the National Institutes of Health.

Susan Turner is a behavioral scientist in the Criminal Justice Program at RAND; Doug Longshore is a behavioral scientist at RAND and is also at the Drug Abuse Research Center at UCLA.

treatment. Central to the TASC program model are several key functions that include identification of drug-using offenders, assessment of their treatment and other needs, placement of offenders in treatment, and monitoring of their progress for reporting back to the criminal justice agencies. By providing these services, TASC programs aim to break the link between drug use and crime and reduce the costs associated with repeated criminal justice involvement and incarceration of drug users. Today, there are more than 150 TASC programs nationwide.

The programs vary widely in terms of the characteristics of their target groups, the services they provide, and their niche in the criminal justice system: they may target juvenile or adult offenders; they may or may not provide services such as AIDS counseling; they may serve as diversion from criminal justice processing or as adjuncts to traditional probation or parole supervision.

TASC programs are often private nonprofit community-based agencies that function as a bridge between treatment providers and criminal justice agencies within a local jurisdiction. Typically, the TASC programs do not provide treatment services themselves, but serve as brokers for such services.

TASC clients are generally nonviolent offenders without serious prior records—offenders more serious than those placed on simple probation and less serious than those whose offenses would result in incarcerative sentences. The most common point of intervention used by TASC programs today is probation. Although TASC programs operate differently in different jurisdictions, the following is a general description of what TASC may mean for an offender.

As part of the presentence investigation, the judge may order the offender to be assessed at TASC for drug and alcohol treatment needs. A TASC case manager conducts the assessment to determine the extent of the offender's drug and alcohol problem, sociodemographic characteristics, prior criminal record, and need for treatment and other services (e.g., education, employment). The assessment is then provided to the judge, who uses this information in the sentencing decision. In this capacity, TASC operates as an adjunct to probation. If the judge sentences the offender to probation with TASC as a condition, the offender then goes to the TASC office. At the TASC office, a more comprehensive assessment may be conducted; a formal treatment plan is developed that lays out the nature and length of treatment and other services recommended for the offender. The case manager makes the referral to a treatment facility. Given the availability of treatment services to criminal justice clients, the offender may be placed on a waiting list until a treatment slot becomes available. Although the main job of the case manager is to refer the offender to drug and alcohol treatment services, the case manager may also help the offender with referrals to other social services agencies, as well.

Monitoring and reporting back an offender's progress is an integral part of the TASC experience. Monitoring generally involves urinalysis testing to determine drug use as well as monitoring of treatment attendance, participation, and progress. Regularly scheduled reports are prepared by the case manager from information gathered from the treatment program and urinalysis tests and are submitted to the judge and/or probation.

Early evaluations of TASC conducted in the 1970s and a few more recent reviews (Inciardi and McBride, 1991, 1992)focused on the operations and process of TASC programs. None has explicitly examined outcomes for TASC participants. To gain a better understanding of how well the programs work, the National Institute on Drug Abuse awarded a multiyear evaluation contract to UCLA and RAND in 1991. The study was conducted between 1991 and 1996 and involved researchers at UCLA, RAND, University of Delaware and Andrews University. This study was the first evaluation of the TASC model that included a research design incorporating explicit comparison groups and measurement of outcomes in a variety of domains. While the evaluation had multiple objectives, one of its primary goals was to assess the effect of the programs on offender drug use, crime, HIV risk behavior, and other outcomes.

OVERALL STUDY DESIGN

The study entailed both a process and an outcome evaluation of five TASC sites across the country:

- Portland, Oregon (adult probation)
- Birmingham, Alabama (adult probation)
- Chicago, Illinois (adult probation)
- Canton, Ohio (adult diversion)
- Orlando, Florida (juvenile probation)

The outcome study measured the background, program implementation, and multiple outcomes (drug use, criminal behavior, psychosocial measures) for over 2,000 offenders, half of whom participated in TASC, the other half in routine criminal justice processing. In two sites, random assignment was used to assign volunteers to either TASC or routine criminal justice processing. In the other three sites, quasi-experimental designs were used. Outcomes were compared at each site for TASC and control/comparison group offenders to determine whether TASC "made a difference."

Types of Data Collected

For each participating study subject, two separate interviews were conducted. The first interview, conducted shortly following recruitment, gathered information on the subject demographics (age, race, sex, marital history, employment, education, etc.); drug use and criminal behavior in the six months before the baseline interview; AIDS risk behaviors during the most recent month; AIDS knowledge and attitudes; and self-ratings related to treatment readiness and motivation. At six months following recruitment, a second interview was conducted. This interview updated the background information as well as drug use and criminal behavior during the six-month period between the initial and follow-up interview. The AIDS risk behavior instrument, AIDS knowledge and attitudes, as well as the self-ratings were gathered for the six-month follow-up. Detailed information on the types of services received during the follow-up period, including measures of intensity and frequency, and helpfulness were also assessed. At both intake and follow-up a urine sample was requested, to help validate self-reported drug use. Follow-up rates were high—across sites, the overall rate was 83 percent.

STUDY OFFENDER CHARACTERISTICS

Reflecting the nature of the offender population, the majority of the offenders—more than three quarters—at each site were male. In Birmingham and Chicago, the vast majority of offenders were African American; in Canton, whites and African Americans were about equally represented. In Portland, the majority of offenders were white. In Orlando, the majority were African Americans; however, more than 10 percent were Hispanic. Across the adult TASC programs, offenders were generally older, averaging 30 years or older. Youth in Orlando averaged 16 years of age.

In terms of prior drug use, approximately 90 percent of offenders in the adult sites had used marijuana, while approximately 80 percent of the juveniles in Orlando had used marijuana. Cocaine (injected or snorted) and crack had been used by a majority of offenders at all sites except Orlando. Amphetamine use varied widely across sites, with more than half of offenders in Canton and Portland having used the drug.

Large percentages had previously been involved in treatment, although sites differed greatly in the extent of such treatment. Almost two thirds of offenders in Portland had prior detoxification or drug treatment. Although the average age of juveniles in Orlando was only 16 years, more than 20 percent of TASC offenders had experienced at least one treatment episode. One primary concern for drug-using groups is their risk for HIV infection. Study interviewers asked offenders if they had ever been told they had the AIDS virus or had AIDS. Very few offenders reported that they had.

To gather information on the extent of prior criminal offenders, interviewers asked offenders to indicate the numbers of crimes they had committed during the past six months. Crimes were described in commonsense phrases such as "broke into a house, building, or car in order to take something" (burglary). The median number of crimes committed during the six months before study recruitment varied greatly across sites, from lows of under ten crimes in Orlando and Birmingham to over thirty for Chicago offenders.

SERVICES RECEIVED DURING FOLLOW-UP PERIOD

To assess the services received by each study subject during the six-month period between baseline and follow-up, we included in the follow-up interview a series of questions on whether the offender received treatment or counseling services, including urinalysis tests, from any provider. If so, the offender was asked to specify the nature of those services. Possible services included: drug detoxification; drug-related medical care; other medical care; urine tests to monitor recent drug or alcohol use; drug counseling; legal counseling; parenting instruction; family problem counseling; AIDS prevention counseling; personal problem counseling; school counseling; school placement; job training; job placement, and other.

In all sites except Canton, TASC offenders were significantly more likely to have received at least one type of service during the six-month follow-up than were comparison offenders. In Canton, although the percentage of TASC subjects receiving services was about 10 percent higher than for comparison offenders, the difference was not significant. This is most likely due to the relatively small sample sizes for this site and the fact that the comparison group was assigned to another treatment program—not a no-treatment condition.

The types of services most frequently received by TASC offenders were urinalysis testing and drug counseling, although a significant percentage of clients reported receiving AIDS counseling in Chicago (53%). The average number of services reported by subjects generally was more than two for TASC offenders, with the exception of Orlando, where the average was just less than one.

Our follow-up time frame was six months, too short to measure full participation in and completion of treatment for all offenders. For this reason, the percent of offenders who had successfully completed treatment by the time of the follow-up would undercount the true effect of TASC on retention. Therefore, we examined the percent of offenders (among those receiving at least one service during the follow-up) who were still enrolled in the four most frequently attended services at the time of follow-up. In Birmingham, a greater percentage of TASC offenders were still receiving drug and alcohol tests than were control/comparison offenders. In Canton, more TASC offenders were still enrolled in drug treatment; slightly more were receiving drug and alcohol tests. In Chicago, slightly more TASC offenders were still enrolled in AIDS prevention counseling. In Orlando and Portland, similar percentages of offenders were still enrolled in the four major types of services at the end of the follow-up.

Overall, the TASC programs in Chicago and Birmingham showed the highest level of service intensity. Differences between TASC and comparison groups in terms of services received were striking at both sites, as shown in Figures 1 and 2.

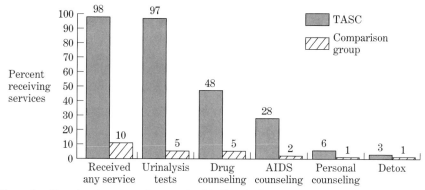

Figure 1. Drug treatment services received in Birmingham.

OUTCOMES

Many different outcomes were examined in the current study. A complete description of the outcomes and the analysis strategy is outlined in Anglin and colleagues (1996). In short, our primary analysis strategy was to compare outcomes using assigned condition, or "intent to treat." That is, at each site, all offenders in the TASC group were compared with all offenders in the control/comparison group, regardless of their "dose" of treatment.[1] Although the outcomes of TASC varied across sites, the effects were gener-

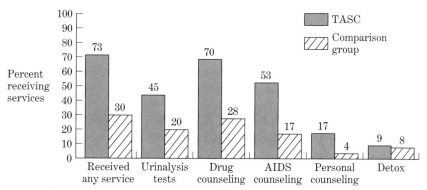

Figure 2. Drug treatment services received in Chicago.

---

[1] An "intent to treat" analysis is more conservative. TASC effects might appear stronger if we had excluded TASC cases who received no treatment services as a result of the TASC referral and cases whose "dose" of treatment services was less than intended or optimal. This approach is the one recommended for experimental field evaluations.

ally more pronounced in Birmingham and Chicago. This might be expected: Both programs are stable, having been in place for over twenty years; and, as noted above, the level of service intensity at these sites is high. We report some of the outcomes for Birmingham and Chicago below.

Drug Use Behavior

The evaluation focused several drug use outcomes, including number of days and number of times drugs were used during the intervention. In many cases, the TASC program seemed to work more effectively for those who might be considered more serious offenders.

In Chicago and Birmingham, TASC was associated with a reduction in the number of drug-use days during the six-month follow-up. In Chicago, however, this effect was dependent upon the number of arrests the offender had prior to age 18. Although all offenders who participated in TASC revealed significant reductions in drug-use days, the reduction in drug-use days during follow-up was greater by almost fifteen days for TASC offenders who had not been arrested before age 18. For those offenders arrested when younger, the impact of TASC was significantly larger—an estimated reduction of over forty drug days during the follow-up period.

Crimes Committed

The study gathered information on three major types of crimes: violent crimes, property crimes, and drug crimes. The total number of violent crimes committed by offenders across sites was very low; thus violent crimes were considered unreliable as a major measure of crime commission for the study. Analyses of property and drug crimes showed divergent findings.

TASC was not associated with a reduction in the numbers of property crimes during the six-month follow-up period. Our analyses showed similar numbers of property crimes being committed by TASC and control/comparison group offenders. However, TASC was associated with reductions in the number of drug crimes committed. In Birmingham, TASC offenders committed an estimated sixteen fewer drug crimes relative to Birmingham control/comparison offenders. In Chicago, the effect of TASC was qualified by the number of prior convictions. If the offender had three or more such convictions, TASC was associated with a reduction of forty drug crimes. If the offender had fewer than three prior convictions, TASC was not associated with reduced numbers of drug crimes.

HIV Risk Behavior

Aside from its potential effects on drug use and criminal activity, TASC may also lead to reductions in HIV risk behavior. The study was able to evaluate the effects of TASC on two high-risk behaviors: unprotected sex and having sex while high on drugs or alcohol.

In Chicago, offenders who scored above the mean on baseline frequency of sex while high showed significantly greater declines in this behavior than those who scored below the mean.

In Birmingham, TASC showed no particular effect on HIV risk behaviors among offenders who reported no incarceration during the baseline period. However, the program did effect a reduction in frequency of sex while high among those offenders who reported being incarcerated for at least one day during the baseline period. These offenders also had more extensive criminal and drug use histories than those who had not been incarcerated during the baseline period.

CONCLUSIONS

Overall, TASC did have favorable effects, both in terms of services received and subsequent outcomes. These favorable effects, however, were qualified by site and offender characteristics. One of the most interesting findings of this study was that many effects depended on the baseline characteristics of offenders. TASC often had a stronger effect among those offenders who were more problematic, whether this characterization was based on the offender's criminal and drug history or sex-risk behavior. This suggests that it might be more cost effective to target TASC resources toward those offenders whose behavior is most problematic.

REFERENCES

Anglin, M. D., D. Longshore, S. Turner, D. McBride, J. Inciardi, and M. Prendergast. 1996. *Studies of the Functioning and Effectiveness of Treatment Alternatives to Street Crime (TASC) Programs: Draft Report.* UCLA Drug Abuse Research Center; Los Angeles.

Garner, J., and C. A. Vischer. 1988. *Policy Experiments Come of Age.* NIJ Reports, 211. Washington, D.C.: Department of Justice.

Inciardi, J. A., and D. C. McBride. 1991. *Treatment Alternatives to Street Crime: History, Experiences, and Issues* (DHHS 91-1749). Rockville, Md.: National Institute on Drug Abuse.

Inciardi, J.A., and D. C. McBride. 1992. "Reviewing the "TASC" (Treatment Alternatives to Street Crimes) Experience." *Journal of Crime and Justice* 15(1):45–61.

CHAPTER **6**

Attitudes of Offenders and the Public Toward Community Corrections

INTRODUCTION

Probation and parole have long suffered from a "soft on crime" image and, as a result, maintain little public support. Their poor (and some believe, misunderstood) public image leaves them unable to compete effectively for scarce public funds. As previously noted, community corrections receives less than 10 percent of state and local government expenditures for correctional services, which includes jails and prisons. And their budgets are declining at a faster rate when compared with other criminal justice components, such as the police and courts.

Why does community corrections fare so poorly? It is not that its services are undervalued. Quite the contrary. Every national study and commission beginning with the President's Commission on Law Enforcement and Administration of Justice (1967) up to the more recent President's *National Drug Control Strategy* (1995) has recommended expanding community corrections. In fact, the National Advisory Commission on Criminal Justice Standards and Goals (1973) referred to community corrections as the justice system's "brightest hope."

But while there is general support for the *concept* of community sanctions, current programs are seen as inadequate. Most of the commissions that endorse community corrections go on to state that current programs are unable to provide effective offender supervision or rehabilitation. Furthermore, the media often report that the public is steadfast against community-based sanctions, believing that no matter how onerous the conditions, they are simply not punishing enough for serious offenders. As John DiIulio states in *No Escape: The Future of American Corrections* (1991:68),

> Most Americans think that criminal sanctions that make little or no use of incarceration fail to protect the public adequately, to deter would-be criminals, and to prevent convicted criminals from finding new victims. They simply do not feel that alternatives to incarceration are an adequate moral

142

response to the pain and suffering imposed upon innocent victims by often calculating and unremorseful victimizers.

The two articles chosen for inclusion in this chapter demonstrate that our concepts of punitiveness are too simplistic. First, as Julian Roberts notes, public opinion surveys show that the public is not nearly as punitive as the media and politicians make them out to be. Rather, when credible public opinion surveys are conducted, the findings reveal a public that distinguishes between violent and nonviolent offenders, repeat and first offenders, and drug addicts and drug dealers. For some groups of offenders, the public endorses community-based rather than incarceration sanctions. He suggests that our misunderstanding of the public's views toward criminal sentencing results from poorly designed public opinion surveys.

The article by Joan Petersilia and Elizabeth Piper Deschenes tackles the question of "punitiveness" from another perspective, that of the offender. Most sentencing laws reflect the notions of how punishing a particular sentence would be, based on the notions of what free citizens believe to be punishing. For them, prison is always the more dreaded sanction. But, as intermediate sanctions have become more onerous, offenders often prefer a short stay in jail or prison to a more cumbersome community-based sanction, which may mandate employment and drug testing. Their article interviews inmates in Minnesota and asks them to rank the perceived severity of a number of community-based versus incarceration sentences. The results show that tough community-based sanctioning can indeed be more punishing than prison in the eyes of offenders.

The results of these articles taken together suggest that there is public support for tough community-based sanctions for nonviolent offenders, and if the sanctions are imposed and monitored closely by corrections professionals, that the offenders themselves judge them more punitive than short prison and jail terms. It is thus no longer necessary to equate criminal punishment solely with prison. The balance of sanctions between probation and prisons has shifted, and at some level, intensive supervision probation and parole is the more dreaded penalty.

American Attitudes About Punishment: Myth and Reality

JULIAN V. ROBERTS

Much of the conventional wisdom about Americans' attitudes toward criminal punishment is wrong. Most Americans believe in rehabilitation, and are willing to spend tax dollars to rehabilitate offenders. Most Americans want

"American Attitudes About Punishment: Myth and Reality" by Julian V. Roberts, from *Overcrowded Times*, Vol. 3, No. 2, April 1992, pp. 1–13, Castine, Maine. Reprinted with permission.

to see criminals punished but for many offenders would rather see community-based punishments imposed than prison sentences.

These findings, which contravene the assumption that Americans want ever more offenders put in prison, is based upon a recent review of public opinion research conducted in the U.S. (and elsewhere) over the past 30 years.

The myth that the public is harshly and single-mindedly punitive results largely from the limits of public opinion surveys. The questions asked are often too simple. The answers are often premised on worse-case stereotypes of offenders and on believes that punishments are much less harsh than they really are.

Table 1 summarizes principal recurring findings from public opinion research concerning sentencing. These findings are drawn from research using different methods and different sample populations in the United States and elsewhere.

SIMPLISTIC QUESTIONS GENERATE SIMPLISTIC ANSWERS

Consider the poll that asks a single question: *"Are sentences too harsh, about right, or not harsh enough?"* For many years, this kind of question was used to investigate public attitudes toward sentencing. Most people respond that sentences are "not harsh enough." And from that response politicians have inferred that sentencing policies in America, Great Britain, Canada, and elsewhere should not be modified to promote greater use of alternatives to imprisonment, for to do so would alienate the public. But is this a correct reading of public opinion? I think not.

The weakness with the interpretation is that it falls to consider three important additional findings from the survey literature. First, when answering a question like this, most people are thinking of violent offenders who have criminal histories. The worst-case scenario, in short. Second, the public has little idea of the actual severity of sentencing practices. Most peo-

TABLE 1
Summary of Principal Findings: Public Opinion and Sentencing

- Public opposition to alternatives to incarceration has been overstated.
- The public knows little about alternatives.
- The public's first response to crime is in terms of imprisonment.
- Informing the public about alternatives reduces support for prison. This is true for a range of crimes, including some violent crimes.
- The American public believes in rehabilitation and favors rehabilitative programs.
- Sentencing stories in the media usually involve violent crimes and sentences of imprisonment.
- Many politicians have misread public views of crime and punishment.
- The public is not more punitive than are judges.

ple *underestimate* the severity of sentencing. Third, and perhaps the most glaring weakness associated with addressing a complex issue like sentencing by means of a single question, is that it fails to take into account that the public knows little about sentencing alternatives such as house arrest, intensive probation, restitution, and community service.

The public tends to think about sentencing exclusively in terms of imprisonment. To many people, the question is not so much whether the offender should be imprisoned, but for how long.

Recent research, using new techniques, shows that public opinions about sentencing are more complicated than is generally acknowledged.

GIVEN ALTERNATIVES, THE PUBLIC WILL USE THEM

What happens when the public is asked questions about sentencing *after* receiving information about sentencing alternatives? Support for imprisonment declines significantly. This important finding emerges from a number of recent studies.

The Public Agenda Foundation carried out research in Alabama and Delaware to determine what would happen to public attitudes if people were given information about sentencing alternatives. The results were remarkably consistent across the two states, and conform to a pattern emerging from surveys in other countries including Canada and Australia. The methodology of the Foundation's research is straightforward. Groups of people are given brief descriptions of crimes. They are then asked to choose between incarceration or probation for the offenders in these descriptions. At this juncture, members of these groups heavily favor imprisonment for most offenders. For example, participants in Delaware were asked to sentence an armed robbery committed by a juvenile with no previous convictions. Four out of five favored incarceration. This is the "before" phase of the study.

Participants are then shown a videotape that describes five alternative sentences: intensively supervised probation; restitution; community service; house arrest; boot camp. A discussion period follows, after which participants are asked to "re-sentence" the offenders they sentenced in the first phase. This second sentencing is the "after" phase of the study. Support for incarceration declined substantially for a number of offenses. For example, in the case of the juvenile first offender who was convicted of armed robbery, only 38 percent of the participants favored incarcerating the offender after learning about alternative punishments.

Of course, the substantial decline in support for incarceration did not occur for every offense. For rape, for example, the 98 percent of respondents who favored imprisonment in the "before" phase declined only to 86 percent. Nevertheless, these offenses were in the minority. In the "before" phase in Delaware, participants wanted to incarcerate 17 out of 23 offenders. This declined to only 5 out of 23 in the "after" phase.

Similar results emerged in Alabama: incarceration was favored in 18 out of 23 cases in the first phase and only 4 cases afterward. Illustrative data for the two studies, showing remarkable consistency in the before and after findings, are shown in Table 2.

DIFFERENT METHODOLOGIES FIND SIMILAR RESULTS

The Public Agenda studies used a "focus group" approach in which relatively small groups of participants focus on a particular problem and discuss the issues involved. The principal alternative approach is to conduct surveys of large, representative samples of the public, in which less information is given, and respondents have less time in which to respond. This is the standard way to measure public opinion in areas such as politics and advertising. What is striking, however, is that similar findings emerge from conventional surveys. For example, Galaway (1984) conducted an experiment that used a representative survey of the public in New Zealand. Half the respondents were simply asked to sentence an offender. The other half were asked to sentence the same offender but were explicitly given the option of court-ordered restitution. Results indicated that the public were willing to accept a reduction in the use of incarceration if offenders were required to pay restitution. Comparable results were found in a Canadian survey by Doob and Roberts (1983), indicating that support for imprisonment is based in part upon ignorance of the alternative sanctions available.

Further evidence of public support for alternatives comes from other questions examined in the Public Agenda Foundation studies. In Delaware, for example, the following question was posed:

> Some states are experimenting with alternatives to prison and probation such as restitution, community service, and house arrest. How do you feel about using alternative sentences?

TABLE 2
Support for Incarceration Before and After Information Was Received About Sentencing Alternatives

	Alabama		Delaware	
Crime	Before	After	Before	After
Theft (5th offense)	90%	46%	83%	47%
Armed robbery	78	47	72	47
Shoplifting	74	22	71	19
Burglary	68	19	70	22
Drunk driving	13	2	16	4
Embezzlement	71	30	71	31

Sources: John Doble and Josh Klein. 1989. Punishing Criminals. The Public's View—An Alabama Survey. *New York: The Edna McConnell Clark Foundation.*
John Doble, Stephen Immerwahr, and Amy Richardson. 1991. Punishing Criminals: The People of Delaware Consider the Options. *New York: The Edna McConnell Clark Foundation.*

More than nine out of ten respondents expressed support for these alternatives. Even more strikingly, support for alternatives was equally substantial among victims of crime. Support for alternatives appears to be particularly strong in the case of juvenile offenders. This is apparent from a number of surveys in the U.S. One recent poll in Ohio by Knowles (1987) found that over 90 percent of respondents approved of use of alternatives for juveniles.

PUBLIC VERSUS THE COURTS

Conventional wisdom suggests that "sentences" preferred by the public would be much harsher than the sentences actually imposed by judges. This is not true. Mande and English (1989) for example show that the public surveyed in Colorado were more, not less, supportive than judges of community-based sanctions. This was true even for some serious crimes.

Aggravated robbery provides a good illustration. The Colorado researchers found that approximately three fourths of offenders convicted of robbery were imprisoned. However, when the views of the public were examined, only 30 percent of respondents favored incarceration; almost half preferred to impose a community-based alternative. Table 3 presents an example of a scenario used in a Colorado study in which public views were contrasted with those held by criminal justice officials. For some crimes the public were close to the public officials in terms of sentencing preferences. The overall result is striking however: *Sentence lengths recommended by this representative sample of Colorado residents were on average twelve months shorter than sentences for the same crimes recommended by criminal justice officials.*

This finding—of a public that is not harsher in its sentencing preferences than are judges—has now been replicated in a series of studies in the U..S., Canada, Great Britain, and Australia. Taken together, these studies

TABLE 3
Sentencing Preferences, Public vs. Criminal Justice Officials

Case: Offender pled guilty to manslaughter, was drinking at the time of the offense, is employed, is 25 years old, married with a three-year old child. He has a prior conviction for assault.

Sentence	Public	Officials
Probation	1%	2%
Probation/jail	19	5
Intensively supervised probation	11	12
Community corrections	20	21
Prison	49	60
	100	100
Median prison term	36 months	48 months

Source: K. English, J. Crouch, and S. Pullen. 1989. Attitudes Toward Crime: A Survey of Colorado Citizens and Criminal Justice Officials. *Colorado: Colorado Department of Public Safety, Division of Criminal Justice.*

do not support the conclusion that the public is considerably more punitive than the courts.

These results suggest that increased use of alternatives to incarceration can proceed without fear of widespread public opposition, so long as the public is provided with enough information.

POLITICIANS MISREAD THE PUBLIC

Public education is only part of the problem, however. It is also necessary to educate criminal justice professionals about the true mood of the public toward sentencing. Criminal justice policymakers fail to appreciate the support among the public for important reforms. For example, Immarigeon (1986) found that a sample of policymakers in Michigan believed that fewer than one resident in four would support an increased use of alternatives to incarceration. In fact, two-thirds of the Michigan public surveyed supported this policy.

PUBLIC SUPPORT FOR REHABILITATION

Another misperception concerns rehabilitation. It is commonly suggested that the public favors punishment over all other sentencing objectives, and that support for rehabilitation has evaporated. This is simply not true. A national survey recently posed the following question:

> In dealing with those who are in prison, do you think it is more important to punish them for their crimes, or more important to get them "started on the right road" (i.e., rehabilitate them)?

There was more support for rehabilitation than for punishment (Flanagan and Maguire, 1990). Support for rehabilitation in the correctional sphere is also manifested in substantial support for parole. A national survey of Americans conducted a few years ago found that eight of ten respondents endorsed use of parole in the criminal justice systems of America.

CONSEQUENCES FOR THE CRIMINAL JUSTICE SYSTEM

The results summarized here have important implications. The first step toward reducing America's alarming prison populations is to reduce public opposition to such a change. The American public is not implacably opposed to alternatives that will lead to a reduction in the number of persons committed to prison. This is true for a wide range of property offenders and also for some offenses involving violence.

Public education is clearly a priority. A substantial degree of public opposition to alternatives is founded upon ignorance of these dispositions. It is imperative that the system educate the public in this regard. Information about "intermediate sanctions" that lie between probation and imprisonment needs to be communicated to the public.

At present, the public tends to respond to the problem of sentencing offenders by considering prison as the primary criminal justice response. For this the media bear some responsibility. Most crimes reported in the news are crimes of violence; most sentences reported are terms of imprisonment. But the public's reflex imprisonment response to crime does not spring from a deep-seated desire to be punitive. Rather, it springs, in part at least, from a lack of awareness of the alternatives available. When the public becomes more aware of alternatives, its enthusiasm for prison declines significantly. There is an important lesson to be learned here.

REFERENCES

Doob, A. N., and J. V. Roberts. 1983. *Sentencing. An Analysis of the Public's View of Sentencing.* Ottawa: Department of Justice, Canada.

Flanagan, T., and K. Maguire. 1990. *Sourcebook of Criminal Justice Statistics—1989.* Washington, D.C.: Bureau of Justice Statistics.

Galaway, B. 1984. *Public Acceptance of Restitution as an Alternative to Imprisonment for Property Offenders: A Survey.* Wellington, New Zealand: Department of Justice.

Immarigeon, R. 1986. "Surveys Reveal Broad Support for Alternative Sentencing." *Journal of the National Prison Project of the American Civil Liberties Union Foundation* 9:1–4.

Knowles, J. 1987. *Ohio Citizen Attitudes Concerning Crime and Criminal Justice,* 5th ed. Columbus, Ohio: Governor's Office of Criminal Justice Services.

Mande, Mary J., and Kim English. 1989. *The Effect of Public Opinion on Correctional Policy: A Comparison of Opinions and Practice.* Colorado: Colorado Department of Public Safety, Division of Criminal Justice.

What Punishes? Inmates Rank the Severity of Prision Versus Intermediate Sanctions

Joan Petersilia and Elizabeth Piper Deschenes

INTRODUCTION AND RESEARCH QUESTIONS

The intermediate sanctions movement of the 1980's was predicated on the assumption that the two extremes of punishment—imprisonment and probation—are both used excessively, with a near vacuum of useful punish-

Dr. Petersilia is a Professor in the School of Social Ecology at the University of California, Irvine. Dr. Deschenes is an Associate Professor, California State University, Long Beach.

"What Punishes? Inmates Rank the Severity of Prison Versus Intermediate Sanctions" by Joan Petersilia and Elizabeth Piper Deschenes, from *Federal Probation*, Vol. 58, No. 1, March 1994, pp. 3–8. Reprinted with permission.

ments in between. According to Morris and Tonry (1990), a more comprehensive sentencing strategy that relies on a range of "intermediate" punishments—including fines, community service, intensive probation, and electronic monitoring—would better meet the needs of the penal system, convicted offenders, and the community than the current polarized choice. The central thesis of the Morris and Tonry proposal is that there are "equivalencies" of punishment and that, at some level of intensity, community-based punishments are as severe as prison terms (i.e., have roughly the same punitive "bite"). They encouraged states to identify these roughly equivalent punishments (or "exchange rates") and allow judges to choose among sentences of rough punitive equivalence. They predicted that in many instances judges would choose to substitute restrictive, intermediate punishments in lieu of a prison term.

Implementing intermediate sanction *programs* within states' broad-based sentencing structure (particularly in states with sentencing guidelines) has proven much easier than developing the comprehensive sentencing *system* that Morris and Tonry envisioned. A major stumbling block has been reaching consensus on the relative severity of different community-based punishments (e.g., house arrest versus community service) and, more importantly, on *which* intermediate sanctions, in what dosage, can be substituted for prison. When the choice was simply prison versus standard probation, most everyone agreed that prison was more severe. But with the emergence of highly restrictive community-based punishments—which often require drug testing, employment, and curfews—it is no longer obvious.

Most law-abiding citizens probably still believe that no matter what conditions probation or parole impose, remaining in the community is categorically preferable to imprisonment, but recent evidence suggests that offenders might not share this view. When Oregon implemented an intensive supervision probation (ISP) program in 1989 and offenders were given the choice of serving a prison term or participating in ISP (which incorporated drug testing, employment, and frequent home visits by the probation officer), about a third of the offenders chose prison instead of ISP (Petersilia, 1990).

It may also be that prison is losing some of its punitive sting. For example, Skolnick (1990) reported that, for certain California youth, having a prison record was no longer seen as stigmatizing, and the prison experience not particularly isolating, since they usually encountered family or friends there. If prison is not judged as severe as we presume it is, this may have important implications for sentencing policy. Since the major purposes of the criminal law are retribution and deterrence, this means that sanctions must be viewed as punitive, to fulfill their goals. And, as Crouch (1993, p. 68) has noted, "Theoretically, for prison to have the punitive and deterrent effect on offenders that the public desires, a fundamental assumption must be met: that offenders generally share the state's punitiveness in the ranking of criminal sanctions."

The unanswered question is, "do they?" If they don't, and if community-based punishments can be designed so that they are seen as equally punitive by offenders, then perhaps policymakers—who say they are imprisoning such a large number of offenders because of the public's desire to get tough with crime—might be convinced that there are other means besides prison to exact punishment.

Despite the importance of the offenders' perspective as noted by Crouch (1993), there have been only three prior attempts to survey the opinions of criminal offenders regarding the perceived severity of sanctions (McClelland & Alpert, 1985; Apospori & Alpert, 1993; Crouch, 1993), and none of these studies included the newer intermediate sanctions (e.g., intensive probation). In addition, most prior research on sanction severity has used either paired comparisons or magnitude estimation to measure judgments, and both techniques have methodological or analytical flaws.[1]

McClelland and Alpert (1985) surveyed 152 arrestees in a midsize western city, following the example of Erickson and Gibbs (1979) who used magnitude estimation techniques to survey policemen and adults in households. Respondents were given a list of penalties (randomly ordered), including different levels of fines, probation, jail, and prison, and instructed to assign a number to each penalty based on the standard of 100 for 1 year in jail. They found that persons who had more experience with the criminal justice system (e.g., more prior convictions) minimized the seriousness of prison in comparison to other punishments. And in later research, Apospori and Alpert (1993) suggested that as the threat of the legal sanction became realized, arrestees raised their perceptions of the severity of sanctions. In a survey of 1,027 incoming prisoners at a Texas institution who were asked if they would prefer probation or prison, Crouch (1993) found that the majority of inmates preferred prison to probation, believing probation was stricter. In addition, Crouch found that those who were married preferred probation to prison, yet minorities and older inmates preferred prison.

This article presents the results of an exploratory study undertaken in cooperation with the Minnesota Department of Corrections and the Minnesota Sentencing Guidelines Commission and funded by the National Institute of Justice to explore these issues. The study developed an instrument and methodology for measuring offender perceptions of sanction severity and, using that method, collected data on the following questions:

1. How do inmates rank the severity of criminal sanctions, and which sanctions are judged equivalent in punitiveness?

2. What background characteristics are associated with variations in the perception of sanction severity?

3. How do inmates rank the difficulty of probation/parole conditions, and how does this affect their ranking of sanctions?

Our research attempted to build upon prior research by adding the newer intermediate sanctions to the survey and including both magnitude estimation and rank ordering scaling techniques. The simpler technique of rank ordering is likely to give a more accurate model of the ratings of various punishments, since offenders may not have the mathematical skills necessary for the magnitude estimation judgment of severity. Besides increasing the simplicity of the task, the use of ordered logistic regression to model the underlying latent scale of sanction severity and test for differences between individuals allowed greater flexibility in the analysis (Agresti, 1990). The basic model being tested assumes that each individual has an underlying scale of the severity of different sanctions. Ordered logistic regression allows us to more easily test whether various sanctions are indeed equivalent with less rigid assumptions about the data.[2] For these reasons, the rank ordering analysis is preferred and this article focuses on those results.

STUDY DESIGN AND RESULTS

Sample Selection

The sample selection criteria were designed to identify offenders who would likely be targeted for intermediate sanctions and therefore whose perceptions about the severity of such sanctions are particularly relevant. We used the same criteria to identify our sample that had been outlined by the Minnesota Legislature in deciding which inmates qualified for the state's Intensive Community Supervision (ICS) program. To be eligible for ICS, offenders must be either a probation violator or a new court commitment with less than a 27-month prison sentence to serve. Offenders with prior convictions for murder, manslaughter, or rape are ineligible. The sample was drawn from incoming inmates who met the ICS eligibility criteria at the two main receiving facilities in Minnesota, St. Cloud and Stillwater. Forty-eight male inmates were so identified during the months of April–July 1992, and all agreed to participate in the study.

The sample of inmates was 50 percent white, and the majority of nonwhites were Afro-American; the average age at the time of the current offense was 26. Inmates tended to be unemployed prior to prison, and about half had less than a high school education. Inmates were serving, on average, prison terms of 17 months, and most had been convicted of property offenses. Inmates averaged seven prior arrests and two prior felony convictions, and one-third had previously served time in prison.

Data Collection

RAND staff coded various demographic and criminal history data from each inmate's official corrections file. Interviews were administered with those who agreed to participate in the study, and respondents received $20 for participating. The interview took about an hour to administer and was divided into four sections:

1) *The Magnitude Estimation Task*. Fifteen legal sanctions were selected for the study (see Table 1). Each sanction description was printed sep-

arately on a 3 × 5-inch card and presented one by one to the respondent in a random order. Respondents were instructed to compare each of the sanctions to the standard of 1 year in jail, which was equivalent to 100 points.

2) Offender Background Interview. About 25 open-ended questions were asked offenders requesting information on employment, housing arrangements, family relationships, present prison experiences, and their perceptions of prison versus community-based sentencing.

3) *The Ranking of Probation Conditions.* Inmates were asked to estimate "the difficulty you would probably experience in trying to meet the (specified) condition." They were asked about 13 commonly imposed conditions and directed to place each "condition card" next to one of five responses (ranging from not difficult at all to very difficult).

4) *The Rank Ordering Task.* To rank order the sanctions, inmates were given a stack of 4 × 6-inch cards (randomly ordered). Each card had printed on it one of the 15 sanctions (see Table 1). Inmates were instructed to simply place the cards on the table, from left to right, in order from least severe to most severe.

Inmate Rankings and Equivalencies of the Severity of Criminal Sanctions

The means and standard deviations for the rank orders of the 15 sanctions presented in Table 1 suggest that inmate consensus is greatest at the low-

TABLE 1
Inmates Rank Ordering of Criminal Sanctions

Criminal sanction	Mean	Standard deviation	Median rank order
Fines			
$100	1.3	1.1	1
$1,000	4.5	3.4	3
$5,000	7.6	3.6	7
Probation			
1 year	4.2	2.0	4
3 years	6.8	2.7	6
5 years	9.8	2.8	10
Intensive probation			
1 year	7.1	2.2	7
3 years	9.5	2.2	10
5 years	11.4	2.6	11.5
Jail			
3 months	4.6	3.1	3.5
6 months	6.4	2.9	6
1 year	9.6	2.8	10
Prison			
1 year	9.7	3.2	11
3 years	13.0	2.0	14
5 years	14.5	1.5	15

est and highest levels—i.e., $100 fine and 5 years in prison. The larger values for the standard deviations on other sanctions suggest there is some variation between individuals, particularly on the ratings of a $5,000 fine, 3 months in jail, and 1 year in prison. Nonetheless, the means and medians provide similar results in the overall rank ordering of the various sanctions. For example, there appear to be "clusters" of sanctions—5 years probation, 3 years intensive probation, and 1 year in jail all have a median rank of 10. To statistically test for significant differences in the rank ordering of various sanctions, further analysis was necessary.

The data were analyzed using ordered logistic regression to model the ordered categorical responses as a function of the type of sanction. In the simplest case the model is of the form:

$$\text{Ranking} = f(\text{sum } \beta(i)^* \text{ sanction}(i))$$

The results of this type of analysis are a collection of parameter estimates or "betas," one for each sanction in the simplest case. The estimated coefficients in this model form a latent variable scale yielding an interval valued "score" for the various sanctions. The betas represent ranking of the sanctions and standards errors for the sanction's position on the latent scale. The statistical test of the difference between the ranking of the sanction and the ranking of the omitted category is a chi-square test with 1 degree of freedom.

The first model tested using ordered logistic regression compared all other sanctions to 1 year of intensive supervision. For this model, the parameter estimate for 1 year ISP was set to zero, and as shown in Table 2, sanctions that are not statistically different from 1 year intensive probation include 6 months jail, 3 years probation, and a $500 fine. The parameter estimates for the other sanctions show results that are consistent with the simple comparison of the median rank orders.

To test for equivalencies in the ratings of the sanctions, the ordered logistic regression analysis was repeated, each time omitting a different sanction, and chi-square tests performed, comparing sanction to the omitted category. The results of this analysis can be used to devise formulas for the substitution of incarceration for community-based punishments as shown in Table 2.

A number of things are worth noting. First, inmates judged 1 year spent in jail as equivalent to 1 year spent in prison. In fact, in the open-ended interviews, several inmates stated that prison time was easier to do because there were more activities to occupy their time and conditions were generally better. Inmates also ranked 5 years of intensive probation supervision as harsher than 1 year in prison but not as harsh as 3 years in prison. Five years in prison was judged more severe than any other sanction and had no equivalent in terms of the intermediate sanctions measured here. Similarly, a $100 fine was judged as significantly less severe than any other sanction measured here, having no other statistical equivalent.

TABLE 2
Inmates' Perceived Severity of Criminal Sanctions

Criminal sanction $100 fine	Parameter Estimate −7.42	Standard Error .68	Chi-square 118.3*
$1,000 fine	−2.14	.38	32.4*
3 months jail	−1.85	.36	25.8*
1 year probation	−1.80	.35	26.5*
6 months jail	−0.49	.34	2.1
3 years probation	−0.15	.34	0.2
1 year intensive probation	0.00		
$5,000 fine	0.24	.36	0.4
3 years intensive probation	1.25	.33	14.2*
1 year jail	1.35	.34	15.4*
5 years probation	1.45	.35	17.4*
1 year prison	1.56	.35	19.5*
5 years intensive probation	2.49	.36	47.9*
3 years prison	4.17	.39	113.1*
5 years prison	7.38	.56	175.1*

* Chi-square test of difference between this parameter estimate and the estimate for the omitted category (1 year ISP) is significantly different at p < .05.

Differences Between Individuals

To test for differences between individuals, ordered logistic regression was used and various models compared by using the chi-square differences from likelihood ratio tests. Only two of the background variables were significantly related to the perceptions of sanction severity: (1) inmates who were married and/or had children tended to rank prison and jail confinement as more severe than those who were single; and (2) inmates who were single tended to rank financial penalties (e.g., fines, restitution) as more severe than inmates who were married. We found no differences in the rankings of sanction severity by race, prior prison experience, employment history, drug dependency, or how safe the inmate felt in prison. It is possible that the sample was too small to detect differences or the characteristics of our sample too homogeneous. On the other hand, it may be that the differences noted in earlier studies reflect the clearer distinctions in the offenders' mind between prison and probation, which because of the inclusion of intermediate sanctions, was not as pronounced in our study as in earlier research.

Rating the Difficulty of Complying With Various Probation Conditions

We were interested in learning how inmates varied in their perception of the difficulty of complying with various probation conditions and whether this perception affected their rankings of different sanctions. Figure 1 presents the results, with the responses averaged over all inmates.

Inmates generally felt they would have little difficulty in complying with various restrictions. The overall rating for the 13 probation conditions was 2.1, which is "relatively easy." They judged the easiest conditions to be payment of a $100 fine and 10 hours per week of community service and the most difficult conditions to be house arrest with 24-hour electronic monitoring and the payment of a $20-per-week probation/parole supervision fee.

It might seem contrary that inmates who judged certain intermediate sanctions as equivalent to prison in harshness would also judge the individual conditions making up those sanctions as rather easy to comply with. Information offered by inmates during the interviews suggests that while each individual condition might be easy to comply with, when conditions are stacked together—*particularly over longer time periods*—they become much more difficult. House arrest sentences are often for periods of 6 months to 1 year, and intensive probation is usually for 1–2 years.

We analyzed the relationship between background characteristics and inmate ratings of probation conditions and found only one significant differ-

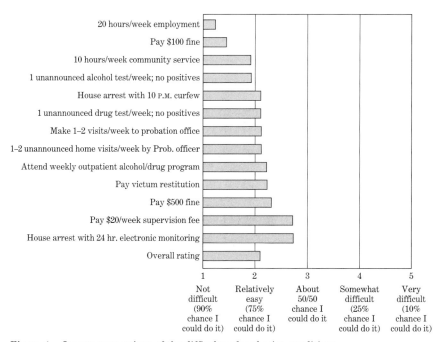

Figure 1. Inmate perceptions of the difficulty of probation conditions.

ence: Those with no history of drug or alcohol use (as noted on their official prison records) reported finding it more difficult to attend a weekly outpatient treatment program than did the users. We also tested whether the inmates' overall rating score on probation conditions was related to the ranking of the severity of the overall criminal sanctions but found no significant differences between those who rated the probation conditions as easy to comply with and those who rated the conditions as more difficult.

DISCUSSION AND POLICY IMPLICATIONS

Our results provide empirical evidence to support what many have suggested: that it is no longer necessary to equate criminal punishment solely with prison. The balance of sanctions between probation and prison appears to have shifted, and at some level of intensity and length, intensive probation is the more dreaded penalty.

These findings have a number of research and policy implications. For one, the clusters of sanctions identified as "equivalent" in severity should be useful to sentencing commissions attempting to incorporate alternatives into sentencing guidelines and to devise formulas showing the equivalency of alternative sanctions to imprisonment.

Ideally, one wants to devise an intermediate sanction that includes enough conditions (but not more than necessary) to exact punishment and protect the public. But since little knowledge exists about how many conditions, or what type, are necessary to achieve those goals, jurisdictions continue to add conditions, thus negating one of the major purposes of intermediate sanctions, which is to provide suitable punishment at less cost than prison. Inmate judgments on punitive equivalence could be useful in setting some boundaries on what types of conditions, imposed for how long, are required to mete out "tough" probation sentences and to suggest some rough ordering that might be used to create a continuum of punishments—from fines through community service, standard probation, intensive probation and house arrest, then moving on to jail, and finally prison.

The study results also have implications for sentencing and deterrence research. Sentencing studies routinely build mathematical models of punishment that treat anything other than prison as "zero" and assign positive values only to increments of imprisonment. Similarly, deterrence studies assign numerical ranks reflecting sanction seriousness and then analyze whether there is a relationship between the severity rankings and some post-treatment outcome (e.g., usually recidivism). Both types of studies rely on scales of sanction severity, which our study suggests are in need of refinement. At a minimum, sentencing studies need to recognize different levels of probation supervision (i.e., not code all probation sentences identically) and that probation terms do not equate to "zero," which implies no sanction at all.

Our findings also have implications for sentencing policy more generally. It is argued by some that the United States has failed to develop a sufficient range of criminal sanctions because the dialogue is often cast as punishment (prison) or not, with other sanctions being seen as "letting off" or a "slap on the wrist." The results of this study show that certain community-based sanctions are not a "slap on the wrist" and are judged quite punitive. This should give justice officials pause, particularly those who state they are imprisoning such a large number of offenders to get "tough on crime." Our results suggest that, in the minds of offenders, community-based sanctions can be severe, and it can no longer be said that incarceration is preferred simply because, as Fogel (1975) stated, "we have not found another satisfactory severe punishment."

NOTES

1. For example, one problem with magnitude estimation is that the validity depends on the adequacy of subjects' mathematical skill, since it requires subjects to rate various stimuli in comparison to the standard numerical value. Although used in numerous psychological experiments on subjects with varying skills, research has shown that the use of magnitude estimation techniques among naive or poorly educated subjects is questionable (Jones & Shorter, 1972).

2. Ordered logistic regression does not depend on the use of an interval level of measurement, as does the magnitude estimation techniques.

REFERENCES

Agresti, A. 1990. *Categorical data analysis.* New York: John Wiley and Sons.

Apospori, E., & Alpert, G. 1993. Research note: The role of differential experience with the criminal justice system in changes in perceptions of severity of legal sanctions over time. *Crime and Delinquency*, 39(2), 184–194.

Crouch, B. M. 1993. Is incarceration really worse? Analysis of offenders' preferences for prison over probation. *Justice Quarterly*, 10(1), 67–88.

Erickson, M. L., & Gibbs, J. P. 1979. On the perceived severity of legal penalties. *Journal of Criminal Law & Criminology*, 70(1), 102–116.

Fogel, D. 1975. *"We are the living proof . . ." The justice model for corrections.* Cincinnati: W.H. Anderson Co.

Jones, B. C., & Shorter, R. 1972. The ratio measurement of social status: Some cross-cultural comparisons. *Social Forces*, 50, 499–511.

McClelland, K. A., & Alpert, G. P. 1985. Factor analysis applied to magnitude estimates of punishment seriousness: Patterns of individual differences. *Journal of Quantitative Criminology*, 1(3), 307–318.

Morris, N., & Tonry, M. 1990. *Between prison and probation: Intermediate punishments in a rational sentencing system.* New York: Oxford University Press.

Petersilia, J. 1990. When probation becomes more dreaded than prison. *Federal Probation*, 54(1), 23–27.

Skolnick, J. H. 1990. Gangs and crime old as time: But drugs change gang culture. *Crime and Delinquency in California, 1980–1989.* Sacramento, CA: Bureau of Criminal Justice Statistics, State of California, pp. 171–179.

CHAPTER 7

Innovative Programs in Community Corrections

INTRODUCTION

Since its beginnings, community corrections has been constantly changing. It has shifted back and forth between emphasizing its social work function versus its law enforcement function. Over the past decade, most reforms have attempted to beef up its law enforcement function—new programs, policies, and procedures have been established to ensure that offenders sentenced to community corrections are monitored more closely and held more accountable for their crimes.

Historically, reform has taken place *within* community corrections agencies. While the pressure for reform has mostly come from outside these agencies, the programs themselves were initiated and implemented mostly within probation and parole structures. But that is changing, and new innovations in probation and parole emphasize the important concept of *partnerships* with other community agencies.

Because probation and parole agencies must now supervise more serious offenders, increased surveillance has become a central concern. Increased surveillance is the basic function of most intermediate sanction programs. However, many jurisdictions would like to keep a closer watch over probationers and parolees without having to establish such programs. In some communities, the police are now helping community corrections agencies supervise their case loads.

It has long been suggested that the police should become more central to the probation function. In the 1980s, many criminologists were recommending that instead of turning a probation officer into a "surveillance officer" who works for the probation department (as is done in many intensive supervision probation/parole programs), the police should be made responsible for part of the supervision. Police are already working in the community, on the streets. They have the arrest power, the training, and the mission to ensure compliance with the law. For them, surveillance does not create the role conflict that it does for many probation and parole officers. And, importantly, law enforcement has been receiving relatively more funding in recent years so that their manpower is not as limited as it is in community corrections.

This chapter profiles four programs that can be considered innovations, in that they are trying new ways of doing business. All of them involve the partnership theme, and in each instance, the program promoters are enthusiastic about the results (although all of the programs are too new to have been formally evaluated). The first two articles talk about partnerships between community corrections agencies and their local communities. A "neighborhood probation" program is being experimented with in Madison, Wisconsin. Similar to the ideals that have reshaped community policing, neighborhood probation attempts to forge stronger links between probation staff and community-based agencies around probationers' surveillance and treatment. Similarly, Project Safety in Cook County, Illinois, attempts to bring probation back to its roots in the community. It has long been recognized that in order to do their jobs, community corrections practitioners need the support of the community—a community that trusts and assists probation and parole officers—as well as relatives, friends, and employers who help keep a community-based offender from relapsing into criminal behavior. Although the inclusion of and commitment to the community is crucial to the mission of community corrections, community corrections has traditionally been offender focused. Its work has been judged and measured by the result of efforts on behalf of or directed toward the offender. In the two profiled programs, the National Institute of Corrections (NIC) describes two probation and parole agencies that are including the community as their client as well as their partner in crime control.

The next two articles describe recently developed partnerships between law enforcement and community corrections. Boston's Operational Night Light is a police–probation partnership designed to implement a targeted curfew program for convicted juveniles and young adults. The Redmond, Washington, police–community corrections partnership routinely informs police officers of the names and conditions of all community corrections clients residing in their neighborhoods. Law enforcement officers help monitor the offenders' conditions, and enter any noticed violations into a computer, accessible to law enforcement and community corrections. These data not only help to connect offenders with new crimes in the community, but is also believed to serve as a deterrent to offenders, because they believe they are being watched more closely than would be possible with community corrections staff alone.

Given the high risks and needs posed by today's offenders, along with declining or stabilized funding, it is clear that future community corrections practice will necessitate greater cooperation and coordination among all agencies responsible for criminal offenders in the community. These four descriptions describe future model community corrections programs.

Neighborhood Probation: Adapting a "Beat Cop" Concept in Community Supervision

DAN NEVERS
Wisconsin Probation and Parole Services

Like many communities, Madison, Wisconsin, is faced with the problem of how to control crime. Traditional approaches have been less than satisfactory in terms of their results. Even in cases where present methods of incapacitation and deterrence seem to be effective, the costs in human and economic terms may be excessive. Consequently, if it is to be part of the crime control solution, the practice of community supervision must be examined to identify new ideas and techniques.

Neighborhood probation is one of these new techniques that holds promise both for crime control and for how we in probation agencies do our jobs. It is also a method of organization that is efficient, focused, and practical. Moreover, it is in keeping with the philosophy that probation supervision should have a strong relationship with the local community.

In this context, there are many similarities between the processes that police jurisdictions have gone through and those that probation is beginning to examine:

- Police departments, like probation agencies, need to develop a method of operation that is closer to the community, more responsive to community concerns, and based on problem solving.

- Police departments also need continued citizen support for funding in a time of intense competition for tax dollars.

- Although police departments, like probation agencies, have developed procedural safeguards for internal accountability, this has not always translated into community accountability or even to the community's perception of increased fairness or protection. When community policing is discussed, it is often this public perception of the control of crime that is cited as a benefit of seeing the beta cop in the neighborhood. This is a tangible result of neighborhood policing that is a quality of life issue with meaning for citizens.[1]

Probation agencies have experienced similar problems. As caseload sizes have grown, officers have been trapped in their offices next to the phone.

"Neighborhood Probation: Adapting a 'Beat Cop' Concept in Community Supervision (Madison, Wisconsin)" by Dan Nevers, from *Topics in Community Corrections*, National Institution of Corrections, U.S. Department of Justice, Summer 1993, pp. 16–19.

Most officers no longer have the opportunity to get out and see what is going on. They may attempt home calls, but these tend to be as hurried as other activities. Officers cannot even interact with the individuals on their caseloads. As they become more responsive to bureaucratic standardization, they resort to report days, seeing fifty or sixty people in a long day, logging in the contacts, and getting on to the demands of court reports, revocations, and violation investigations. As a result of further violations, offenders are often next seen in the jail.

Other problems have developed from a "response mentality." Responding to an area without boundaries, officers lose focus and become inefficient. Officers assigned to a large area of the city lose time in trying to organize, leaving little time to gain familiarity with distinct characteristics of individuals or neighborhoods. The consequence is that officers are remote from the daily activities and patterns of offenders.

Finally, it is difficult to obtain information about an area when twenty officers go into a particular neighborhood. Sometimes it is even difficult to estimate how many offenders live in a given neighborhood, much less develop information about various needs that may have an effect on their criminality.

Under the old system, probation and parole officers saw each other on the street, sometimes discovering that offenders they supervised lived in the same housing complex, but they had very little sense of what was really happening in the community.

Clearly, the current approach to probation and parole supervision needs to be examined in relation to several problems:

- Community supervision is at present not organized to use the experiences of rank and file officers to get to know a community and address problems at the most appropriate level—the front line, or community, level.

- Officers are easily overwhelmed by the numbers they must supervise and are unable to respond to the demands of offenders spread around a large city.

- Community supervision, as traditionally organized, lacks sensitivity to the community and may, in fact, cause more problems by overreacting to the behavior of unfamiliar offenders.[2]

NEIGHBORHOOD SUPERVISION IN THE BROADWAY-SIMPSON AREA

In his book, *Problem-Oriented Policing*, University of Wisconsin law professor Herman Goldstein pointed out,

> In a democracy in which complex social problems will always place heavy demands on the police, we have an obligation to strive constantly—not periodically—for a form of policing that is not only effective, but humane and

civil; that not only protects individual rights, equality, and other values basic to a democracy, but strengthens our commitment to them.[3]

This concept became the basis for many community policing or "beat cop" programs.

In turn, another University of Wisconsin law professor and former Division of Corrections Administrator Walter Dickey met with Wisconsin Probation and Parole staff to develop a community orientation in relation to probation and parole supervision. What has developed is in contrast to traditional practices in a number of ways (see Table 1).

The Broadway-Simpson area, where we first developed neighborhood probation, is geographically isolated from the rest of Madison. Its boundaries are defined by water and a beltline highway. It is an area with a high concentration of rental properties, approximately 900 apartments within a one-half mile square; its population is predominately low-income, single parent families. More than 500 children live in the area. There is a high incidence of victimization from crime.[4]

Although the area appears to be relatively quiet, statistics from the Department of Corrections show an alarming number of offenders in the neighborhood. Police calls in the area tripled between 1989 and 1991. The first move to stabilize the neighborhood came in 1989, when the Madison police stationed a police officer there.

Initially, the presence of the police officer did not have a significant deterrent effect on offenders. By 1991 there was a recognition of the correlation between the mounting crime rate and the equally high rate of probation violations in the neighborhood. In January 1991, an experienced African-American probation officer, Cheryl Knox, volunteered to take responsibility for the neighborhood and moved her office to the Broadway-Simpson neighborhood center. With the help of the Madison Police Department's computerized listing, we identified more than 100 offenders living in the area.

Our agency quickly became familiar with the neighborhood because of the large number of offenders living there. We also became acquainted with other service providers and began doing home visits in teams. This led to innovative approaches to supervision, such as coordinating with the county health nurse to supervise a mother who had previously abused her children. Under our authority and as part of our case plan, the nurse checked for phys-

TABLE 1
Contrasting Traditional and Neighborhood Probation

Traditional supervision	Neighborhood probation
General assignment	Geographic focus
Offender focus	Community focus
"Professional" problem solving	Community involvement
Office bound	Community presence
Diffuse agency responsibility	Individual responsibility

ical or psychological signs of abuse, provided literature, and gave advice on parenting. Similar networking has developed in other areas, including assisting in the formation of a citizens' patrol group and organizing area property owners to solve common problems.

Of course, the project has not been without problems:

- We are trying to reorganize a system with very limited resources in an already overburdened system. Progress has been painfully slow, resulting in considerable stress for the supervisor and officer.

- There is a real as well as a perceived threat to worker safety. Officers need training in safety awareness and strategies for protection. For example, Ms. Knox identified safe apartments and exit routes in the apartment complexes. She knows where the trouble spots are and takes precautions. She carries a radio that is dispatched to the Madison Police Department, and she has learned to work with the police for protection.

- It is clear that we need a neighborhood-based information system, although we have overcome this lack to some extent by working with the police department. As we have learned more about the neighborhood, we have had to revise the project. We now understand that there is a critical need to recognize that all neighborhoods are different and that workers must have flexibility to respond to these differences.

- It is difficult but important to protect the worker from the constant experience of the overwhelming needs of the community. We allow the agent to "retreat" to the confines of the unit office to do paperwork and interact with fellow officers. We are also trying to develop a team of officers that can provide backup, share responsibilities, and offer support to each other. At present, six officers are assigned to neighborhood responsibilities in various areas of the city; four of them work in teams.

- We continue to struggle to broaden our focus from the individual offender to the needs of community. Our agency's authority and workload credit are focused on the individual, which makes it difficult to emphasize the community. At the same time, we need to refine our role beyond policing and to educate the community about the unique functions of community supervision. We have discussed developing community advisory groups composed of local residents and family members of offenders as a way to reach the neighborhood and develop trust.

SUMMARY

Richard Faulkner, Program Specialist at the National Institute of Corrections, summarized the development of neighborhood probation as follows:

The idea of "beat probation" is not new, but the concept as a formal and sanctioned program is a departure from what we often call supervision. Prior to having the heavy caseloads of today, superior Wisconsin probation and pa-role agents maintained a network of contacts in the community, knew the po-lice officers, community leaders and in point of fact had an active role in the community. We have lost sight of that type of activity and it is at the cost of the community as well as government agencies. It seems that every few years someone comes along . . . with the revolutionary idea to "get back to basics" to better accomplish our daily tasks. So here we go with "beat probation."[5]

There have been some payoffs to our approach in Madison. We have in-creased our visibility in the community and are part of community-funded initiatives such as "Weed and Seed" that give us a chance to coordinate with other agencies. Because of our positive experience, we have increased the number of officers devoted to neighborhood probation and have targeted new areas.

Neighborhood probation is a low-cost, visible attempt to bring correc-tions and the community together. Our hope is that it will continue to de-velop as a means to strengthen our commitment to become part of a com-munity solution to crime control.

NOTES

1. George L. Kelling, "Police and Communities: The Quiet Revolution," *Perspec-tive on Policing* (June 1988): 5.

2. Walter J. Dickey, "Reflections of a Former Corrections Director: Are Offend-ers Tougher Today?" *Federal Probation* 56 (June 1992): 39.

3. Herman Goldstein, *Problem Oriented Policing*, (New York: McGraw-Hill, Inc., 1990), xiii.

4. Joe Balles, "Neighborhood Intervention Task Force Survey Results" (City of Madison interdepartmental correspondence, January 1993).

5. J. Richard Faulkner, personal correspondence, May 1991.

Chicago's Project Safeway: Strengthening Probation's Links With the Community

ROBIN LEAF, ARTHUR LURIGIO, AND NANCY MARTIN

Large numbers of offenders moving into and out of the criminal justice sys-tem have taxed correctional agencies throughout the country. One conse-quence of rampant jail and prison crowding is that probation has become

"Chicago's Project Safeway: Strengthening Probation's Links With the Community" by Robin Leaf, Arthur Lurigio, and Nancy Martin, from *Topics in Community Corrections*, National In-stitute of Corrections, U.S. Department of Justice, Summer 1993, pp. 19–22.

more than just an alternative to incarceration—it is now the most prevalent sentence in the United States. Unless a crime requires mandatory prison time, probation is the most likely sentence for a broad range of criminals.

In Illinois and throughout the country, probation departments are monitoring not only more cases but more high-risk cases. Clearly, probation is no longer a sentence reserved for first-time misdemeanants or petty criminals. Current probation caseloads in most urban departments consist of serious offenders who previously would not have been considered for community supervision.

Intermediate sanctions were created to remedy the institutional crowding problem and to protect the public against high-risk felons on community release. These programs, including intensive probation supervision, home confinement, and electronic monitoring, were intended to give judges greater latitude in their sentencing decisions by providing options on the punishment continuum that lie between prison and routine probation. Most intermediate sanctions emphasize the enforcement aspects of probation, which have begun to permeate probation casework in general.

Although these programs have shown tremendous promise for reducing prison populations and for monitoring serious offenders, they essentially represent a closed system of probation that has minimal impact or influence on the surrounding community. Most contemporary modes of probation supervision have taken probation farther from its roots in the community and have made it less responsive to community needs and concerns. In effect, probation has become "prison-in-the-community" with an overriding focus on incapacitation and deterrence. This change in perspective has eclipsed probation's more traditional goals of rehabilitation and offender reintegration. Recent research has demonstrated, however, that enhanced surveillance programs have limited effects on offender behavior when they are implemented without a substantial community treatment or service component.

RETURNING PROBATION TO ITS ROOTS

In addressing these issues, probation administrators must consider two basic questions. First, why is it essential for probation to return to a community orientation? The answer lies in the common goal shared by both the community and probation: ensuring that offenders become law-abiding and productive members of society. Probation offenders attend school, seek employment, work, and serve their sentences in the communities where they live. Those who continue to commit crimes and who fail to lead productive lives exacerbate the problems of impoverished neighborhoods. The community and the probation agency must support each other's activities to meet the mutual goal of offender reintegration. Whenever possible, they must also combine their efforts and share relevant information and resources.

Second, how can probation respond to the challenge of returning to its roots? The response of the Cook County Adult Probation Department, in

Chicago, Illinois, has been to create a community-based probation center called Project Safeway. Functioning under the auspices of the Circuit Court of Cook County, the project is designed to forge a working partnership among the Adult Probation Department, not-for-profit service providers, and the community.

PROJECT SAFEWAY

Project Safeway is housed in a facility located on the west side of Chicago. We selected this area because of the large offender population living near the center and the availability of local community resources. Project Safeway became operational on November 1, 1991. The center serves only offenders who reside in the immediate community; it is open for extended hours to meet program and offender needs. During its first full year of operations, project staff supervised approximately 700 cases from the geographic catchment area.

Project Safeway has three main goals:

- To strengthen probation's linkages with the community;
- To offer a "full-service" model of probation; and
- To effect substantial and lasting change in offenders' lives through personal, family, and neighborhood interventions.

As a first step in meeting these goals, we convened a local advisory council consisting of community residents, business persons, and police representatives. The council assists project staff in identifying needs of the community and offender, communicating project goals and objectives to the larger community, addressing issues regarding program development and implementation, and recruiting community volunteers to work with offenders. We have undertaken a variety of activities to achieve these goals. The project has also implemented a number of specific programs.

Community Contact   The daily responsibilities of Project Safeway staff require them to visit community service providers, organizations, clubs, businesses, and churches to develop support and communication networks throughout the community. Staff are also encouraged to participate in community assistance efforts, especially those that directly serve project offenders and their families, e.g., collecting food and clothing for the needy.

Staff have pursued a number of other efforts to increase community understanding and participation in Project Safeway. We distribute a quarterly news letter to highlight project goals, accomplishments, and activities and have held open houses for the public. We also hosted local business people, judges, and politicians at a leadership breakfast to apprise them of the project's endeavors and gain their endorsement of its programs. Moreover, Project Safeway hosted an Opportunity Day, an occasion for offenders and neighborhood residents to learn about different employment and educational avenues.

Offender Programs Project Safeway conducts on-site offender programs that draw on community resources to assist offenders in their efforts to avoid criminal behavior. The following are some examples of these programs:

- We developed an orientation program that prepares offenders for the probation experience. The program encourages participants to view probation as a positive force and an opportunity for change, and it provides training in life management and communication skills.

- Local community college faculty are available on-site to teach G.E.D. classes. We have expanded educational classes to address the different needs and skill levels of offenders.

- Treatment Alternatives for Special Clients (TASC) is on-site to do substance abuse evaluations, make referrals to treatment agencies for treatment-ready offenders, and conduct substance abuse education classes for offenders waiting for treatment or those refusing to recognize their drug problems.

- Offenders with community service mandates often fulfill their hours within the project's geographic boundaries, which emphasizes the importance of community involvement. For example, we have initiated a neighborhood clean-up program with community residents and offenders working together to clear trash-ridden vacant lots. We have placed other probationers with community service requirements in local churches, not-for-profit service agencies, and neighborhood organizations.

- Project Safeway provides offenders with training in readiness skills and job placement services through the Safer Foundation and other community agencies. We are working with local political and business leaders to promote job opportunities because unemployment is one of the major social problems in the catchment area.

- We are collaborating with other county and state agencies and service providers to develop strategies to address a variety of offender needs, such as HIV prevention, training in parenting skills, and health education. For example, project staff and local health care experts have designed a wellness program for offenders that communicates information on pertinent health issues and encourages the adoption of healthier lifestyles.

Field Services Link Project Safeway is also the base of operations for the Cook County Adult Probation Department's field services units, which include an intensive probation supervision program and a home confinement program. These programs have greatly strengthened the public safety aspects of Project Safeway. Field service officers carry weapons and radios and make frequent home visits. The presence of these officers at Project Safeway exerts a forceful, visible, and continual probation presence in the area. The field service units communicate regularly with the Chicago Police Department, the Cook County Sheriff's Office, and the State Parole Authority to strengthen further our surveillance and enforcement capacity.

SUMMARY AND CONCLUSIONS

The community's general response to Project Safeway has been favorable but cautious. Residents within the project's boundaries realize that they must solve their own problems. Nonetheless, we have enlisted the cooperation of several community organizations in joint initiatives to assist probationers in their attempts to make the successful transition from being convicted criminals to becoming free and productive members of society.

Although it is too early to evaluate Project Safeway's effectiveness or its impact on the community, the Cook County Adult Probation Department is committed to expanding the project and to launching other, similar efforts. Across the country, probation professionals are recognizing that they must create new supervision strategies that include community-based components to meet the challenges of the growing and evolving probation population. Probation agencies and the community are joining forces to offer opportunities and support that will foster offenders' growth and change. We also hope that these efforts will ultimately reduce recidivism and reverse the deterioration of neighborhoods.

Redmond, Washington's SMART Partnership for Police and Community Corrections

TERRY MORGAN AND STEPHEN D. MARRS

One of the primary aims of an officer engaged in Community Policing is to gain familiarity with the people on his or her beat. It is considered advantageous for the police officer to develop personal relationships with business owners and ordinary citizens. While this is a worthy goal, we believe that it is even *more* important for the officer to know the *supervised offenders* that live in his or her beat. *This* type of familiarity is what this partnership is all about. The Supervision Management And Recidivist Tracking (SMART) Partnership was begun between the Redmond Police Department and The Washington State Department of Corrections in an effort to develop this kind of awareness among police. Even more important, this and other partnerships signified the transformation of the involved departments into "mission driven" rather than "turf driven" agencies. Each agency seized the chance to increase public safety, even though it meant stepping slightly out of its traditional role.

In October of 1992, the Redmond Washington Police Department (RPD) and the Washington State Department of Corrections (DOC) started a dynamic and unique partnership. In accordance with their community policing/community corrections philosophies, both agencies moved to forge closer community ties and closer ties with other agencies where synergistic relationships could be developed. Both agencies realized the enormous potential benefit in partnerships between probation and police. In a two-part program, police officers received training and actually began direct monitoring of felons who were under DOC supervision and who lived in their patrol district. These twice-a-month contacts were logged and forwarded to DOC. The second part of the program involved developing a system of routine information exchange regarding random police contacts with persons who were under DOC supervision. Police were able to tell, during a field contact, if the subject was under supervision because every person who is DOC active is entered in the Washington State Crime Information Computer and their DOC status is accessed during a routine warrant check. Each such contact was then documented on 3×5-inch field interview report (FIR), and all of these were forwarded on a weekly basis to DOC for follow-up, to determine if the circumstances of the contact indicated a violation of supervisory conditions. The program gave DOC an enhanced twenty-four hour capability, made police officers familiar with the felons living on their beat, and sent a strong message to the offender population that they had better abide by the conditions of their release and not commit new crimes. *While providing these benefits, the program has been nearly cost free to both agencies.*

The SMART Partnership that was pioneered between the RPD and the DOC has remained the centerpiece of both agencies' efforts to forge closer ties between police and probation agencies. The program has now been instituted by many other police agencies in Washington State, including Seattle, Bellevue, King County, Port Angeles, Olympia, Aberdeen, and Tacoma police, to name a few. The National Institute of Corrections is working on promotion of the program on the national level and on its integration with other community policing strategies.

DEVELOPMENT OF THE SMART PARTNERSHIP

Redmond is a city of 40,000 people, a metropolitan area located across Lake Washington from Seattle. Redmond is a relatively affluent city. It is headquarters for the Microsoft Corporation and is known for its bicycle races, hot air balloons, and excellent park system. With fifty-seven commissioned officers, the city has one of the lowest officer-to-population ratios of any police department in King County, yet it has traditionally enjoyed a relatively low crime rate. While still a very livable city, Redmond has not escaped an increase in crime that has impacted the entire Eastside. Auto prowls and auto thefts have become common, and violent crimes that were once a rarity, such as robbery and rape, have also increased. Given the staffing and budget levels, the police department has responded to these challenges.

In January of 1992, the RPD held its annual goal-setting meeting under the cloud of citywide budget cuts. There was little chance of gaining approval for any new program that required additional staff or money. Still, a goal emerged from this meeting that would have a positive effect on policing in Redmond and potentially the entire state. This goal was the creation of a mutually beneficial partnership between the Redmond Police Department and the Washington State Department of Corrections. The program supporting this partnership was to be developed and implemented without significant costs or staffing requirements for either agency. The program would also become a model that could be implemented in any size police agency. A night-shift sergeant and patrol squad were assigned as a team to develop the program that would fulfill this goal.

The team contacted the Bellevue office of the DOC and found that one of the community corrections officers had been actively working with local police departments to foster better relationships. His supervisor was also very supportive of efforts in this area. The team also learned about the Volunteer Community Corrections Monitor Program, which is a program to train police officers to assist in monitoring those persons classified as community custody inmates (CCIs),who are on the highest level of supervision by DOC. The CCI classification is unique among DOC supervisory levels in that each person has a mandatory eight-hour curfew. Violation of curfew *can* result in a felony escape charge with a sentence measured in years, rather than a civil violation that carries a warning or shorter commitment. The community monitoring law was new and had been used sporadically, with small numbers of detectives having received training. Never had patrol officers been placed in this role. A one-hour course would qualify an officer as a community monitor, able to assist the DOC in monitoring CCIs in their homes. While the law empowered police to assist with direct monitoring, it is important to note that police would act only in a reporting capacity, advising DOC of known or suspected violations. Police would not take independent enforcement action based only on supervisory violations, unless acting on authority of a warrant. Any violations of law that came to an officer's attention while he or she was functioning as a community monitor would be handled as a police function, the same as any other violation of law.

Armed with knowledge of the community monitoring law and DOCs desire to participate, the team developed a two-part program for information exchange and offender monitoring. The first part consisted of setting up a formal system of information exchange and follow-up. Redmond officers were to document any contact they had with a person whose warrant check showed that he or she was under active supervision by the DOC. Unless the subject was arrested for a new crime or warrant, the contact would be documented on a 3×5-inch FIR; otherwise the arrest report would be used. The goal was to keep the paperwork as simple as possible, without creating new forms. Every department uses FIRs, and since these pocket-size cards record a wealth of information on a subject and his or her activities, such as date, time, location of contact, address, phone number, vehicle, and associates, they would be an excellent way of recording incident-driven or suspicious contacts with persons who were under DOC supervision.

The department's crime analyst would also have a critical role. While screening crime reports, arrest reports and FIRs for statistics and crime bulletin information, part of the normal job, he or she would also make copies of any of these documents showing police contact with a person under DOC supervision. These copies would be forwarded on a weekly basis to the program's community corrections liaison officer at the Bellevue office of DOC. The reports would then be forwarded from Bellevue to community corrections officers anywhere in the state, who in turn would investigate the incident to see if it constituted a violation. One possible scenario follows.

> Subject X is stopped for defective taillights as he exits a business park at 0300 hours. A warrant check shows that he is under active supervision for burglary. Finding no evidence of a crime, the officer fills out a FIR, and the subject is released. In this hypothetical case, the subject is supervised out of nearby Everett, Washington, where he resides.
>
> The FIR is forwarded through Crime Analysis, where it may also make the weekly crime information bulletin; it is then sent to the Bellevue DOC office and on to the Everett corrections officer, who discovers that X committed two documented violations: (1) Leaving his county of residence, and (2) violation of his 11:30 p.m. curfew. X now faces a wide range of sanctions, *and this situation, even though it involved police contact, would never have come to the attention of DOC in the past!*

While the above example is hypothetical, it is representative of many violations that have been brought to the attention of DOC through random police contacts and forwarding of FIRs. These violations have consisted of violations by association with forbidden persons, being under the influence of drugs or alcohol, as well as curfew and travel violations such as shown in the previous example. Statistics have not been tracked over the four years that the program has been operational; however, DOC hired an intern in 1996 to accomplish this task. Limited research that was completed showed that in a one-year period from September 1993 to September 1994, the Eastside police departments that participated in the program (primarily Bellevue, Redmond, and King County) forwarded 359 FIRs to DOC to be screened for violations. With far more departments now participating, with no overtime expenditure or extra field work, DOC is receiving many hundreds of documented offender contacts a year. For persons who are under supervision, in an ever-increasing number of jurisdictions in Washington, being contacted by a police officer at 2:00 a.m. is just like being contacted by their community corrections officer. Between this part of the program and the direct monitoring segment described below, DOC has truly been given an enhanced twenty-four-hour capability, and persons who are under supervision have been held increasingly accountable to their conditions of release.

The second part of the program involves assigning officers to assist in monitoring community custody inmates who live in their patrol beats. This would be done only with those subjects believed by DOC and the police department to have a high probability of reoffending or who have served time for committing a very serious crime. To accomplish this part of the program, the nighttime patrol team that was developing the program as well as the city prosecutor attended the one-hour Community Corrections Monitor training. (A few months later the training and monitoring portion of the program were expanded to the entire patrol division). Officers from this squad could now be assigned CCIs and engage in direct monitoring. A system was set up where DOC would send a packet of information to the squad sergeant when they desired police assistance in monitoring a CCI who lived in Redmond. The sergeant would then assign the district officer as the CCI's monitor. The officer would be given a copy of the information and would begin twice monthly visits, two phone calls per month were also authorized. The number of visits and phone calls could be increased with cause and they would always occur during the subject's hours of curfew. To prevent the program from interfering with other duties, no officer would be assigned primary monitoring duties for more than two CCIs. A simple form was developed, called a contact log, so that calls and visits could be documented. If the subject was home and cooperative, documentation would consist of a one- or two-line entry. At the end of the month these contact logs would be forwarded to the sergeant, who would file a copy and send the original to the subject's CCO in Bellevue. If, during a visit, a violation were observed, the matter would be brought to the immediate attention of the sergeant, and DOC would be notified as soon as possible (usually the morning of the next working day). (One of the problems brought to light by the program, which DOC is working to correct, is that except to verify warrants there is currently no twenty-four-hour link between DOC and local police.) During a monitoring visit police had the same authority as a CCO to verify compliance with release conditions. They could request entry and in some cases conduct a routine inspection, for instance if the subject were forbidden from possessing alcohol, police could enter and look in the normal places where alcohol containers would likely be found, such as the refrigerator and kitchen garbage container. If the subject refused entry or was uncooperative, the officer would simply advise the subject that his or her actions constituted a violation and that a report would be forwarded to his or her CCO. If during a visit an officer observed a criminal violation, then normal police enforcement action would be taken. It was made very clear to officers during training what the limits of their authority were when acting as community monitors.

Concerns that police would overstep these limits appear to be unfounded. In fact there are many examples of positive relationships developing between police and the persons they monitor. For instance: During the early period of the program, an officer had been assigned to monitor a subject who had a criminal and prison history dating back twenty years. He had recently been released from prison for burglary and was living in a local apartment complex. One evening he and his girlfriend got into a loud argument, which prompted neighbors to call the police. The resulting investigation revealed that there had been no assault or any other violation that would necessitate an arrest; however, the communications center advised that there was a warrant for the subject's arrest. Upon being informed of this fact, the subject became hostile, swearing that he could not possibly have a warrant and that an old associate must have used his name when *he* was arrested. The warrant was confirmed and the officers had legal cause to arrest the subject. However, the officer who was the subject's monitor had responded to the call and he offered to return to the station and pull the booking photo for the case on which the warrant was issued. The booking photo revealed that the subject was telling the truth. The subject was not arrested and the warrant was reissued for the right person along with a new obstructing charge. The subject was extremely grateful that he had not been arrested. He stated that it was the first time in his life that he had ever gotten a break from the police. After this incident, he would refer to his monitoring officer and the other officers that he was familiar with as "his police officers." The subject was always cooperative on subsequent monitoring visits, and in fact surprised the police and his CCO by successfully completing his term of supervision.

There are many examples that illustrate the effectiveness of police monitoring. Whenever a monitoring officer made a visit to an offender's residence, he or she was required to take a second officer along, preferably a different officer on each visit. This way over a period of time, everyone on the squad became familiar with the subject and his or her conditions. It became nearly impossible for a monitored subject to violate curfew without being detected. A female CCI, who was under supervision for narcotics trafficking, had received permission from her community corrections officer to leave town on a holiday weekend to visit her parents. On one of the nights that she was supposed to be out of town, she was identified as a passenger in a vehicle that had been stopped because the driver was intoxicated. She was known to the officer at the scene of the stop because he had gone to her residence with her monitoring officer on a prior occasion. In another incident in nearby Bellevue, whose police department was the first to adopt the Redmond program, Bellevue police were assisting in monitoring a subject who had a long and violent criminal history, which included an incident where he was wounded in a shoot-out with police. On the first night that Bellevue officers went to his residence he was gone. His CCO was immediately notified and a warrant was issued for his arrest. The subject was arrested on authority of the warrant in Oregon three days later. After his arrest, investigators learned that since leaving his residence he had committed felonies in Washington, Idaho, and Oregon. The subject's "escape" from community custody was discovered much sooner by the Bellevue police than would have been the case without community monitoring. These examples serve to illustrate the effectiveness of the community monitoring program and the importance of police/corrections collaboration.

In Redmond, this collaboration has exceeded the scope of the original program. The two CCOs who work the Redmond area have been provided part-time work space in the Redmond Police Department. They are known to all of the officers in the department. This fact has allowed far greater information exchange than could be accomplished through any formal program. Two high-profile cases serve to illustrate this point. Both subjects involved had been placed on parole in other states and chose to move to Washington. Under current law the state must accept these people and their supervision is transferred to the Washington State Department of Corrections. The first subject had been convicted of falsifying autopsy reports when he was a coroner in Texas, and the case had been featured on the show "60 Minutes." The subject had moved to Redmond and one of the Redmond Detectives had received a tip that he was in possession of a number of guns, which is a violation of law for anyone who is under DOC supervision. Due to the working relationship that had been established with these two DOC officers, the tip was immediately passed on to them, and an investigation was launched, which resulted in a mutual search of the subject's residence by DOC and Redmond Police. They recovered 122 firearms, including one fully automatic M-16 rifle. The subject was arrested. He has been convicted of firearms violations and faces parole revocation in Texas.

The other incident involved a martial arts instructor who had been convicted of three separate murders in California. He had killed a rival martial arts instructor with a sword and had shot and killed two other people. He served eight years in California for these crimes and was paroled. The subject moved to unincorporated King County and opened a martial arts academy in Redmond. The Redmond area DOC officers learned that the subject had begun drinking heavily and was becoming increasingly hostile to family members and associates (behavior that had preceded his earlier crime spree in California). He was also experiencing financial problems and was the subject of a six-figure extortion investigation. Finally the DOC officers learned that he had flown to another state without permission. A warrant was issued for his arrest and King County, Redmond, and Port of Seattle Police were notified. Because of the subject's criminal history and combative expertise, police and DOC wanted to dictate the place and circumstances of the arrest. The preparation paid off and Port police were able to learn of his return flight. As he stepped off the plane, he found himself at a severe tactical disadvantage and peacefully surrendered.

These are examples of proactive police and corrections work that most likely prevented serious crimes. In the last example the cooperation may have prevented the subject from committing another homicide.

THE HITS CONNECTION

In the summer of 1995, representatives of the DOC and Redmond Police Department met with members of the Washington State Attorney General's Office Homicide Investigative Tracking System (HITS) unit. Out of this meeting emerged a dynamic plan to link all of the police departments in the state who adopt the SMART Partnership. These departments will be linked directly with DOC and with each other. This will be done through the HITS computer system. To understand how this will work, it is first necessary to have a basis understanding of the HITS unit:

HITS began in 1987 as a result of the cross jurisdictional difficulties encountered during the investigations of the infamous Green River and Ted Bundy serial murders. Since that time HITS has become an invaluable and indispensable computerized clearing house, responsible for the collection, collation, and dissemination of vital information regarding homicides, sex crimes, and serious assaults. HITS solicits case reports on unsolved crimes of the type listed above from all of the police departments in the state, and compares the known facts and MO of each individual case against all of the unsolved cases, solved cases, and other data contained in its computer data base. HITS has thus been able to provide clues and suspect information that has helped solve many of these most serious cases.

Under the plan, several police departments that are already participating in the SMART Partnership, starting with Redmond, will establish a direct computer link with HITS through their crime analyst. The only equipment necessary will be a PC and a modem (which most departments already possess). Any FIR generated on a person who is under DOC supervision would be electronically transferred by the crime analyst directly into the HITS computer, where it would become part of the HITS computer data base. HITS would also e-mail the FIR to the subject's DOC community corrections officer for follow-up. Historically, local DOC offices had to collect FIRs from participating police departments and then forward them to the correct CCO. Once this system is in place and has gone through a troubleshooting period, all law enforcement agencies in the state will be invited to participate. This new system will be much more efficient and will have four very important additional advantages: (1) DOC and any police department in the state will be able to access HITS FIR file. The value of every police agency's FIR will be greatly increased, since the information on the FIR will no longer be limited to the department where it originated. This will be a tremendous aid to investigators who are searching for critical information, such as possible addresses, associates, or vehicles. Since HITS computer data base already contains information on everyone in the state who is under DOC supervision, all of the community corrections officers in the state will be able to access and update these fields as well as access the FIR field. This will in effect provide a new computer system for DOC, at virtually no cost. The system will also make statistical research on police of-fender contacts, violations discovered, and so on much easier. (2) DOC will receive automatic notification when a subject is FIRed. This will mean that for someone who is under DOC supervision, a police contact at 2:00 a.m. by any officer who works for a participating department will be nearly the same as being contacted by his or her community corrections officer. (3) The FIR file will become part of the data base used by HITS to solve homicide, rape, and assault crimes. If the person who is the subject of a FIR is a suspect in a major crime that is being investigated by HITS, the FIR could provide evidence that creates an even stronger link between the suspect and the crime, such as a vehicle match or being FIRed in a location that contradicts the suspect's alibi. (4) If most of the police departments in Washington state participate, HITS data base will be significantly increased with a continu-ous source of information on persons who, as the beginning of this article il-lustrated, are at high risk of reoffending. Due to their advanced computer capability, HITS believes that very little programming time and expense would be required to implement this system. This will be an important tool for law enforcement and corrections, and will provide a tremendous incen-tive to every police department in the state to join the SMART Partner-ship. This system could also be duplicated in any of the twenty-two other states that have computer-based investigative units similar to HITS.

THE FUTURE

The partnership that started with a graveyard patrol squad of Redmond po-lice officers and a single community corrections officer continues to grow and evolve. The partnership won the Association of Washington Cities Award for Innovation in 1994, and was featured in one of the workshops at the Police Executive Research Forum's Sixth Annual Problem Oriented Policing Conference in San Diego, California. Both agencies have developed other types of partnerships with other police and probation agencies. For instance: DOC and the Seattle police have created a very successful joint emphasis patrol called Operation Street Sweep that targets a high-crime area of the city and sends CCOs and police on patrol together to enforce laws and violations of supervisory conditions. Persons found to be in seri-ous violation of either law or supervisory conditions are arrested on the spot. This program has proven to reduce crime in some of the highest crime dis-tricts of Seattle. The Redmond Police Department recently developed a three-way partnership between local schools and Juvenile Probation. This program allows the schools to know which students are on probation and what their conditions are. Thus incidents of truancy and other violations can be immediately reported to the student's probation officer. Police are also provided information on juveniles who are on probation who live in the city. The information is kept in a file in the patrol division and is also entered into the police department's own computer system. This program allows police to be aware of and report juvenile probation violations. In the past there was no way for an officer in a field situation to even know whether a juvenile was on probation. As in other jurisdictions, juvenile crime is a serious matter in Redmond. Juvenile Probation routinely handles supervision of cases where the underlying crime was very serious, including burglary, car prowl, and assault with a weapon. RPD has also developed a partnership with the U.S. Probation Service. This program, though strongly supported by both agencies, has been hindered by the fact that there is no computer inquiry available to an officer during a field contact that will tell the officer whether the subject of the inquiry is under federal supervision. This deficiency makes it impossible for officers to do FIRs on these subjects. It is also an officer safety issue. The next upgrade of NCIC (called NCIC 2000), may improve this situation.

New laws and policies are needed to facilitate SMART Partnerships between police and probation agencies. These will vary from state to state, due to differences in state law regarding police powers and the structure of corrections agencies, as well as the level of computer support. In Washington we are working to expand the Community Monitoring law to allow police assistance in monitoring persons on other levels of supervision besides just CCIs. We are also working on developing a twenty-four-hour link with DOC that would allow authorization, in an emergency, for police detention of a supervised person who is encountered in a situation involving a serious violation of release conditions. On the federal level, police organizations and executives need to lobby to make sure that when NCIC is upgraded, that a person's federal supervisory status will show during a routine warrant check.

With a national failure rate of 56.6 percent for parole, and approximately 70 percent of violent crime being committed by a small percentage of hardened criminals, it is clear what group is responsible for most of our crime. The effort to make patrol officers aware of probationers who live in or frequent their beats, and the creation of close partnerships with the agencies responsible for their supervision, needs to be an integral part of every police department's community policing strategy. There is a great demand on police agencies to do more than just enforce the law and on corrections agencies to do more than just enforce probation conditions. Both of these agencies have an expanded mission of community safety. Collaboration between police and corrections is one of the best and most cost-effective strategies for fulfilling this mission. Isn't it time for your agency to develop a SMART Partnership?

Boston's Operation Night Light:
An Emerging Model For
Police-Probation Partnerships

RONALD P. CORBETT, JR., AND BERNARD L. FITZGERALD
Massachusetts Probation Dept.

JAMES JORDAN
Boston Police Department

> Probation departments must learn to think strategically about
> the nature of the crime problem they are facing. Operation
> Night Light provides an excellent example of pro-active re-
> sponses to the increasing risk profile of those on probation.
>
> > Donald Cochran
> > Commissioner of Probation
> > Commonwealth of Massachusetts

> Our mission is prevention of crime and fear of crime in our
> neighborhoods. To achieve it, we seek to work in new ways
> with partners from across the spectrum of community and in-
> stitutional stakeholders. This project is significant also be-
> cause it involves an innovation created by first-line officers
> and their peers. By working in partnership with Probation, we
> are tailoring tactics down to the level of the individual offender
> who is most likely to be the next offender or the next victim.
> Night Light represents the future of public safety and criminal
> justice in Boston.
>
> > Paul F. Evans
> > Police Commissioner
> > Boston Police Department

INTRODUCTION

Communities across the country are experiencing a worrisome surge in the
amount of serious violence committed by juveniles, reflected in a growing
rate of homicides committed by teenagers. In the face of this disturbing
trend, these communities have been searching for policies that will stem the
bloody tide. The problem becomes more urgent in the face of predictions
from Professor James Fox of Northeastern University, among others, who
foresees a major increase in juvenile violence occurring by the end of the
decade due to demographic imperatives.

In their search for weapons to employ in the effort to decrease violence, some communities have considered and some have implemented citywide curfews. The notion is that prohibiting teenagers from being on city streets during the evening hours will have a deterrent effect on juvenile violence.

The turn toward curfews is understandable, and the early results, though questioned by some, seem encouraging. But there are some potential difficulties, which a *targeted* curfew program such as Boston's Operation Night Light can overcome. First, general curfews, by blanketing all juveniles, can strain the resources of the local police in the process of stopping, questioning, and detaining a large number of juveniles. Second, in the process of targeting all youth, those who are engaged in positive, constructive, or at the least harmless activities will be stopped, creating frustration on all sides. Last, if only a certain segment of kids (i.e., those identified as potential or "suspected" troublemakers) have curfews enforced against them, charges of discrimination or harassment will inevitably follow.

Operation Night Light has proven to be a sensible and workable form of targeted "curfew." In essence, Night Light focuses on high-risk offenders who are believed to need the kind of restraint that a curfew involves to deter the associations, activities, and temptations that are likely to permeate their lives. By restricting enforcement to *convicted* juveniles and young adults, the enforcement task becomes manageable and the complaints about harassment essentially disappear.

BACKGROUND AND HISTORY

Operation Night Light is a partnership between police and probation that provides the court with a tool to enforce the terms of probation in meaningful ways.

A simple way to capture the innovation is to note that Night Light has police engaging in community corrections and probation officers addressing community problems while probation officers (POs) remain POs and cops remain cops.

Night Light is driven by knowledge acquired by practitioners. The project developed from a collaboration in 1992 between probation officers in the Dorchester District Court and Boston police officers in the Anti-Gang Violence Unit. They rethought their mission and strategy as a consequence of their frustrations on the street. Their success and innovation were recognized and pushed forward by the executives in both police and probation. The recognition led to the establishment of Night Light as a formal partnership between the Boston Police Department and the Office of the Commissioner of Probation for Massachusetts.

Night Light is now a central tactic in Boston's multijurisdictional, highly collaborative strategy to deter and prevent youth gang firearm violence. In addition, a dozen other probation jurisdictions throughout Massachusetts have implemented similar programs.

OPERATIONS

A typical evening in Night Light would include the matching of a one- or two-person probation team with a similar team from the police department. The team would meet at Strike Force Headquarters to prepare for the evening's work. The probation officers involved would have identified some ten to fifteen probationers they wanted to see that evening, concentrating on those cases thought to be "active" on the street at a given time or on those who had been slipping in terms of their compliance with probation conditions. Operating in an unmarked car and in plainclothes, these teams would go to the first scheduled curfew check. The police team is responsible for safety issues and will be sensitive to the manner in which the home is approached and also to exit areas, should the probationer seek to evade the contact. Once the security issues, which are not monumental in most cases, are addressed, the probation officer(s) will approach the door and seek entry. Once inside the home, the contact proceeds as would any typical probationary home visit. Every effort is made to ensure that the parents and other family members are not alarmed by the presence of probation and police officers, and courtesy and a friendly manner are emphasized.

The purpose of the visit is to ascertain whether the probationer is home in observance of the curfew, to reinforce the importance of strict observance of all conditions, and to inquire of any parents present about the behavior of the probationer, both in the home and in the community. After those basic objectives are accomplished, and any other issues of concern to any of the parties are addressed, the team will thank everyone for their cooperation and go on to the next scheduled contact.

It is not uncommon for a team to stop at a park or street corner where youth are congregated to both determine whether any probationers are present and demonstrate to the youth of the city that the probation and police departments are working together in the evening and are interested in the whereabouts and activities of young people on probation. We have learned that word spreads fast that there is a new mode of operation in probation and a new level of jeopardy for those who would ignore their probationary obligations.

> We can use Night Light to target community concerns. If we have a rash of shootings, drive-bys, drug dealing, community complaints, we can call the court, be it Roxbury or Dorchester Court and make all our area checks down here. So besides the added uniform presence, drug unit, detectives, and everybody else from here, we have probation officers down there to start shaking everybody's tree too. If nothing else, it just defuses it.
>
> Boston Probation Officer

MUTUAL BENEFITS FROM NIGHT LIGHT

The partnership between probation and the police would not have been sustained were it not the case that both sides were reaping tangible and significant benefits. From the probation point of view, the presence of the police now made it possible to enter the most crime-ridden areas of the city into the late evening. That is, the police provide a high degree of security for probation officers who are not armed or equipped with telecommunications capacity. Also, because of the familiarity between both departments that has grown out of Night Light, there is now routine sharing of information between departments on a citywide level regarding the identities of those on probation so that any information obtained by any police officer concerning the activities of a probationer (whether the subject of Night Light or not) can be passed on to probation. While it may seem an obvious strategy, it does not seem to be the practice in most jurisdictions to routinely exchange information between probation and law enforcement. This failure robs probation of access to the contacts and observations made by police who are working the community on a twenty-four-hour, seven-day-per-week basis and therefore have more "eyes and ears" working the streets than even the most proactive probation department can muster. This increased flow of information and intelligence regarding probationer activities has been one of the greatest by-products of Night Light.

In sum, from probation's point of view, there is a new credibility to probation supervision and the enforcement of curfews and area restrictions that was not present when probation activities were limited to the 9 to 5 p.m. time frame. Feedback from offenders, police, parents, and community members alike indicate that the kids are aware that things have changed and have become more cautious, not to say more compliant, in their behavior. This is a breakthrough.

From the police perspective, they now have a tool available to them that significantly enlarges their own power. Many police officers will speak of the frustration that comes with knowing certain offenders are active in a community but being unable to control them due to the difficulties involved in crime detection and apprehension. While not all offenders being targeted by the police are on probation, both common sense and the available data suggest that probationers account for upward of 20 percent of all serious crime. Therefore, any strategy that can legally target this group through closer surveillance and supervision can have a deterrent effect not available to the police. Deterrence is achieved through incapacitating probationers by requiring that they avoid certain areas and also be in their homes at a reasonable hour each evening and not on the streets at times when gang-related violence flourishes. The understanding among probationers that, while they will most often not be detected undertaking criminal activity, their failure to abide by court-ordered conditions can put them in jeopardy of incarceration just as certainly as if they were arrested for a new offense, is a point not lost on them. Put differently, the threshold for depriving them of their liberty is much lower than it is for the nonprobationer and permits their removal from the street for a variety of noncriminal behaviors.

The police both marvel at and appreciate the power of probation officers in this respect. Members of the police department have often commented on how the kids fear their PO more than they fear a uniformed officer. Provided this broader power is used fairly and judiciously, it does put a formidable crime-fighting technique on the street as a supplement to that which is achieved through conventional police strategies.

THE FIRST NIGHT

Some of the unique value to the police of Night Light can be seen in the events of the very first night of operations in November 1992. No sooner had the police car left the station than a call was received of a shooting in the area to which the Night Light team was headed. At the scene, the team discovered that one of the probation officer's clients was the victim, still conscious with a gunshot wound to the chest. A large crowd of young people had gathered and the two probation officers present began to work the crowd. Because of their familiarity with many of the kids present, they were able to gather names and leads in a fashion that, by the account of the police present, would have been difficult if not impossible if left only to law enforcement.

This capacity of probation to obtain information not generally or as easily available to police does raise the issue of "boundary management" in the program—that is, the importance of remembering who has what job with which responsibilities. Without care and caution, probation officers *could* utilize the trust available to them to perform investigatory functions beyond the scope of their duties. It has been the experience of those in the program that both sides have been respectful of the professional constraints on their actions, which has prevented any abuse. More importantly, the greater though regulated sharing of information between police and probation has, by all accounts, increased probation's ability to keep close taps on their case loads and the police department's ability to successfully investigate serious incidents.

> There's a greater fear of probation officers in the streets by these kids. We can take away their liberty for a *few hours*. There's a great fear that the probation people are going to violate them for a *few years*.
> Boston Police Detective

BALANCING SURVEILLANCE WITH SERVICE

There is no question that Operation Night Light puts a sterner face on probation in the eyes of offenders, families, and the community. The risk presented by some young offenders more than warrants this increased oversight. Nonetheless, both probation and the police are cognizant of the fact that if either department's activities are restricted to the "get tough" aspect of its responsibilities, both our moral authority and the community support on which we depend will erode.

Accordingly, both sides have taken great pains to sponsor a number of treatment and prevention programs that accent the desire to reach kids at all stages of their careers—from both the nonoffender up through the kid deeply immersed in a criminal lifestyle—in the hope of promoting law-abiding behavior and productive lives in the future.

On the police side, the same officers involved in Night Light have established both a summer jobs program and a camp scholarship program that reaches literally hundreds of disadvantaged kids each summer. A number of the youth who are the beneficiaries of these programs are kids who have turned their lives around by getting out of the gang life, thereby earning the right to participate in these programs.

On the probation side, a drug court has been sponsored whereby first offenders can get immediate access to intensive treatment for substance abuse in the hope that they can be diverted from further trouble. The department also sponsors a "Changing Lives Through Literature" program, whereby high-risk offenders are offered a college-level seminar concentrating on literature, which speaks through the medium of plays, short stories, novels, and essays to the issues confronting young inner-city residents. This last effort has been both a surprising and resounding success.

The probation and police have jointly reached out to an organized group of city clergy known as the 10 Point Coalition. The Coalition has dedicated itself to bringing the attention and resources of the city's churches to the toughest problems facing urban America. Through regular meetings and joint sponsorship of seminars and training programs, police, probation, and the clergy have worked together to collectively address both individual cases and citywide issues. The success of this effort was embodied in the Coalition's decision to present commendations to the Night Light staff for their efforts on behalf of the community.

The strong bonds existing in this partnership became clear under potentially tragic circumstances. A leading member of the Coalition, the Reverend Eugene Rivers, had his house shot up one evening in a drive-by. The room in which his two young children were sleeping was hit, though they were not injured. Reverend Rivers had been working closely with the Night Light crew, who immediately turned their full efforts to identifying the perpetrator. Within a very short time, they were able to gain information leading to an arrest and a successful prosecution. Strong ties with the 10 Point Coalition continue to the present.

PROGRAM IMPACT

What difference have the over 5,000 Night Light contacts (home visits, street contacts, etc.) made in the last three and one half years.? While direct impact is notoriously difficult to prove with absolute certainty, the trends in the impacted areas, in terms of declining rates of homicide and other violent crimes, are encouraging. To point to some recent data, there was one juvenile homicide during the first six months of 1996, compared with ten for the same time period in 1995. Moreover, all of the staff involved believe strongly that compliance with probation as well as lessened levels of gang-related violence are at least partially attributable to the efforts of the Night Light staff. In addition, court personnel believe that probationary sentences have gained a new and enhanced credibility due to the stricter enforcement of key conditions that Night Light provides. It is clear now, as it has not always been in the past (the word is on the street, so to speak) that those on probation must take their obligations seriously or they will be detected in not doing so and consequences will ensue.

There is also the hard to measure but real reassurance that comes to those neighborhoods where Night Light takes place. The knowledge that probation officers are around with the police ensuring that probationers are off the streets in the evening brings a measure of relief to hard-hit communities. It is also very clear that the parents of these young people, who are often in a losing battle to keep their (usually) sons from responding to the lure of the streets, genuinely appreciate the support they receive through curfew enforcement. While this program is designed primarily to deter these young offenders from committing any new crimes, their parents recognize that it also serves to keep these same young people from being victimized themselves in the mortal combat that envelops their streets.

CHAPTER **8**

Considering the Future of Community Corrections

I find the great thing in this world is not so much where we stand as in what direction we are moving.

Oliver Wendell Holmes

INTRODUCTION

The 1990s will likely be remembered as a time when prison populations exploded and the nation's attitude toward crime and criminal offenders became particularly punitive. But, it is also likely to be remembered as a time when major changes took place in community corrections. Technology, particularly the use of drug tests and electronic monitoring equipment, will continue to spread as their costs decline. But much more important than the change in gadgetry is the change in management, goals, and professionalism that is taking place within probation and parole agencies.

Led by the increasingly important American Probation and Parole Association (APPA), community corrections leaders are becoming proactive. No longer are they willing to sit by and let the media and political hype put them on the defensive. As Alan Schuman, past president of the APPA recently put it, "For once, we will be the drivers instead of the driven." No longer will they promise to deliver rehabilitation services and close offender surveillance, all while having their funding cut.

Instead, they are developing leadership around a vision of what community corrections can and should be by the year 2000. What are the outcomes their programs can and should realistically deliver? Is offender recidivism the measure by which they should be evaluated? How can they best garner public support for their programs? Which partnerships are critical for effective offender programming and surveillance? What kinds of skills should the "new" probation or parole officer possess? Given the risk of today's offender, should probation and parole officers be armed? These and other issues are being debated among corrections professionals, and rightly so, the answers are being provided by those who work in the field.

Thinking hard about how to design a community corrections system that works is critical. We have become so preoccupied with debating who to imprison, for how long, and under what conditions that we have all but ignored community corrections. It is currently true—and has always been so—that three fourths of all convicted criminals will continue to reside in the community. And for those who are initially sent to prison, they too will return to the community, usually within a period of less than two years. So the future of community corrections has major implications for public safety and the offender's prospects for rehabilitation.

The articles in this chapter consider the four issues that I believe are particularly important in charting community correction's future: ethics, program structure, organizational management, and outside pressures and influences.

The first article, written by Andrew von Hirsch, considers an issue we have disregarded recently, and that is the ethical considerations involved in sentencing convicted offenders to such punitive community-based programs. He discusses the need to balance the community's desire to exact retribution from the offender with the seriousness of the offender's original criminal conduct. He cautions against creating a community-based sentencing system that is far more intrusive and punishing than justified by the offender's crime.

Paul Gendreau and his colleagues outline a "second generation" model of intermediate sanctions, based on what has been learned from the earlier studies (reviewed in Chapter 4). This article is a particularly useful one, not only because it succinctly outlines the principles for effective programs, but also demonstrates the cumulative way in which corrections evaluations should proceed. The authors examine past programs and identify the factors that differentiated the successful programs from the failures. They conclude that there are several basic techniques that have proven effective in promoting positive behavior change in offenders.

Rather than abandoning intermediate sanctions as another corrections experiment that failed, we need to learn from the evaluation evidence and use the results to redesign the program model and better target programs with clientele. Corrections has never had a history of knowledge building. Instead, the field is littered with one fad after another, which is usually tried and found wanting. This haphazard approach to research and development circumvents any chance for success, and the common belief that "nothing works" in offender rehabilitation is a result. Gendreau and co-workers, provide concrete information that something *does* work in intermediate sanction programs. We should quickly implement revised program models, which should be subject to continued evaluation.

The third article, written by Ronald Corbett, Deputy Commissioner of Probation in Boston, addresses the management concerns surrounding community corrections. Corbett notes that the future of probation and parole looks bleak without major reform. But he believes that many of the "reinventing" themes now popular in business can be usefully applied to community corrections agencies. Principles like publicly identifying relevant missions, orienting services toward results, and recognizing the importance of customers are critical to community correction's future.

The last article is by Todd Clear and Anthony Braga. They summarize the external pressures that will continue to influence community corrections. Crowded prison conditions will continue to put pressure on community corrections, and it is likely that funding will continue to be insufficient. The substance abuse problems of offenders will continue to increase, and job and work opportunities will likely decline. Community corrections will be the last resort some offenders have to link up with needed programs and services. These authors end by noting that justice demands balance in terms of crime and sanctions, and that although the public is in no mood to coddle criminals, quality community corrections gives them exactly what they most want: increased public safety.

The Ethics of Community-Based Sanctions

ANDREW VON HIRSCH

The reviving interest in noncustodial penalties makes it urgent to explore the ethical limits on their use. This article explores three kinds of limits: proportionality (desert) constraints, restrictions against humiliating or degrading punishments, and concerns about intrusion into the rights of third parties. In connection with the second of these limits, the concept of "acceptable penal content" is developed.

Imprisonment is a severe punishment, suited only for grave offenses. Crimes of lesser and intermediate gravity should receive nonincarcerative sanctions. Such sanctions long were underdeveloped in the United States, and it is

Andrew von Hirsch is professor, School of Criminal Justice, Rutgers University, Newark, New Jersey.

"The Ethics of Community-Based Sanctions" by Andrew von Hirsch, from *Crime and Delinquency*, Vol. 36, No. 1, pp. 162–173, © 1990 by Sage Publications, Inc. Reprinted by permission of Sage Publications, Inc.

gratifying that they are not attracting interest. Noncustodial penalties, however, raise their own ethical questions. Is the sanction proportionate to the gravity of the crime? Is it unduly intrusive, upon either defendants' human dignity or the privacy of third persons?

In the enthusiasm for community-based sanctions, such issues are easily overlooked. Harsh as imprisonment is, its deprivations are manifest—and so, therefore, is the need for limits on its use. Noncustodial penalties seem humane by comparison, and their apparent humanity can lead us to ignore the moral issues. As Allen (1964) warned us two decades ago, it is precisely when we seem to ourselves to be "doing good" for offenders that we most need to safeguard their rights.

This essay will address two kinds of ethical issues involved in noncustodial sanctions. One concerns just deserts: that is, the proportionality of the sanction to the gravity of the crime of conviction. The other issue—or, as we will see, cluster of issues—concerns the "intrusiveness" of the sanction, that is, the constraints that are needed to prevent punishments in the community from degrading the offender or threatening the rights of third parties.

PROPORTIONALITY AND DESERT

The issue of proportionality in community-based sanctions has suffered a double neglect. Desert theorists, when writing on proportionality and its requirements, tended to focus on the use and limits of imprisonment, paying little attention to community sanctions. Reformers involved in developing these sanctions, meanwhile, gave little thought to proportionality.

The disregard of proportionality has reinforced a tendency to assess community-based sanctions principally in terms of their effectiveness. If a program (e.g., an intensive supervision scheme) seems to "work" in the sense of its participants having a low rate of return to crime, then it is said to be a good program. Seldom considered are questions of the sanction's severity and of the seriousness of the crimes of those recruited into the program.

Imprisonment is obviously a severe punishment, and its manifestly punitive character brings questions of proportionality into sharp relief. Noncustodial measures, however, are also punishments—whether their proponents characterize them as such or not. A sanction levied in the community, like any other punishment, visits deprivation on the offender under circumstances that convey disapproval or censure of his or her conduct. Like any other blaming sanction, its degree of severity should reflect the degree of blameworthiness of the criminal conduct. In other words, the punishment should comport with the seriousness of the crime.

The punitive character of noncustodial sanctions, however, is often less visible to those who espouse them. Because these sanctions are often advertised as more humane alternatives to the harsh sanction of imprisonment, the deprivations they themselves involve are often overlooked. Because the offender no longer has to suffer the pains of confinement, why cavil at the pains the new program makes him or her suffer in the community?

Such attitudes are particularly worrisome when it comes to the newer noncustodial sanctions, which include such measures as intensive supervision, community service, home detention, and day-fines. These sanctions often involve substantial deprivations: intensive supervision and home detention curtail an offender's freedom of movement, a community-service program exacts enforced labor, a day-fine may inflict substantial economic losses. Part of the attraction of these programs has been that their more punitive character gives them greater public credibility than routine probation and, hence, makes them plausible substitutes for imprisonment. In short, these are sanctions of intermediate severity. But then it *must* be asked: Are the offenses involved serious enough to make the sanction a proportionate response? Often, the answer to this question is no. Clear points out that intensive supervision programs tend to be applied to offenders convicted of the *least* serious felonies because program organizers feel that such persons would be more likely to "cooperate."

When devising community penalties, reformers should ask themselves about the proportionality of the sanction. They might begin by posing a few simple questions. First, how serious are the crimes that the proposed sanction would punish? Seriousness is a complex topic (see von Hirsch, 1985, ch. 6), but rough-and-ready assessments should be possible. For example, several sentencing commissions (most notably, those of Minnesota, Washington, and Pennsylvania) have explicitly ranked the gravity of crimes on a rating scale (von Hirsch, Knapp, and Tonry, 1987); those rankings could be drawn upon, supplemented by common-sense arguments about the appropriateness of particular rankings.

Second, how severe is the proposed sanction? Severity is likewise a complex topic (see von Hirsch, Wasik, and Greene, 1989), but, again, a commonsense assessment is possible. If one assumes routine probation to be lenient and imprisonment to be severe, one can make a comparative judgment of the onerousness of the proposed sanction. This would involve inquiring about the extent of restriction of freedom of movement, of monetary deprivation, etc., and it should yield a rough assessment of whether the sanction is mild, intermediate, or more severe. In assessing severity, the preventive as well as punitive aspects of the sanction should be considered. An intensive supervision program that, for example, involves curfews or periods of home detection invades personal liberty to a significant extent, and is therefore quite severe. This holds true whether the purpose of the detection is to punish or to restrain or cure.

Asking such questions will put reformers in the position to begin to make judgments about commensurability. Potential mismatches will begin to become apparent, for example, the imposition of sanctions of intermediate or higher severity on lesser crimes.

COMMON FALLACIES OF "INTRUSIVENESS"

When we consider the potential intrusiveness of sanctions, we enter less-explored territory. Whereas an extensive literature on desert exists, less thought has been devoted to what makes a punishment unacceptably humiliating or violative of others' privacy. We might begin by clearing away the underbrush, that is, putting aside some commonly heard fallacies.

One fallacy is the *anything-but-prison theory*. Intervention in the community is tolerable irrespective of its intrusiveness, this theory asserts, as long as the resulting sanction is less onerous than imprisonment. This is tantamount to a carte blanche: Because imprisonment (at least for protracted periods) is harsher than almost any other community punishment, one could virtually never object.

The anything-but-prison theory is a version of the wider misconception that an individual cannot complain about how he or she is being punished if there is something still worse that might have been done instead. The idea bedeviled prison policy for years: Prisoners should not complain of conditions because they might have fared worse—been held longer or in nastier conditions, or even been executed. The short answer is that a sanction needs to be justified in its own right, not merely by comparison with another—possibly more onerous—punishment.

The theory also rests on the mistaken factual supposition that all those who receive the proposed community sanction would otherwise have been imprisoned. That is almost never the case. Many, if not the bulk, of those receiving the new community sanctions are likely to be persons who otherwise would have received a conventional noncustodial sanction such as probation instead.

A second fallacy is that *intrusiveness is a matter of technology*. The installation of an electronic monitor on an offender's telephone elicits comparisons to "Big Brother," but no similar issues of privacy are assumed to arise from home visits by enforcement agents. The mistake should be obvious: Orwell's totalitarian state may have relied on two-way television screens, but the Czarist secret police achieved plenty of intrusion without newfangled gadgetry. The same point holds for noncustodial sanctions. Intrusion depends not on technology but on the extent to which the practice affects the dignity and privacy of those intruded upon. Frequent, unannounced home visits may be more disturbing than an electronic telephone monitor that verifies the offender's presence in the home but cannot see into it.

A third fallacy is *legalism*. Intrusiveness, in this view, is a matter of whether the practice infringes on specific constitutional requirements. The U.S. Constitution does not give much consideration to the treatment of convicted offenders, and such provisions as are germane have been restrictively interpreted. Those provisions do not exhaust the ethical requirements the state should abide by in the treatment of offenders. This has been understood where proportionality is concerned. The Eighth Amendment (as now construed) outlaws only the most grossly disproportionate punishments, but the state should (and some jurisdictions have) gone further in safeguarding desert requirements. The same should hold true for the present issues of "intrusiveness." When a program is developed, its sponsors should ask themselves not only whether it passes constitutional muster but whether there are any substantial ethical grounds for considering it humiliating or intrusive.

DIGNITY AND "ACCEPTABLE PENAL CONTENT"

The idea of "intrusiveness" is actually a cluster of concepts, and we need to identify its component elements. One important element is the idea of *dignity*—that offenders should not be treated in a humiliating or degrading fashion. We need to inquire why convicted criminals should be punished with dignity and how this idea can be put into operation in fashioning punishments.

The Rationale for "Dignity" in Punishment   To inquire into the rationale for the idea, we might begin with a passage from the philosopher Jeffrie Murphy:

> A punishment will be unjust (and thus banned on principle) if it is of such a nature as to be degrading or dehumanizing (inconsistent with human dignity). The values of justice, rights and desert make sense, after all, only on the assumption that we are dealing with creatures who are autonomous, responsible, and deserving of the special kind of treatment due that status. . . . A theory of just punishment, then, must keep this special status of persons and the respect it deserves at the center of attention. (Murphy, 1979, p. 233)

What this passage reflects is the idea that convicted offenders are still members of the moral community and that they remain *persons* and should be treated as such. Someone's status as a person would ordinarily militate against *any* sort of insulting or demeaning treatment. With offenders, however, there is a complication—the nature of punishment itself. Punishment not only serves as a deprivation but also conveys blame or censure (von Hirsch, 1985, chap. 3). Blame, because it embodies disapproval of the offender for his or her conduct, is necessarily unflattering. What is left, then, of the idea that punishment should not humiliate its recipient?

The answer lies in the communicative character of blaming. Blame, Duff (1986) has pointed out, conveys disapproval addressed to a rational agent. The function of the disapproval is not only to express our judgment of the wrongfulness of the act but to communicate that judgment to offenders in the hope that they will reflect upon it and reevaluate their actions. We may wish offenders to feel ashamed of what they have done, but the shame we are trying to elicit is their *own* shame at the conduct, not merely a sense of being abased by what we are doing to them. The more one treats wrongdoers in a demeaning fashion, the more this entire moral process is short-circuited. When prisoners are made to walk the lockstep—to shuffle forward, with head down and eyes averted—they are humiliated irrespective of any judgment they might make about the propriety of their conduct. The shame comes not from any acceptance of the social judgment of censure but simply from the fact that they are being treated as inferior beings.

Punishments, therefore, should be of the kind that can be endured with self-possession by persons of reasonable fortitude. These individuals should be able to undergo the penalty (unpleasant as it inevitably is) with dignity, protesting their innocence if they feel they are innocent or acknowledging their guilt if they feel guilty—but acknowledging it as a *person*, not a slave, would do. A person can endure the deprivation of various goods and liberties with dignity, but it is hard to be dignified while having to carry out rituals of self-abasement, whether the lockstep, the stocks, or newer rituals.

Acceptable Penal Content How do we apply this idea of dignity? One way would be to try to identify and list the various kinds of intrusions we wish to rule out as undignified. But as intrusion on dignity is a matter of degree, this would be no easy task. It would be particularly difficult for noncustodial sanctions because these may be so numerous and variable in character.

A better approach, I think, is through the idea of "acceptable penal content." The penal content of a sanction consists of those deprivations imposed in order to achieve its punitive and preventive ends. Acceptable penal content, then, is the idea that a sanction should be devised so that its intended penal deprivations are those that can be administered in a manner that is clearly consistent with the offender's dignity. If the penal deprivation includes a given imposition, X, then one must ask whether that can be undergone by offenders in a reasonably self-possessed fashion. Unless one is confident that it can, it should not be a part of the sanction.

Once we have specified the acceptable penal content of the sanction, we may also have to permit certain ancillary deprivations as necessary to carry the sanction out. Imprisonment, for example, involves maintaining congregate institutions and preventing escapes or attacks on other inmates and staff. Segregation of some violent or easily victimized offenders for limited periods may be necessary for such purposes, even if not appropriate as part of the intended penal content in the first place. But these ancillary deprivations must truly be essential to maintaining the sanction.

Can these ideas be carried over to noncustodial penalties? I think they can. The first step would be to try to identify the acceptable penal content for such penalties. Certain kinds of impositions, I think, can be undergone with a modicum of self-possession, and thus would qualify. These would include deprivations of property (if not impoverishing); compulsory labor, if served under humane conditions (community service, but not chain-gang work); and limitation of freedom of movement. Clearly excluded, for example, would be punitive regimes purposely designed to make the offender appear humbled or ridiculous. An example is compulsory self-accusation, e.g., making convicted drunken drivers carry bumper stickers indicating their drinking habits. There is no way a person can, with dignity, go about in public with a sign admitting himself or herself to be a moral pariah. We may wish the offender to feel ashamed of what he or she has done—but not act as though he or she is ashamed, whatever he or she actually feels. This list of acceptable and unacceptable intrusions is far from complete, and I shall not try to complete it. I am merely suggesting a mode of analysis.

That analysis should be applied not only to the expressly punitive but also to the supposed rehabilitative features of a program. Deprivations administered for treatment are still penal deprivations and can be no less degrading than deprivations imposed for expressly punitive or deterrent ends. I would, for example, consider suspect a drug program in the community that involves compulsory attitudinizing. One may wish to persuade the offender of the evils of drug use and, for that purpose, deny him or her access to drugs or other stimulants. But if we try to *compel* the offender, as part of the program, to endorse attitudes about drug use that he or she does not necessarily subscribe to, we are bypassing his or her status as a rational agent.

After we have specified the acceptable penal content, there comes the question of ancillary enforcement measures. These are measures that are not part of the primary sanction—the intended penal deprivation—but are necessary to ensure that that sanction is carried out. An example is home visits. Such visits are not a part of acceptable penal content: It is not plausible to assert that, without any other need for it, the punishment for a given type of crime should be that state agents will periodically snoop into one's home. The visits could be justified only as a mechanism to help enforce another sanction that *does* meet our suggested standard of acceptable penal content.

What might such a sanction be? Consider the sanction of community service, which I have suggested does meet the primary standard. To assure attendance at work sites and check on excuses for absences, occasional home visits may be necessary and indeed are part of the enforcement routine of the Vera Institute's community service project (McDonald, 1986). Because home visits are justified only as an ancillary enforcement mechanism, their scope must be limited accordingly, that is, be no more intrusive than necessary to enforce the primary sanction. If home visits are ancillary to community service, they should occur only when the participant has failed to appear for work, and their use should be restricted to ascertaining the offender's whereabouts and checking on any claimed excuse. The less connected the visits are with such enforcement and the more intrusive they become, the more they are suspect. General, periodic searches of the offender's home could not be sustained on this theory.

THE RIGHTS OF THIRD PARTIES

The prison segregates the offender. The segregation, whatever its other ills, means the rights of third parties are not directly affected. If X goes to prison, this does not restrain Y's right of movement, privacy, etc. Granted, Y still suffers if he or she is attached to X or economically dependent. But Y, nevertheless, is not restrained.

Noncustodial penalties reintroduce the punished offender into settings in which others live their own existence. As a result, the offender's punishment spills over into the lives of others. Home visits, or an electronic telephone monitor ringing at all hours of the day, affects not only the defendant but any other person residing at the apartment—and it is *their* as well as his or her dwelling place.

The third-party question is distinct from the issue of the offender's dignity, as discussed earlier. That is true even when the latter issue is affected by the presence of third parties. Consider home visits. Such visits may be potentially shaming to the defendant in part because of the presence of unconvicted third-party witnesses, that is, the other residents of the home. But the visits also affect those other residents, diminishing *their* own sense of privacy.

However, such other persons are often affected because they have some consensual relation to the defendant, for example, they share the defendant's home. Here lies the difficulty: Granted that the quality of their lives may suffer, but have they not in some sense assumed that risk? When A chooses to live with B, will not A inevitably suffer indirectly from whatever adverse consequences legitimately befall B as a consequence of his or her behavior? It is *this* issue—the extent to which third parties lose their right to complain—that requires more reflection. I have not been able to think of a general answer to this relinquishment-of-rights question. The following modest steps, however, might help to reduce the impact of noncustodial punishments on third parties:

1) Often, it is not the primary sanction itself but its ancillary enforcement mechanism that intrudes into the lives of third parties (to cite a previous example, home visits used to enforce community service). In such cases, the enforcement mechanism should be limited to enforcing the primary sanction and should not be used to investigate the general extent to which other persons abide by the law. When the defendant's home is visited to check on his or her excuse for being absent at the work site, for example, that should *not* be used as an occasion to gather evidence of law violations by others in the apartment.

2) The impact on third persons should be one of the criteria used in choosing among noncustodial penalties. Often, the sanctioners may have several sanctions of approximately equal severity to choose from, any of which would comport with crimes of a given degree of seriousness. Where that choice is available, the sanctioner should, other things being equal, choose

the sanction that affects third parties least. Suppose, for example, that the choice lies between home detention (enforced by a telephone monitor) and a fairly stiff schedule of community service (enforced by home visits to check the offender's presence, but only when he or she fails to appear at the work site). Suppose, for the sake of argument, that the penalties have been calibrated to be of approximately equal severity (see von Hirsch et al., 1989). If we conclude that the occasional home visits used to enforce community service are less disturbing to other residents than a (frequently ringing) telephone monitor used with home detention, that would be reason for preferring community service.

CONCLUSIONS

This essay provides more questions than answers. Concerning the first issue, that of proportionality, I have some sense of confidence because there has been an extensive literature on desert. Concerning the second issue, that relating to dignity and humiliation, I have tried to offer the rudiments of a theory, but it stands in need of development. Concerning the third, intrusion into the rights of third parties, I have done little more than raise some issues.

Because innovative noncustodial penalties are only beginning to be explored in this country, little thought has been devoted to limits on their use. Such thinking is now urgently necessary. With adequate ethical limits, community-based sanctions may become a means of creating a less inhumane and unjust penal system. Without adequate limits, however, they could become just another menace and extend the network of state intrusion into citizens' lives. We should not, to paraphrase David Rothman, decarcerate the prisons to make a prison of our society.

REFERENCES

Allen, Francis A. 1964. *The Borderland of Criminal Justice.* Chicago: University of Chicago Press.

Duff, R. A. 1986. *Trials and Punishments.* Cambridge, England: Cambridge University Press.

Green, Judith A. 1988. "Structuring Criminal Fines: Making an 'Intermediate Penalty' More Useful and Equitable." *Justice System Journal* 13:37.

McDonald, Douglas C. 1986. *Punishment Without Walls: Community Service Sentences in New York City.* New Brunswick, NJ: Rutgers University Press.

Murphy, Jeffrie G. 1979. *Retribution, Justice, and Therapy.* Dordrecht, Netherlands: D. Riedel.

Singer, Richard G. 1979. *Just Deserts: Sentencing Based on Equality and Desert.* Cambridge, MA: Ballinger.

von Hirsch, Andrew. 1976. *Doing Justice: The Choice of Punishments.* New York: Hill & Wang. Reprinted 1986, Boston: Northeastern University Press.

von Hirsch, Andrew. 1985. *Past or Future Crimes: Deservedness and Dangerousness in the Sentencing of Criminals.* New Brunswick, NJ: Rutgers University Press.

von Hirsch, Andrew, K. A. Knapp, and M. Tonry. 1987. *The Sentencing Commission and Its Guidelines.* Boston: Northeastern University Press.

von Hirsch, Andrew, M. Wasik and J. A. Greene. 1989. "Punishments in the Community and the Principles of Desert." *Rutgers Law Journal* 20:595.

Intensive Rehabilitation Supervision: The Next Generation in Community Corrections?

PAUL GENDREAU, FRANCIS T. CULLEN, AND JAMES BONTA

Since their inception in the early 1980's, "intensive supervision programs" (ISP's), which emphasize the close monitoring of offenders in the community, have spread rapidly across the United States. Today, virtually every state has some form of ISP for the supervision of parolees and probationers (Petersilia & Turner, 1993). It is estimated that over 120,000 offenders are now placed in ISPs (Camp & Camp, 1993).

The growth of ISP's attests to their political attractiveness, but now, after a decade of experimentation, it is time to assess whether they have lived up to their promise. As we review below, the existing evaluation research suggests that ISP's with a strong focus on control are not an effective correctional intervention. However, there is beginning evidence that supervision programs which merge control with rehabilitation achieve more favorable results. When seen in the context of the growing evidence demonstrating the effectiveness of correctional treatment, these latter ISP findings provide a basis for considering a new generation of community corrections programs that not only supervise but also rehabilitate offenders. These programs, which we call *intensive rehabilitation supervision* (IRS), should be informed by the existing knowledge base on offender classification and on the principles of effective correctional treatment.

Dr. Gendreau is professor of psychology and director of the graduate unit at the Saint John Campus of the University of New Brunswick. Dr. Cullen is distinguished research professor, Department of Criminal Justice, University of Cincinnati. Dr. Bonta is chief, Corrections Research, Ministry Secretariat, Solicitor General, Canada.

"Intensive Rehabilitation Supervision: The Next Generation in Community Corrections?" by Paul Gendreau, Francis T. Cullen, and James Bonta, from *Federal Probation*, Vol. 58, No. 1, March 1994, pp. 72–78. Reprinted with permission.

IRS: THE SECOND GENERATION OF
COMMUNITY SUPERVISION PROGRAMS

Based on the existing empirical evidence, a persuasive case can be made for abandoning intensive supervision programs that seek only to control and punish offenders in favor of programs that give equal primacy to changing offenders. ISP's, moreover, may provide a unique opportunity for effective rehabilitation. Given their extensive contact with offenders, probation and parole officers should have the time needed to enhance the delivery of services and to monitor their clients' progress. We might also add that intensive rehabilitation supervision programs have a good prospect of receiving political support. By retaining "intensive supervision," the programs would not weaken surveillance over offenders, and by systematically incorporating treatment, intensive rehabilitation supervision (IRS) could offer the realistic hope of lower recidivism rates. More generally, research is clear in showing that the public favors correctional interventions that both control and rehabilitate (Cullen, Skovron, Scott, & Burton, 1990).

Who Gets into IRS: Risk/Needs Assessment

A glaring weakness of the first generation ISP's is that there is no unifying theoretical basis for the selection of offenders for program participation. On the face of it, one would expect that ISP's would be reserved for the higher-risk offender who would supposedly benefit from increased control. However, after yielding to political pressure to get touch on everyone, using subjective as opposed to objective risk assessments, and allowing judges' discretion in sentencing to ISP's, many ISP's are left with a limited range of offenders who fall in the lower-risk categories.

    While reviewers of the rehabilitation literature may debate the overall potency of treatment, they do not dispute the fact that some treatment programs are effective in reducing recidivism for some offenders. The trick is identifying for *which* offenders treatment is most effective. Andrews, Bonta, and Hoge (1990) described a number of general principles that guides the matching of offender to treatment. The first two principles, the risk and need principles, are particularly relevant to our proposal to marry ISP with treatment in the form of IRS.

    The risk principle states that treatment will more likely be effective when treatment services are matched with the risk level of the offender. That is, intensive services should be provided for higher-risk offenders and minimal services for lower-risk offenders. Mismatching level of service with offender risk has seldom shown reductions in recidivism (Andrews & Bonta, 1994; Andrews, Zinger, Hoge, Bonta, Gendreau, & Cullen, 1990). As we have noted, many ISP programs do not target higher risk offenders, although they provide a structural setting for sustaining intensive services. More frequent monitoring and supervision, however, are simply not equivalent to intensive rehabilitation services. After all, hypochondriacs may visit doctors daily, and they do not necessarily get better. What becomes important is what the doctor does with the patient during those visits, and part of the answer comes from the second principle.

The need principle recognizes two types of offender needs: criminogenic and noncriminogenic (e.g., Andrews & Bonta, 1994). Criminogenic needs are actually *dynamic* risk factors. A dynamic risk factor is one that can change over time. Some examples in this regard are an offender's attitudes toward employment, peers, authority, and substance abuse. The importance of criminogenic needs is that they serve as treatment goals: when programs successfully diminish these needs, we can reasonably expect reduction in recidivism. Some examples of noncriminogenic needs are anxiety, depression, and self-esteem; when programs target these types of needs, reductions in recidivism are negligible (Andrews & Bonta, 1994).

From our description of the risk and need principles, we hope that the reader sees the important implications for the design of IRS programs. Basically, IRS programs should target higher-risk clientele and provide rehabilitation services aimed at reducing criminogenic needs. In order to achieve these goals, the first step requires systematic risk-needs assessment.

Most offender assessment/classification instruments are simply risk instruments composed of items measuring an offender's past criminal history (Bonta, 1993). An example is the Salient Factor Score (Hoffman, 1983). All but one of the seven items are historical; that is, they relate to an offender's past, e.g., number of previous convictions, age at first arrest, rather than his or her current behavior and attitudes. Although they may achieve reasonable predictive accuracy and could be helpful in directing higher-risk offenders into IRS programs, they fail to provide the dynamic risk factors needed for effective treatment planning.

In contrast the more recently developed risk-needs assessment instruments include not only criminal history items but also information of a dynamic quality. The criminogenic needs information can then provide staff assistance in identifying problematic aspects of the offender's situation requiring attention in order to reduce the risk of reoffending.

To our knowledge, there are only three risk-needs classification instruments in widespread use. These three instruments are the Level of Supervision Inventory (LSI) (Andrews & Bonta, 1994), the Wisconsin classification system (Baird, 1981), and the Community Risk/Needs Management Scale used by the Correctional Services of Canada (Motiuk, 1993). Only the LSI and the Community Risk/Needs Management Scale were developed specifically with the risk and needs principle considered. At this point in time, only the LSI has shown post-probation dynamic risk validity. That is, changes in offender needs, as measured by the LSI, were associated with changes in recidivism. Analyses of the two other systems show some promise with respect to dynamic risk (Bonta, Andrews, & Motiuk, 1993), but more direct evidence is still lacking.

In short, systematic risk-needs assessment should be used to guide the selection of offenders into IRS programs. Interventions developed for these offenders should be based on specific treatment principles, with risk and need principles forming the general context for treatment.

Principles of Effective Correctional Treatment

Even though the anti-rehabilitation "nothing works" rhetoric took firm hold in the United States for a variety of sociopolitical reasons (Cullen & Gendreau, 1989), dedicated clinicians and researchers have continued to generate data on the effectiveness of offender rehabilitation programs. For the interested reader, this evidence can be found in a variety of published critical narrative reviews and meta-analyses of the offender-treatment outcome literature (Andrews & Bonta, 1994; Andrews et al., 1990; Cullen & Gendreau, 1989; Garrett, 1985; Gendreau, 1993; Gendreau & Andrews, 1990; Gendreau & Ross, 1979, 1984, 1987; Gottschalk, Davidson, Mayer, & Gensheimer, 1987; Izzo & Ross, 1990; Lipsey, 1992; Losel, 1993; Palmer, 1992).

What are the results from these studies? First, if one surveys all the treatment studies that had control group comparisons, as Mark Lipsey (1992) did for 443 studies, 64 percent of the studies reported reductions in favor of the treatment group. The average reduction in recidivism summed across the 443 studies was 10 percent. Secondly, according to Lipsey, when the results were broken down by the general type of program (e.g., employment), reductions in recidivism ranged from 10 to 18 percent.

It is not enough, however, simply to sum across studies or to partition them into general programmatic categories. The salient question is, what are the characteristics that distinguish between effective and ineffective programs? What exactly is done under the name of "employment"? Therefore, based on the literature reviews and to a lesser extent on the documented clinical wisdom of our treatment colleagues, we have discovered that programs which adhered to most of the characteristics to be described below, reduced recidivism in the range of 25 to 80 percent with an average of about 40 percent. A summary of these characteristics is provided. As well, we also include a listing of the principles of ineffective programs. Such knowledge is likely just as important as knowing "what works."

Principles of What Works

1. *Risk principle: Intensive services, behavioral in nature, are provided to higher risk offenders.*
   a. Intensive services occupy 40–70 percent of the offender's time and are of 3 to 9 months duration.
   b. Behavioral programs range from radical behaviorism (e.g., token economies) to cognitive social learning strategies that employ mod-

eling, cognitive restructuring, and explicit reinforcement of alternatives to antisocial styles of thinking, feeling, and acting.

2. *Need principle: The goal of treatment is to reduce criminogenic needs.*
   a. Therapist and program providers must clearly differentiate criminogenic from noncriminogenic needs and ensure that the program targets criminogenic needs.
   b. Program success is partly measured by the reduction of criminogenic needs.

3. *Responsivity: The style and mode of treatment is matched to the offender.*
   a. The learning style and personality of the offender are matched with the program. For example, impulsive offenders and those who prefer a high degree of structure may benefit from a token economy program.
   b. Offenders are matched with the therapist, e.g., "anxious" offenders may respond better to more relaxed and calmer therapists.
   c. Therapists are matched with the type of program, e.g., therapists who have a concrete conceptual level for problem solving may function best in a radical behavioral program.

4. *Program contingencies/behavioral strategies are enforced in a firm but fair manner.*
   a. Reinforcement contingencies are designed with meaningful input from offenders but remain under the control of the staff. Nondirective counseling programs do not seem to work with offenders.
   b. Positive reinforces outweigh punishers by a 4:1 ratio.
   c. Internal controls are established to maintain prosocial behaviors and discourage antisocial behaviors in the absence of external contingencies.

5. *Therapists relate to offenders in interpersonally sensitive and constructive ways and are trained and supervised appropriately.*
   a. Therapists have at least an undergraduate degree or equivalent, with knowledge of the theories of criminal behavior and of the prediction and treatment literature.
   b. Therapists receive 3 to 6 months of formal and on-the-job/internship training in the application of behavioral interventions generally and specific to the program.
   c. Therapists are reassessed periodically on quality of service delivery.
   d. Therapists monitor offender change on criminogenic needs.

6. *The program structure and activities should disrupt the criminal network.*

7. *There is a high level of advocacy and brokerage as long as the community agency offers appropriate services.*

a. Community services should be assessed in as objective a manner as possible, for example, the Correctional Program Assessment Inventory or CPAI (Gendreau & Andrews, 1993), so as to ensure that quality services applicable to the offenders and their problems are provided. All too often this is not the case. In a recent survey of 112 offender substances abuse programs using the CPAI, only 10 percent had programmatic elements that would lead one to believe that an effective service was being provided (Gendreau & Goggin, 1990).

Principles of What Does Not Work

1. *Programs, including behavioral, that target low-risk offenders.*
2. *Programs that target offender need factors not predictive of criminal behavior (e.g., anxiety, depression, self-esteem).*
3. *Traditional Freudian psychodynamic and Rogerian nondirective therapies.* These programs, at least in the offender treatment literature, have been characterized as follows:

   - "talking" cures
   - good relationship with the client is the primary goal
   - unraveling the unconscious
   - gaining insight as the major goal
   - resolving neurotic conflicts and self-actualizing
   - externalizing blame to parents, staff, victims, society
   - ventilating anger

4. *Traditional "medical model" approaches.*

   - diet change
   - pharmacological, e.g., testosterone suppressants for sex offenders
   - plastic surgery

5. *Subcultural and labeling approaches.* For a more complete review of these approaches see Andrews and Bonta (1994). Briefly, they note that interventions based on the following views are ineffective:

   - Respect offenders' culture
   - Provide legitimate opportunities only.
   - Rely on incidental learning. Somehow offenders will "get it" with minimal guidance.
   - Divert offenders from the stigmatization of the criminal justice system. This will be sufficient to reduce criminal behavior.

- Use alternative sanctions with lower levels of punishment; these punishments are supposedly dignified and just, while treatment is coercive and does an injustice to offenders.

6. *Deterrence or "punishing smarter" strategies.* This category includes the first generation ISPs described in this column, as well as boot-camps, electronic monitoring, scared straight, and shock incarceration. Gendreau and Little (1993) have conducted a preliminary meta-analysis of this literature. Their analysis consisted of 174 comparisons between a "punishment" group and a control group. The punishment/deterrence strategies produced slight increases in recidivism. Also of note is that both Cullen et al.'s (1993) narrative review of this literature and Andrews, Zinger et al.'s (1990) meta-analysis reached similar conclusions.

INTENSIVE REHABILITATION SUPERVISION: THE FUTURE

The empirical evidence regarding ISP's is decisive: without a rehabilitation component, reductions in recidivism are as elusive as a desert mirage. This leaves community corrections somewhat at a crossroad. The choice is between (1) abandoning ISP's and returning to regular probation and parole supervision or (2) incorporating effective rehabilitation programming into the intensive monitoring conducted within ISP's. The first choice would be difficult: too much is invested politically in these programs.

The second choice, a new generation of intensive community programming, is more palatable. IRS holds the hope of reduced recidivism within a context of public support. The switch, however, from ISP's to IRS's will not be easy.

First of all, program developers must familiarize themselves with the extensive rehabilitation and punishment literature. For many, this will be foreign territory. Second, for staff who have become accustomed to a "law enforcement" role, incorporating a therapeutic role may bring confusion and conflict. Tonry (1990) has outlined some of the areas of resistance in this regard. Third, the temptation will be to provide IRS to all clientele instead of targeting the higher-risk offender. Not only would this be in contradiction to the risk principle, but it also would widen the net of state control. Finally, there is the question of costs. Training staff to adopt new roles and learn new skills will certainly require the expenditure of resources.

There are probably other unforeseen obstacles, but they are not, in our view, insurmountable. The principles of effective rehabilitation can be taught, staff supported in the transition to new roles, and objective risk-needs assessments adopted to guide the identification of offenders for IRS.

In terms of costs, traditional ISP's along with their adjunct programs (electronic monitoring, urinalysis) are extremely expensive. Diverting this money to rehabilitation programs at least has the promise of producing reduced recidivism. There already seems to be a modest movement toward incorporating treatment into ISP's and targeting higher-risk offenders (see the New Jersey studies), but it is more haphazard rather than planned. We think the time for this movement to accelerate in a systematic and proactive manner is now opportune. To maintain the status quo is clearly unacceptable.

REFERENCES

Andrews, D. A., & Bonta, J. 1994. *The psychology of criminal conduct.* Cincinnati, OH: Anderson.

Andrews, D. A., Bonta, J., & Hoge, R. D. 1990. Classification for effective rehabilitation: Rediscovering psychology. *Criminal Justice and Behavior, 17,* 19–52.

Andrews, D. A., Zinger, I., Hoge, R. D., Bonta, J., Gendreau, P., & Cullen, F. T. 1990. Does correctional treatment work? A psychologically informed meta-analysis. *Criminology, 28,* 369–404.

Baird, S. C. 1981. Probation and parole classification: The Wisconsin model. *Corrections Today, 43,* 36–41.

Bonta, J. (1993, November). *Risk-needs assessment and treatment.* Presentation at a conference of the International Association of Residential and Community Alternatives, Philadelphia, PA.

Bonta, J., Andrews, D. A., & Motiuk, L. L. (1993, October). *Dynamic risk assessment and effective treatment.* Paper presented at the annual meeting of the American Society of Criminology, Phoenix, AZ.

Camp, G. M., & Camp, C. G. 1993. *The corrections yearbook: Probation and parole.* South Salem, NY: Criminal Justice Institute.

Cullen, F. T., & Gendreau, P. 1989. The effectiveness of correctional rehabilitation: Reconsidering the "Nothing Works" debate. In L. Goodstein & D. MacKenzie (Eds.), *American prisons: Issues in research and policy* (pp. 23–44). New York: Plenum.

Cullen, F. T., Skovron, S. E., Scott, J. E., & Burton, V. S. 1990. Public support for correctional rehabilitation: The tenacity of the rehabilitation ideal. *Criminal Justice and Behavior, 17,* 6–18.

Cullen, F. T., Wright, J. P., & Applegate, B. K. (1993, November). *Control in the community.* Presentation at a conference of the International Association of Residential and Community Alternatives, Philadelphia, PA.

Garrett, C. J. 1985. Effects of residential treatment on adjudicated delinquents: A meta-analysis. *Journal of Research in Crime and Delinquency, 22,* 287–308.

Gendreau, P. (1993, November). *The principles of effective intervention with offenders.* Presentation at a conference of the International Association of Residential and Community Alternatives, Philadelphia, PA.

Gendreau, P., & Andrews, D. A. 1990. Tertiary prevention: What the meta-analysis of the offender treatment literature tells us about "what works." *Canadian Journal of Criminology, 32,* 173–184.

Gendreau, P., & Andrews, D. A. 1993. *The correctional program assessment inventory* (3rd ed.). University of New Brunswick, Saint John, N. B. and Carleton University, Ottawa, Ontario.

Gendreau, P., & Little, T. 1993. *A meta-analysis of the effectiveness of sanctions on offender recidivism.* Unpublished manuscript, Department of Psychology, University of New Brunswick, Saint John.

Gendreau, P., & Goddard, M. 1994. *The realities of punishment.* Manuscript submitted for publication.

Gendreau, P., & Ross, R. R. 1984. Correctional treatment: Some recommendations for successful intervention. *Juvenile and Family Court Journal, 34,* 31–40.

Gendreau, P., & Ross, R. R. 1979. Effective correctional treatment: Bibliotherapy for cynics. *Crime and Delinquency, 25,* 463–489.

Gendreau, P., & Ross, R. R. 1987. Revivication of rehabilitation: Evidence from the 1980s. *Justice Quarterly, 4,* 349–407.

Gottschalk, R., Davidson, W. S., Mayer, J., & Gensheimer, R. 1987. Behavioral approaches with juvenile offenders: A meta-analysis of long-term treatment efficacy. In E. K. Morris & C. J. Braukman (Eds.), *Behavioral approaches to crime and delinquency: A handbook of application, research, and concepts* (pp. 399–422). New York: Plenum Press.

Hoffman, P. B. 1983. Screening for risk: A revised salient factor score (SFS 81). *Journal of Criminal Justice, 11,* 539–547.

Izzo, R., & Ross, R. R. 1990. Meta-analysis of rehabilitation programs for juvenile delinquents: A brief report. *Criminal Justice and Behavior, 17,* 134–142.

Lipsey, M. W. 1992. Juvenile delinquency treatment: A meta-analytic inquiry into the variability of effects. In T. D. Cook, H. Cooper, D. S. Cordray, H. Hartmann, L. V. Hedges, R. J. Light, T. A. Louis, & F. Mosteller, (Eds.), *Meta-analysis for explanation* (pp. 83–127). New York: Russell Sage Foundation.

Losel, F. (1993, November). *Evaluating psychosocial interventions in prison and other contexts.* Paper presented at the Twentieth Criminological Conference, Strasbourg, Germany.

Motiuk, L. L. 1993. Where are we in our ability to assess risk? *Forum on Corrections Research, 5,* 14–19.

Palmer, T. 1992. *The re-emergence of correctional intervention.* Newbury Park, CA: Sage.

Petersilia, J., & Turner, S. 1993. Intensive probation and parole. In M. Tonry & N. Morris (Eds.), *Crime and justice: An annual review of the research* (Vol. 17). Chicago, IL: University of Chicago Press.

When Community Corrections Means Business: Introducing "Reinventing" Themes to Probation and Parole

RONALD P. CORBETT, JR.
Deputy Commissioner of Probation, Boston, Massachusetts

Does community corrections really need to be "reinvented"? While perhaps not the definitive answer to that question, Osborne and Gaebler's comments on the state of the criminal justice enterprise might be instructive: "Perhaps the only public system in worse shape than education and health care is criminal justice" (1992, p. 319).

Probably not a fair or accurate statement but nonetheless a sobering one for all who care about the public perception of criminal justice and its component parts. Few would argue that community corrections should somehow exempt itself from the kind of intense self-scrutiny that the reinventing process requires. There is ample evidence that, absent significant reform, the future of probation and parole is bleak. The public debate on crime has ignored or diminished the role of community corrections. The recent federal crime control legislation has all but eliminated consideration of probation and parole, and funding levels have remained stagnant nationally during a period when the community corrections population has soared (Petersilia, 1995). While these trends are ideological and political in large part and should not be taken as a product of some considered judgment on the effectiveness or efficiency of community corrections operations, all government agencies must recognize that they are in a "change or perish" atmosphere where only the strong will survive. That is, in light of both cutback mentalities and a get-tough-on-crime mood, probation and parole agencies will need to take the offensive in demonstrating to a skeptical public that they can be serious allies in the effort, as Vice President Gore put it, to make government "work better and cost less." If President Clinton is correct in suggesting that "People will regain confidence in government if we make it work better" (Gore, 1995, p. 7), then much can be gained from acting now.

The balance of this article will explore four reinventing themes for their meaning and application to community corrections. We will look at the relevance of *mission*, an orientation toward *results*, the importance *of customers*, and the role of *prevention*.

"When Community Corrections Means Business: Introduction 'Reinventing' Themes to Probation and Parole" by Ronald P. Corbett, Jr., from *Federal Probation*, Vol. 60, No. 1, March 1996, pp. 36–42. Reprinted with permission.

MISSION-DRIVEN COMMUNITY CORRECTIONS

If anything comes through clearly in the welter of books written in recent years on cutting-edge practice in management, it is the understanding that all successful enterprises are characterized by a clear sense of mission. It may seem self-evident and a mere commonplace to suggest that organizations need a commonly shared set of beliefs and a well-communicated sense of purpose, yet it is unmistakable that, particularly in the public sector, little concerted attention is given to this fundamental point. Certainly, many organizations will somewhere have articulated their overall credo, but too often this exists on a plaque in the lobby of headquarters and not in the minds and hearts of the employees. Moreover, traditional company philosophies are vague, "feel-good" statements, not living documents that drive strategic plans or day-to-day decisions.

Done correctly, the development of a mission statement engages key members of an organization in a painstaking effort to define the essential purpose and goals they mean to pursue. It is meant to be both more than a collection of platitudes but less than an enumeration of organizational objectives. Osborne and Gaebler put it this way:

> The experience of hashing out the fundamental purpose of an organization—debating all the different assumptions and views held by its members and agreeing on one basic mission—can be a powerful one. . . . It can help people at all levels decide what they should do and what they should stop doing. (1992, p. 131)

Many organizations that undertake to develop a new mission statement find that getting consensus on the basics proves to be harder work than was imagined and exposes "fault lines" in the fundamental beliefs system within the organization. This is bound to be true in corrections, where philosophies are continually in flux and there is much contested terrain, ideologically speaking. For example, should the principal goal of probation and parole be public safety? Offender reintegration? Victim services? Most observers would argue that a community corrections mission statement properly should reflect a composite of all these and perhaps more. Perhaps so, but serving one goal may undermine another, and a scarcity of resources requires tough decisions about priorities, all of which becomes complicated in the fact of a diffuse and omnibus mission statement.

The point is that arriving at a mission statement is hard but vital work, and it cannot be done in the absence of a consensus about the chief purpose(s) of an organization. Once the mission statement is promulgated, all major decisions should flow from and reinforce the mission statement. The "tough calls" that all executives face should be resolved in the light of the mission statement, and common organizational practices should be aligned with the values inherent in the statement.

Though it is devilishly difficult work, community corrections organizations have successfully developed and published mission statements in recent years. After inviting the input of a substantial portion of its membership, the APPA has recently published a vision statement and has commenced the practice of bringing all of its activities (training, research, advocacy, etc.) into alignment with its vision. (Management aficionados will argue that mission and vision statements are distinguishable, with a mission statement reflecting the status quo in an organization and a vision statement reflecting a hoped-for future state. To the extent that both define what an organization *should* be about, they come to the same thing.) The APPA core statement is as follows:

> We see a fair, just, and safe society where community partnerships are restoring hope by embracing a balance of prevention, intervention, and advocacy.

The Georgia Department of Corrections, nationally recognized for its innovations in the community corrections area, also underwent an organization-wide process to develop its mission statement, which reads in part as follows:

> The mission of the Georgia Department of Corrections is to protect the public and staff by managing offenders either in a safe and secure environment or through effective community supervision according to their needs and risks. In collaboration with the community and other agencies, we provide programs which offer offenders the opportunity to become responsible, productive, law-abiding citizens.

In addition to clarifying an organization's fundamental business and giving direction to decisionmaking, a well-crafted mission statement that addresses both beliefs and values can inspire staff members in a way that can motivate them and earn their commitment.

RESULTS-DRIVEN COMMUNITY CORRECTIONS

As a companion piece to mission-driven government, results-driven agencies not only declare their purpose through a mission statement but promise specific outcomes based on it. They define what the "deliverables" are and are committed to being judged by their success in achieving them. In short, a results-driven government promises "bang for the buck."

In *Common Sense Government*, Vice President Gore reports that, in his own research on the management of federal agencies, "most agencies were hard pressed to tell you what their performance goals were, let along if they were achieving them" (p. 116). In a related point, Osborne and Gaebler (1992) note that the majority of legislators, on whom government agencies depend for continuing support, have "no idea which programs they fund are successful and which are failing" (p. 147). Whatever other failings the private sector may have, it is impossible to imagine any company being unable to measure its success!

Government agencies have not focused on results because they have not had to. Funding streams have been driven not by outcomes but rather by inputs. A government agency generally gets funded by the numbers of clients it has or the number of activities it undertakes. For example, school funding is driven by enrollment, not by measurable improvements in student academic performance. Public works departments get funded by the amount of trash hauled or parks cleaned—not by the quality or efficiency with which those tasks are undertaken.

Concentrating on results has never been imperative to monopolies, and government agencies (until recently) have all the features of monopolies. But that is changing. *Reinventing Government* first documented the trend toward privatization or "outsourcing," and then its very publication acted as a catalyst for many levels of government to consider introducing competition in the delivery of public services. If public agencies would not commit to a bottom line, then legislators and executives would consider forcing the issue by creating a marketplace for the provision of public services. Hence the advent of, for example in Massachusetts, privately run charter schools which compete with public schools for students. Or the contracting out of prison health services formerly provided by state employees.

In an example from criminal justice, Commissioner Bratton of the New York City Police Department, on that job for only 2 years, has been unexcelled in his propensity for not only publishing results but predicting them! For the last 2 years, he has publicly promised the citizens of New York decreases in crime (the ultimate "outcome" in the criminal justice world) *and has achieved them.* Having delivered a 27 percent decrease in serious crime in the last 2 years, he began 1996 by promising an additional 10 percent reduction for the year. Commissioner Bratton and the New York City Police Department are becoming the gold standard in results-driven government (Pooley, 1996).

With the publication of *Results-Driven Management* (1995), APPA has given the community corrections field a tremendous opportunity to commit the profession to well-defined outcomes. Traditionally, probation and parole have measured their contribution to the public good in terms of presentence reports written, individuals supervised, and monies collected. Osborne and Gaebler have helped the profession understand that these are *activities* rather than *results, inputs* rather than *outputs.* Intended objectives must be concretely defined in terms of the mission of the agency and reflect what taxpayers might reasonably wish that agency to accomplish.

Results-Driven Management is the product of a great deal of thought about how to translate the mission of community corrections into concrete "deliverables." For example, in lieu of the usual reporting of restitution collected, it is recommended that agencies report on the percent of overall restitution orders which were collected. Any collection agency in the private sector measures its effectiveness not in total dollar amounts but in recovery rates, and the same is now recommended for probation. Presentence work would no longer be measured principally in terms of volume and timeliness but rather in terms of instances where a recommendation for probation was accepted and then followed by successful completion of probation. The APPA report contains several additional examples of specific results that can be measured.

THE GREAT RECIDIVISM DEBATE

The public, which pays the bill for probation, wants, more than anything else, that those placed on probation do not reoffend. Straightforward as that seems, the community corrections profession nonetheless has been split on the validity of recidivism as a measure of effectiveness. A good deal of the debate on this subject has been carried out in the pages of *Perspectives*, and no consensus seems imminent.

Part of the reluctance to commit to recidivism as a main measure is due to the recognition that many of the forces that affect an offender's behavior—family, neighborhood, job market, availability of treatment services—are beyond the control of a probation and parole officer. While that is undoubtedly true, the average fair-minded citizen would still want to believe that the intervention of a probation or parole officer increases the odds of a favorable outcome, compared either to no intervention or to incarceration. And the profession ignores this expectation at its peril.

One way to frame the recidivism question can be drawn fro Commissioner Bratton's approach described above. He does not promise an elimination of crime; rather, he talks about improvements in the overall crime rates that he expects to make from year to year. While he does not promise that the current reductions will continue indefinitely, his goal is to return to the kind of rate that was common, say, 30 years ago. Similarly, community corrections agencies should be willing to publish current recidivism rates and then commit to deliver at least modest reductions from year to year. Such a campaign would force agencies to work smarter than ever before and possibly unleash a wave of creativity the likes of which the profession has rarely seen. If it works (and I believe it would) the gains in public support would more than repay the effort.

CUSTOMER-ORIENTED COMMUNITY CORRECTIONS

Tom Peters, arguably the best known of contemporary management gurus, has made the phrase "staying close to the customer" a mantra among leading corporations. The phrase connotes the importance of paying relentless attention to the needs, wants, and opinions of those who are paying for the product and responding to changing tastes and preferences in a flexible and timely manner. The idea of serving the customer is at first a vexing and awkward one when applied to the public sector, where arguably there are multiple customers (e.g., legislators, clients, and taxpayers) whose wishes will often conflict. Nonetheless, as part of the *Reinventing Government* revolution, some government agencies have worked through these real difficulties and are making the idea of customer service relevant in the public domain.

In the community corrections world, efforts to become more sensitive and responsive to a variety of customers has led, in Phoenix, Arizona, to the practice of surveying parents regarding their degree of satisfaction with the supervision exercised over their children on probation or, in Illinois and Massachusetts, to surveying probationers regarding their experience of supervision and their contact with probation officers. Clearly, these practices could be extended to assessing the satisfaction of victims with the timeliness of restitution payments or the opinion of municipal administrators regarding the value of the community service received in their localities. In addition, something as seemingly trivial as the degree of telephone courtesy extended to those who must call probation and parole offices can be a very telling indication of the "face" that community corrections is presenting to is public.

PREVENTION-ORIENTED COMMUNITY CORRECTIONS

It has been said that a smart person solves problems and a genius prevents them. By this standard, criminal justice—until recently—has been replete with wise men and short of geniuses. Prevention has not been seen traditionally as in the province of criminal justice; the system was designed instead to deal with prevention's failures. Public health, schools, and most of all families would have to perform the preventive function—everyone else was too busy mopping up the mess!

Nevertheless, it has become respectable to speak of prevention in recent years. The hallmark of the prevention spirit is the willingness to look beyond mandates and job descriptions to a new, different, and broader conceptualization of the task at hand and redirect some resources currently devoted to reacting to problems over into a preventive mode.

The Massachusetts Probation Department has initiated "Fatherhood" programs designed to reach young fathers on probation with a skill-building training program aimed at developing their capacity to act as responsible parents. This course is offered to young offenders regardless of their offense as a way not so much to deter their criminal behavior (though it is expected to contribute to that goal), but to improve their ability to raise healthy and responsible children whose own lives will remain trouble-free.

Thinking in terms of prevention is truly a paradigm shift for courts and corrections. Financial support for this reorientation toward prevention may be hard to come by. Joan Petersilia (1995), in a recent article on trends in crime policy, comments with alarm on the fact that prevention funding originally included in recent federal legislation—the Violent Crime Control and Law Enforcement Act of 1994—was removed altogether in subsequent revisions. Despite these setbacks, in the end the financial imperatives may well be inexorable. Simply put, it is cheaper to prevent crime than to treat it. While an emphasis on prevention may not currently carry the correct political or ideological charge, getting serious about prevention carries the best hope of reversing the public expenditures on prisons that threaten to bankrupt governments across the country.

In the face of the current climate, there is a real danger that those who believe in the value of publicly provided goods and services will retreat into a defensive, fatalistic posture and miss the substance that is sometimes hidden in this politically charged atmosphere as well as the opportunities that present themselves. The American public *has* lost confidence in too many places in the ability of government agencies to deliver a good and economical product. Yet there are many signs that, where there is a commitment to put the public's business on a strong business footing and to introduce the kind of discipline that all private concerns must adhere to in order to survive, public support and confidence can be regained. Osborne and Gaebler's *Reinventing Government*, along with the many innovations that is has spawned, points the way to a more confident future. Those of us who care about the future of community corrections should follow that lead.

REFERENCES

Boone, H. N., & Fulton, B. 1995. *Results-driven management.* Lexington, KY: American Probation and Parole Association.

Gore, A. 1995. *Common sense government.* New York: Random House.

Osborne, D., & Gaebler, T. 1992. *Reinventing government.* Reading, MA: Addison-Wesley.

Petersilia, J. (1995, Summer). A crime control rationale for reinvesting in community corrections. *Spectrum*, pp. 16–29.

Pooley, E. (1996, January 15). One good apple. *Time*, pp. 54–56.

Traub, J. (1996, January 15). Dollface. *The New Yorker*, pp. 28–35.

Challenges for Corrections in the Community

TODD R. CLEAR
Florida State University

ANTHONY A. BRAGA
Rutgers University

There can be no question that, for the forseeable future, most offenders will be managed in community supervision programs. Given this recent evidence

"Challenges for Corrections in the Community" by Todd R. Clear and Anthony A. Braga, excerpted from *Crime*, edited by James Q. Wilson and Joan Petersilia, Chap. 18, pp. 440–444, 1995, Institute for Contemporary Studies, San Francisco. Reprinted with permission.

about these programs, what are the prospects for community-based programs? What challenges do they face? We suggest there are five, described below.

THE PROBLEM OF PRISON CROWDING AND ITS COSTS

It seems safe to say that unless the existing programs are revamped in extraordinary ways, community corrections agencies will remain of only marginal importance as solutions to problems of institutional crowding. This may seem at least ironic or even preposterous, but our review shows that for the most part community-based programs are designed and run in ways that make them virtually predestined to exacerbate rather than ameliorate prison crowding.

For one thing, most programs articulate a target group that leads to *enhanced* levels of control and costs, not reduced levels. Most ISPs are probation-enhancement programs rather than confinement diversion programs. They seek a "tougher" probation to replace traditional methods, and they target the "toughest" probation cases. This approach can reduce crowding and related costs only by substantial reductions in failure rates compared to traditional probation. As evaluations have shown, stringent conditions and strict enforcement means ISPs actually produce a *higher* failure rate by promoting revocations that may have little to do with crime.

Similarly, most shock incarceration programs target first time offenders and most exclude violent or previously incarcerated offenders. Often, boot camp programs are limited to persons under a certain age, no older than early 20s. In most correctional systems in the United States, first-time property offenders do not go to prison anyway. The only first-time offenders who receive terms of confinement are drug offenders—in today's negative attitude toward drugs, these offenders are often excluded from program eligibility as well. By designating such a limited target group, boot camps often guarantee irrelevance to the problems confronting institutional corrections systems.

Not only does the target group cast doubt on these programs, but their methods do as well. What has been called "catch 'em and snatch 'em" probation is oriented toward maximum surveillance and minimum tolerance. It is not surprising that these programs lead to high rates of return to prison. But the net effect of these programs, then, can be extremely damaging. For example, probation enhancement programs take offenders that would otherwise *not* be prison bound and place them in programs that actually *increase* their exposure to confinement.

If community corrections were to be able to confront with any durability the problem of prison crowding, three changes would be needed in the design of these programs.

First, the target groups for these programs would have to be narrowly defined so as to maximize the probability that the program is getting only prison- or jail-bound offenders. Because most jurisdictions experience considerable sentencing disparity, this is not an easy task, since many offenders have a moderate chance of either prison or non-prison sentences. The two "safe" target groups, in terms of diversion, are offenders whose crimes are serious (particularly violent offenders or drug distributors), and persons who are seriously failing under regular community supervision. Because of the obvious political considerations attaching to the first choice, most programs opt for community failures.

Second, the methods used to supervise these offenders must change. Adjectives like "tough," and "no-nonsense" sound good and inspire public confidence. But these methods often do not fit well to the lives of the people under community supervision. For many of those under community supervision, increased structure and controls may ultimately be helpful, but expecting an easy adjustment to those changes is unrealistic. When these programs adopt a stance which seeks any opportunity to remove a person from the streets, they can be assured of finding plenty of them. What is needed instead is a philosophy that offenders will be retained on the streets by whatever means are available. Under this idea, occasional rules violations are to be expected and worked through with the client.

Third, the consequences of program failure will need to be mediated. Often, the reverse is true: program failures are "taught a lesson," by receiving expanded prison terms. Not only are these terms often undeserved, because they are disporportionate to the conduct for which they are imposed, they are counterproductive. For example, if a person who would have received a 6 month penalty is diverted to one of these programs, we know chances of failure increase. But even if this were not true, when the costs of failure increase as well—say, to a 1 year term—the chances the program achiving prison savings is made even more remote, for a even a 50% reduction in failure would amount to a wash in resources, overall.

THE PROBLEM OF SURVEILLANCE AND ITS EFFECTIVENESS

Of what good is the close contact, if its only rationale is to identify the malfeasant and take firm action? Surveillance and control are not values in themselves; they are useful only if they lead to positive results. We have seen that closer surveillance increases program failure rates in ways that do not seem to be associated with crime reduction. Indeed, the use of electronic monitors seems unrelated to rates of programs compliance—the tighter the monitor the more frequent the failure—also in ways unrelated to crime. Thus, the logical reason for watching people so closely—that it will prevent crime or increase compliance—is not supported by the data.

If close supervision is not necessarily effective, is it perhaps benign? There is no direct way to answer this question, but most of us might admit to an uneasiness with the expanded use of surveillance and control by government agency when the payoff seems so unclear. Putting government agents in peoples' homes in order to find reasons to remove them from the home should strike all of us as a bit troubling, and a wholesale advancement of this technical capacity might be more than troubling.

The emphasis on surveillance and control also detracts from the time and attention devoted to service delivery. Since both the RAND evaluation and an earlier evaluation of Massachusetts' IPS reported significantly lower recidivism rates when offenders received treatment (for substance abuse, employment, and family problems), an emphasis on treatment seems to be a promising avenue for crime control in the community.

Ultimately, the question comes down to "why?" That is, what is the reason for the control, and what value is obtained by more perfect knowledge of the person's behavior? In the case of offenders whose crimes become more frequent (or more likely) when drugs are in their system, a program of urine testing makes intuitive sense as a preventive measure. This can be especially well argued when the resulting offense is likely to be serious, such as a sex offense against a child. However, without an attitude change about how requirements are enforced, a general program of urine testing is likely to expose the ordinary offender to sanctions that decrease our chances of achieving goals of cost containment and community adjustment.

A case can be made, then, that program requirements need to be tailored to individual cases and their circumstances, not applied accross the board. Moreover, sanctions need to be designed in ways that promote compliance by trial and error, not by simple threat.

THE PROBLEM OF PROGRAM DESIGN AND OFFENDER RISK

One of the ironies of the changes in community corrections is that the most powerful programs are being front-loaded on the least risky offenders. Boot camps are reserved for youthful first-time offenders; ISPs are restricted to property offenders; Electronic monitors are given only to the employed. It is understandable that new programs seek "safe" clients with whom to demonstrate their impact, but a growing body of evidence suggests this is not a wise use of these resources.

Put in another way, New Jersey's ISP, which provides daily contact with offenders and eligibility for teatment programs that otherwise have waiting lists, is reserved for the *very best risks* in the New Jersey prison system. The worst risks eventually come out onto regular parole, in case loads of 100 or more. We might wonder if this is not an upside-down use of resources.

Meta-analyses find that intervention programs work best with high-risk clients. The reasons are simple: it is not easy to affect a base expectancy failure rate of 5%—low risk—but even a moderately well-designed program of structure stands a chance to reduce a 50% base rate of failure—high risk. Yet again, these new programs routinely select from the lesser risk clients in the system. Is it any surprise that the evaluation results seem always to suggest little impact with small sample sizes?

If these programs are to provide maximum bang for the buck, we must recognize that they need to target high-probability-of-failure cases, and bring the rates down (not the contemporary strategy, which is too often to target low-probability cases and bring failure rates up).

THE PROBLEM OF OVERALL COMMUNITY SAFETY

Studies of offenders in the community find that they account for a minor portion of overall crime in the community. This is counterintuitive, but true. As Geerken and Hayes estimated, Louisiana probationers and parolees accounted for only 7% of felony arrests in a given year. Beefing up probation and parole they concluded would have little overall effect on levels of crime in the community. Likewise, the National Research Panel of the National Academy of Sciences has estimated that the tripling of time served by violent felons since 1975 has only produced a reduction in violent crime of between 10 and 15%.

Clearly, the number of felons under supervision in the community has only marginal implications for the safety of the communities in which they reside. A full review of the evidence on this question is not possible here, but it appears that the way the question has been posed in the past has been wrong. We should not ask *whether* the offender should be on the streets, but *how* the offender should be managed on the streets. In this regard, it appears that

- Intervention programs are promising when applied to higher risk offenders;
- Expanded use of non-prison alternatives does not need result in expanded criminal behavior, if low-risk offenders are diverted from prison;
- The relaxation of stringent program requirements for low-risk cases need not be associated with increased criminality; and
- The levels of criminality, as indicated by arrests, in traditional community programs are low in most jurisdictions.

These are all good indicators that an increased investment in and policy emphasis on community-based methods will not lead to decreases in community safety, and may well increase community safety.

THE PROBLEM OF JUSTICE

In the 1970s, and debate occupied the penological community about the meaning of the term justice, and how it was best achieved through the sanctioning process. It is testimony about the distance we have taken from that debate that in this last section we finally raise the question of justice. It is a sad demonstration of the field of public policy that a lengthy discussion of the offender in the community could be provided with so little discussion of the problem of what is just.

In the 1980s, the calibration of penalties in this country has changed. The advent of three-strikes legislation, the example of the Federal Sentencing Guidelines, the ubiquity of mandatory penalties has meant that what is seen as "right" or "fair" is different on a matter of scale from what was true 20 years ago. The irony is that while the popular public idea has it that this is a lenient nation, we have become markedly less so for two decades.

It is hard for community penalties to compete with confinement when the question is punishment and the standard is measured in years and even decades. Certainly, some research suggests that some prisoners would rather stay in prison than be released on the most stringent supervision programs—the dubious distinction of being more onerous than prison is an odd badge for a community program to wear.

Perhaps in the future, the justice question will no longer be dominated by images of harshness, discipline, loss, and suffering. In its place might be appeals to the capacity to make amends to victims and their communities, the maintenance of family ties and parenting possibilities, the opportunity to contribute to society rather than merely be a net drain on its resources.

When—if ever—the popular idea of justice loses its current mean-spirited distortion and becomes broad enough to embrace these ideas of basic social justice, community-based methods will have the potential for a sustained importance and a central place in the scheme of policymaking.